D0912959

THE ART OF MEMBERSHIP

About the ASAE-Wiley Series

All titles in the ASAE-Wiley Series are developed through a publishing alliance between ASAE: The Center for Association Leadership and John Wiley & Sons to better serve the content needs of member-serving organizations and the people who lead and manage them.

THE ART OF MEMBERSHIP

How to Attract, Retain, and Cement Member Loyalty

SHERI JACOBS, CAE

The Center for Association Leadership

JB JOSSEY-BASS™

A Wiley Brand

A Wiley Brand
One Montgomery Street, Suite 1200, San Francisco, CA 94104-4594
www.josseybass.com

Jossey-Bass books and products are available through most bookstores. To contact Jossey-Bass directly call our Customer Care Department within the U.S. at 800-956-7739, outside the U.S. at 317-572-3986, or fax 317-572-4002.

Wiley publishes in a variety of print and electronic formats and by print-on-demand. Some material included with standard print versions of this book may not be included in e-books or in print-on-demand. If this book refers to media such as a CD or DVD that is not included in the version you purchased, you may download this material at http://booksupport.wiley.com. For more information about Wiley products, visit www.wiley.com.

Library of Congress Cataloging-in-Publication Data

Jacobs, Sheri.
    The art of membership : how to attract, retain, and cement member loyalty / Sheri Jacobs. — First edition.
        pages cm
    Includes bibliographical references and index.
    ISBN 978-1-118-63310-6 (hardback); ISBN 978-1-118-63311-3 (pdf);
    ISBN 978-1-118-63308-3 (epub)
        1. Associations, institutions, etc.—Membership.   2. Membership campaigns.
    I. Title.
    AS6.J33   2014
    060—dc23
                                                                2013032685

Printed in the United States of America
FIRST EDITION
HB Printing   10 9 8 7 6 5 4 3 2 1

To my husband and daughter, Matt and Jillian Getter, to whom I am eternally grateful for their patience, love, and support.

And to my parents, Allan and Jodie Jacobs, who inspired me with their own commitment to making the world a better place through their volunteer work and contributions.

Contents

Part Four   Personalize the Process

List of Tables, Figures, and Exhibits

Tables

Figures

Exhibits

Preface

It was late in the evening when the call came in over the police scanner. There had been an accident on Route 81, about ten miles north of the small town in New York where I was working as a photojournalist on a daily newspaper. A driver entering the highway on the wrong side of the road had hit another car head-on. An important detail in this story is that this wasn't just an isolated, unfortunate accident. It was the third time in as many months that someone had made a wrong turn there and entered the highway on the wrong side. It was the first time, however, that this action had caused a fatality.

I had been on the job for four short months, yet because I was on the late shift, I was called to the scene of this accident. This was my first full-time position after college, though I had spent nearly three years working at other newspapers. I felt prepared to put aside my emotions and cover the events that unfolded in front of me. As I moved around the cars, staying out of the way of the first responders, I tried to capture images that would tell the story. It was a devastating scene, yet one that I felt could be best portrayed through the lens of a camera.

As I was developing my film, I was approached by one of the editors. He informed me the newspaper was going to run a small item about the "incident," but there would not be room for a photo; the decision had been made to run a different photo, from an altogether different story, on the front page.

Of course there was room for a photo! I thought—especially for a story as important as this one. I protested. I was quickly overruled.

I strongly felt this was not the right approach. However, I was twenty-three years old and had very little experience, and I had no authority over the stories we covered in the newspaper. I mentioned the incident to one of the other staff photographers, asking him whether he didn't agree that we had an obligation, as journalists, to share this story with others and warn them about the dangers of this intersection.

His response took me completely by surprise. For most events, he told me, especially very public ones, the newspaper provides fair coverage and will inform the public. But sometimes the decision regarding the importance of a story is solely in the hands of a small group of people, experienced professionals—who may or may not understand the whole story. I was surprised, because I thought it would be important to gain input from those who were closest to the situation.

Over the years, I've thought about this experience many times. The journalistic landscape has changed dramatically. If you have a story to tell, there are many ways to get the message out. From blogs to photo-sharing websites like Reddit to YouTube, user-generated content is being created and shared every day.

The newsrooms that existed twenty years ago could not function in today's world. Yesterday's technology would be out of date, and the editorial staff would be out of sync with today's potential audiences.

Why am I sharing this story as the introduction to a book about the art of membership? Because although organizations have a mission, a vision, and a story to tell, they can no longer rely on tried-and-true methods that worked ten years ago. Membership, like storytelling, is an art. You've got to skillfully recruit members who will remain members throughout their careers. And during those careers, you've got to successfully provide for them exactly what they need, when they need it. When you accomplish this, they will tell your organization's story to their colleagues and peers.

With concern growing about how to address advances in technology, changing workforce demographics, and a flood of information and resources, I decided it was time to tackle the entire situation through my own lens. Although the experiences, research, and information used for this book come primarily from organizations, the challenge of recruiting, engaging, and retaining members is faced by many different types of organizations and nonprofits—from museums to alumni organizations and chambers of commerce to cause-related organizations. I believe many people will find the content in this book and recommendations suitable and relevant to their situation as well. In this book I identify many of the underlying reasons that associations are struggling to recruit and retain members and the steps you can take to grow your membership. These are my Membership Rules: a set of bedrock principles that should form the basis of every membership program.

What's in This Book?

I've structured the book with twelve chapters grouped in four parts. The first part explains how organizations can find their value. The second will help you define your audience. The third will help you sell your organization. And the fourth provides you with the information you need to succeed within your own organization.

Part One: Find Your Value

• *Chapter One: Understand the Value Before You Start Selling* goes through the steps necessary to conduct a thorough assessment of your organization's various value points. I introduce a key tool that can be used to determine the actual value of a product. I also explain how to (1) conduct market research to measure value; (2) identify a variety of audience segments based on psychographics, demographics, and other factors; and (3) identify gaps in value, weaknesses in the price/value equation, and opportunities to increase profits through bundling of products.

• *Chapter Two: Value Is in the Eye of the Beholder* explains why classifying individuals based only on demographics such as birth year (generation), gender, work setting, or title may be of little use, because these groups sometimes have little more in common than the defining trait. The chapter includes an action plan for creating a customized membership structure for any size organization.

• *Chapter Three: Sell What Matters* explains the difference between features and benefits by looking at advantages and outcomes. I explain why promoting a long tail of programs, products, and services (such as free and discounted offerings) does more harm than good. This chapter includes a questionnaire for readers to complete to help them narrow the selection of benefits to promote in the marketing collateral (that is, print and digital).

• *Chapter Four: Charge More or Less—And Other Alternative Pricing Strategies* addresses the often-debated issue of pricing. Regardless of the current economic climate, members and prospects will continue to scrutinize purchasing decisions even if they can afford it and they've been satisfied with the product in the past. This chapter includes the six most common pricing objectives, along with the types of strategies that are most effective to achieve the objectives. I also identify the four factors that affect price sensitivity. Pricing strategies are accompanied by a case study.

Part Two: Who Are Your Members?

• *Chapter Five: Members or Customers? Developing the Most Qualified Prospect List* will help organizations understand the underlying reasons why some individuals decide to join and others do not. This chapter will help organizations understand and identify the low, medium, and high drivers of membership based on different audience segments. Finally, I provide the pros and cons for various types of marketing tactics, along with case studies to support each viewpoint.

• *Chapter Six: Behavior and Preference Are Very Different Things* explains one of the major weaknesses of most membership surveys. Although preference questions may provide important data on how a member would act or respond when few or no barriers (such as cost or time) exist, they often do not reflect the realities most people and organizations face. In this chapter I provide sample questions and supporting data to demonstrate the importance of asking the right preference and behavior questions. I also provide case studies to illustrate how to apply the findings to strategic decision making as well as marketing membership, programs, products, and services.

• *Chapter Seven: Look at Where Your Members Are Going* shows how luck, good and bad, is more often the result of planning (or the lack thereof) than chance. I show how organizations committed to collecting and analyzing data through market research are more likely to perform better than others that are not, despite facing comparable opportunities and circumstances. This chapter includes a detailed checklist of the specific types of research and data points collected by organizations that demonstrate a commitment to preparing and anticipating events rather than reacting to them.

Part Three: Sell Your Organization

• *Chapter Eight: Be a Problem Solver* explains why it is important to answer the question: "Why should I join?" when describing an organization's benefits. This chapter focuses on how to market an organization and its offerings in a way that resonates with members, prospects, and customers. It includes a list of Dos and Don'ts for describing the benefits of membership.

• *Chapter Nine: Prove It!* makes the case for eliminating clichés such as "The premiere organization for . . ." or "Top-notch speakers on cutting-edge topics." This chapter will help organizations understand how to collect the proof and create messages that leverage the unique selling points of the organization, and how to move people to action.

Part Four: Personalize the Process

• *Chapter Ten: Overcome Objections* explains why organizations must raise objections and address them if they are to transform prospects into members. This chapter provides a list of the ten most commonly heard objections and recommendations on how to overcome them. I also include two examples of organizations that incorporated market research they collected into their marketing messages to help overcome objections.

• *Chapter Eleven: Engagement, Onboarding, and the First Ninety Days* explains how to implement a ninety-day new member onboarding program. Why is this important? My research has shown that a key predictor for new member retention is creating a second, meaningful interaction between the member and the association within the first three months of joining the association. In addition, I believe an organization must develop a relationship with a new member before it can begin "selling" its programs, events, publications, and products.

• *Chapter Twelve: Be Flexible* lays out my premise that a rigid set of policies regarding member or customer transactions creates unnecessary barriers to growth. In this chapter I address how associations can build flexibility into policies by taking into consideration the operational complexities required for implementation.

This book is based on a considerable amount of research conducted with more than one hundred local, state, national, and international associations. From benchmarking studies conducted by Avenue M Group to explore the effective practices of organizations, to a series of *Decision to...* publications that came from research conducted by ASAE: The Center for Association Leadership, this book synthesizes the data and provides primary tenets behind the art of membership.

To take into account a diversity of budgets, size (in terms of members), geographic scope, industries, and other factors, I introduce a variety of case studies and research to support each idea.

The lessons shared in this book are intended to provide guidance to the following audiences who should be actively engaged in growing their membership:

- Chief executive officers
- Membership and marketing directors whose primary responsibilities include membership recruitment and retention
- Board members and other volunteer leaders engaged in strategic decision making at any type of membership or charitable organization
- Membership managers, coordinators, and customer service representatives who are responsible for implementing the tactical suggestions included in this book

Regardless of your knowledge or experience, this book is designed to help you address the problems your organization faces today and prepare for a robust future.

Acknowledgments

To the following individuals, listed in alphabetical order, I extend my sincere appreciation for sharing their time, stories, and support.

Michael Alter	Jami Kral
Patricia Banks	Gary LaBranche
Chris Bluhm	Colleen Lawler
Paula Cleave	Jim Lecinski
Jennifer Deters	Steve Lieber
Monica Dignam	Scott MacKenzie
Mark Dorsey	David Martin
Gregory Fine	Tom Morrison
Debra Jacobs	Stephen Phelan
Scharan Johnson	Keith Skillman
Jay Karen	Steve Smith

I also wish to acknowledge the Avenue M Group team for all of their contributions: Caitlin Palagi, Maria Berg-Stark, Roya Meshulam, and Linda Wing.

Finally, I am grateful to Suzi Wirtz, the editorial advisor on this book. I could not have written this book without her enthusiastic support and advice.

Bannockburn, Illinois   Sheri Jacobs
December 2013

About the Author

Sheri Jacobs is president and CEO of Avenue M Group, a marketing consulting agency. A senior executive and an association management veteran with more than seventeen years of experience, Sheri applies her experience in research, marketing, strategy, and branding projects to create a unique firm that helps associations meet their goals.

Sheri started her nonprofit career in the development office of the Chicago Children's Museum and moved into marketing after becoming a founding officer of Picture This Projects, a nonprofit group that teaches photography to inner-city children as a means of expression and empowerment. She transitioned from the philanthropic community to the association community in 1994 when she became the director of membership and marketing at the American Academy of Implant Dentistry. She expanded her knowledge when she joined the staff at the American Bar Association in 1999. In 2002, Sheri joined the Association Forum of Chicagoland as the chief marketing officer and director of membership. During her tenure at the Association Forum, she built award-winning campaigns that resulted in double-digit membership and meeting attendance growth.

Sheri is a top-rated speaker and a contributor to various associations and publications, including the ASAE: The Center for Association Leadership publication *Decision to Join*. Sheri is also a past chair for the ASAE Membership Council and the Marketing Council. She is the coeditor of and contributor to ASAE's best-selling membership book, *Membership Essentials* (ASAE, 2007) and the author of the marketing book *199 Ideas: Powerful Marketing Tactics That Sell* (ASAE, 2010). Sheri earned her BA in history and journalism from Indiana University and became a Certified Association Executive in 2003.

When Sheri is not at work, you can usually find her spending time with her daughter, husband, and yellow lab—or training for her next marathon.

THE ART OF MEMBERSHIP

PART ONE

FIND
YOUR
VALUE

Understand the Value Before You Start Selling

WHEN I STARTED WORKING at a small specialty health care association more than fifteen years ago, I asked the executive director why individuals joined our association. This was my entrée into working for professional membership organizations, and my primary responsibility at this particular association was to help grow membership; I felt if I could understand why people joined, I'd have a good handle on how to persuade others to join. The executive director had an interesting perspective, as he had been with the organization for more than ten years, and he was also married to one of the members. He told me that individuals typically joined because they had expanded their practice and needed the specialty information that the association offered. He also said that some members joined because they wanted to earn our credential.

At the time, there were three significant events that appeared likely to impede our ability to grow as an organization. The first was the emergence of the Internet and the potential of newly created, web-based communities that could connect our members to each other without our involvement. A few of our volunteer leaders raised the idea that at some point we could lose members because they simply no longer needed us to connect with one another. The second area of concern was tied to a recent drop in graduate school enrollment in this field. The third was the increasing number of organizations and individuals who were offering continuing education programs, workshops, and conferences.

As I sat in my office, one week into the job, I thought about what my executive director had said. I tried to understand what would motivate nonmembers to join the organization. I also did my homework by examining past research. According to a recent membership study, our members rated our credential program as the most important benefit of membership. As was true of many of our competitors, however, most of our recruitment letters promoted our annual conference, advocacy, and the prestige of belonging to our group—none of these the #1 benefit. We also promised to help members to stay up-to-date on the latest research and techniques through our journal and newsletter— again, not the #1 benefit. Sure, membership included a discount on our educational programs and a frame-worthy certificate, but nonmembers could register and attend our events and subscribe to our journal as well. Some members, of course, joined because they believed in our mission, and they supported our efforts to ensure that they had the right to practice and the tools to be effective and successful. But this reason simply didn't motivate most of the prospective market to join. If we were going to increase our market share not by a little, but by a lot, we needed to better understand what would prompt nonmembers to join.

Since that time, many years ago, I've asked countless association professionals: Why should someone join your organization? Regardless of the organization's size or geographic scope, or the industry, the answers are almost always the same.

We offer *exclusive, members-only benefits* including:

- Advocacy at the state and national levels, including legislative updates and reports
- Print and digital subscription to the professional magazine and/or journal
- Discounts on books, periodicals, and research and trend reports
- Discounts on a wide variety of continuing education offerings— online and in person
- Weekly or monthly email newsletters filled with news and information
- Opportunities to volunteer, take a leadership role, or contribute to the knowledge base

- Networking either for business development or to expand your peer group for professional development
- Career assistance and job placement
- Personal and financial services

But think about it. How many of these benefits are truly unique, exclusive, and, most important, valuable? Sometimes it isn't the benefits themselves that are unique, but how they are bundled. Or the unique benefit could be the prestige of belonging to the organization. Although some individuals will strongly believe in your organization's mission and support your efforts to influence legislation that affects their ability to practice (or work or educate or do business), this will not compel every single person to join. The challenge is compounded by the fact that these days the decision to join may no longer be in the hands of the actual member. As organizations begin to offer new membership models, such as a group billing model, the benefits of belonging to an organization may need to reach beyond the individual and extend to the employer.

Many organizations have gravitated toward the less-is-more concept in recruitment and retention campaign messaging. Consider the ever-popular and simple phrase: *Join today!* And then the subhead: *There are three easy ways to join: sign up online or by phone, or mail your application with payment.* Two words—*join today*—offer a concise call to action, urging prospective members to be a part of your community.

Some organizations focus on the emotional benefits they have identified as "exclusive" to their organization and their members. For example, one association suggests that joining could make you a hero at your company or organization. Another promotes the opportunity to help shape the future. A third invites you to become part of an essential community of peers.

If your organization uses these tactics or similar ones in its marketing collateral and on its website, you are certainly not alone. And you are not wrong in doing so. Many organizations tell prospective members it is easy to join—just sign on the dotted line and submit payment, and you can be a part of the community. If the process is more complex at your organization because you require prospective members to meet certain qualifications, or if they need to join through a state or regional chapter, what I am about to share is relevant to you as well.

Although simplifying the process of joining your organization is helpful, getting prospective members to complete an application form and submit payment is not where the real challenge lies. The real issue for most organizations isn't the process of joining; the challenge is being able to answer the question *why*.

So I'll ask again: Why join? Why renew? What does your association offer that is so unique and so valuable that an individual will pay for membership out of his or her own pocket if the employer stops paying? What does your organization offer that is so essential that members will maintain their dues even if they are in transition or facing a financial hardship? What differentiates members in your community from nonmembers? What are the most compelling reasons to join your organization? Not renew, but join. If you don't know the answer to these questions, you certainly are not alone. The good news is, there is help.

Did You Really Want Lasagna Anyway?

The American workforce is changing. Corporations are acquiring small and mid-sized businesses and practices, and some professionals are becoming employees rather than owners, partners, or practitioners. Of course, this isn't occurring in every field or industry, but there appears to be a significant shift in the workforce today.

How does a changing workforce affect associations? Members and prospects can obtain the continuing education credits they need through work-sponsored education programs. And even the highly valued member discount and members-only access to information on the website can be shared with nonmembers.

If you remove the actual *decision to join* from the hands of the individual, you dramatically change the value proposition. If an organization were to create a group billing program that provided a significant incentive for companies to enroll all of their employees in the organization, the value of its benefits could change, because the price that is being paid to obtain those benefits has changed. For example, let's say your organization offers Company A the opportunity to pay a membership fee that will include unlimited memberships in the organization for its employees. It may also include discounts to your professional development programs. The individuals who are now members of your organization did not have to pay anything to join your organization. As such, if you ask them how much they value different benefits of membership, their perceptions are not based on a fair exchange of fees for services.

Understanding *the primary drivers of membership* goes beyond simply identifying which of your organization's offerings are most *important* to members and prospects. Asking members to rank the importance of the programs, products, and services offered by your association will tell you which of your organization's offerings interest current members, but it will not tell you why you've been unable to convince some prospective members to join. Satisfaction may identify your strengths and weaknesses, as well as areas for improvement, but it will not provide the information you need to determine what actually motivates people to join.

When I explain how measuring interest and satisfaction may not provide you with the information you need in order to determine value, I often share "the lasagna anecdote." Imagine you are invited to a friend's house for dinner. When you arrive, the two of you sit down to a meal that includes a salad and lasagna. When the meal is finished, your friend asks: Did you enjoy everything? Are you satisfied? Are you full? You may have enjoyed the meal (interest may have been high because you were hungry). You may have been very satisfied with what she served (in fact, the meal was delicious!). However, your host didn't ask whether lasagna was what you wanted for dinner. In other words, asking members to rate the importance of your offerings and their satisfaction with those offerings may not give you the insight you need to determine what specifically will prompt nonmembers to join.

Understanding the *primary drivers* of membership helps you communicate the value you offer and what is unique about your organization.

Consider the organization Mothers Against Drunk Driving (MADD). Its mission is to stop drunk driving, support the victims of this violent crime, and prevent underage drinking. All three are worthy goals. In 2011, individual contributions to MADD totaled nearly $6 million. With 197 field locations throughout the United States, MADD has been able to extend its programs to many communities. Although the organization has demonstrated that it has had a successful impact on the problem, and in 2011 the number of alcohol-related driving fatalities was down from prior years, the problem is far from being solved. "About one-third of all drivers arrested or convicted of driving while intoxicated or driving under the influence of alcohol are repeat offenders" (Mothers Against Drunk Driving, 2012, para. 2). And "over 1.41 million drivers were arrested in 2010 for driving under the influence of alcohol or narcotics" (Mothers Against Drunk Driving, 2012, para. 3).

Success, for MADD, is measured in the number of lives saved, and you'd be hard-pressed to find many adults who don't support or agree with the group's important, life-saving legislative initiatives. While many support their efforts to stop drunk driving, individual contributions to MADD don't reflect the general population's support of the organization. MADD seeks financial support through donations rather than from membership dues; therefore, it presents a good example of how individuals may strongly believe in a cause yet not provide financial support in the form of dues.

Simply put, support for your organization's cause or mission may be highly valued and important, but it isn't necessarily essential. In most cases, perceiving that value and importance alone isn't enough to make someone join.

The most convincing evidence that being an advocate for the profession, while important to many, does not motivate everyone to join an organization can be found in the research I've conducted with more than fifteen associations. In each study, we asked participants to select the primary reason they *originally joined* the organization. In each case, the list contained no fewer than ten items (see Table 1.1). The results were not surprising. In fact, most of the associations that participated in the study could have easily predicted the outcome of their survey. Although advocacy was ranked high in terms of importance, on average, less than 20 percent of the member respondents selected advocacy as the primary reason they originally joined their professional association. Our research showed that the primary reason individuals join an organization varies greatly. Using Table 1.1 will help you answer the question *why join?* Notice that we asked the primary reason for *joining* and the primary reason for *renewing*. There is a difference.

Table 1.1.   Primary Reasons to Join and Renew

Value	Primary reason for joining	Primary reason for renewing
Access to specific information		
Advance my career		
Colleague recommendation		
Expand my professional network		
Employer paid my dues		
Gain leadership experience		
Join my local community of peers		
Join my national community of peers		
Join both my local and national community of peers		
Obtain required education credits		
Stay up-to-date		
Support advocacy efforts		
Obtain credibility or prestige		

In the studies we conducted, we found that the most common reasons cited for *joining* a professional organization were to realize *personal benefits* related to accessing job-related information, taking advantage of professional development opportunities, and networking with peers. However, once an individual gains experience, and the need for specific education and information diminishes, I've seen an increase in the value placed on intangible benefits such as advocacy or foundation-related activities.

Understanding the fundamental difference between benefits that are important and the primary drivers of membership is the first step to understanding the marketable value of your organization.

Case Study: The American Physical Therapy Association

Scharan Johnson is the director of membership development for the American Physical Therapy Association (APTA). She heads a team of three people who together undertake the efforts to recruit new members and retain and engage current ones. Over the years, Johnson and her team have learned that physical therapists are most likely to join the organization while they are students. Once they have the exposure to APTA, the first two years after graduation are also most critical to attracting and retaining members. As the team has narrowed the scope of their prospect pool, they understand how important it is to create messages that are most likely to resonate with this audience.

To help APTA address the recruitment challenges they were facing, they engaged my company, Avenue M Group. The first thing we examined was the price sensitivity of students and young professionals. Past research had revealed that although a majority of members are employed full-time, nearly 70 percent pay their own dues. APTA members scrutinize the value they receive, because there is an opportunity cost to joining the association.

"The price of dues is a common objection—in fact, two-thirds of those lapsed members stated this was the primary reason they would not renew their membership," said Johnson (personal communication, January 10, 2013). She also acknowledged that most physical therapists graduate with a significant debt load due to extensive education and clinical training requirements.

As we looked at the APTA's list of benefits, I suggested we label each item based on the criteria shown in Table 1.2.

Next, to simplify matters, I established a simple ranking system for benefits based on whether they were a low, medium, or high driver of membership. In this scenario, I established 1 = Low driver of membership, 2 = Medium driver of membership, and 3 = High driver of membership. To assign the appropriate values,

Table 1.2.   Defining Member Benefits

A	The benefit is **available** to members and nonmembers.
O	The benefit is available to members **only**; nonmembers cannot access the benefit.
F	The benefit is **free to members**; nonmembers can purchase or access the benefit for a fee.
D	The benefit is offered **to members at a discounted price**; nonmembers must pay the full price.

we examined data collected from market research and the results of past membership recruitment campaigns.

Finally, we combined the pricing and the product valuation in a chart (see Table 1.3). Ideally, an association has at least three to four benefits that are high drivers of membership, and either these are exclusive to members or nonmembers must pay a substantial fee to obtain them. A recent graduate of a physical therapy program may appreciate APTA's advocacy efforts, yet it is very unlikely he or she will pay even a nominal fee for this benefit. Therefore, advocacy is assigned a 1 or low driver ranking. On the other hand, information that is easily accessible and highly relevant to their daily work was significantly more likely to be highly valued, so the website and online journal were assigned a 3 or high driver ranking. By promoting only the items of high value and use to this specific audience segment, the APTA has a greater likelihood of recruiting new members and retaining current ones.

Once we completed the process of evaluating the low, medium, and high drivers of membership, APTA could begin to craft statements that truly captured the benefits of joining the organization—not just the "stuff" that new members would receive once they joined. "I think the process really helped us understand how to customize our messages. Looking at your benefits in this one page—a lot of things click—where your benefits really matter," Johnson explained. "You struggle with the idea of trying to sell benefits that advance the profession and those that help the

Table 1.3.   Drivers of APTA Membership

APTA offering	Benefit definition	Physical therapist driver ranking	Student or new grad driver ranking
Association website	O	3	3
Advocacy	A	1	1
Practice and patient care materials	A	3	1
Online journal	F	3	3
Certification program	A	3	2
Public relations tools	O	2	1
Print journal	F	2	2
Annual conference	D	2	2
Consumer website	A	2	2
Volunteer opportunities	O	2	2
Find a PT	O	1	1
Jobs career center	A	1	3

Note: 1 = low driver, 2 = medium driver, 3 = high driver. See Table 1.2 for benefit definitions.

members, but it's finding that balance" (Scharan Johnson, personal communication, January 10, 2013).

The Next-Best Alternative

Understanding the specific value of your benefits—that is, whether they are low, medium, or high drivers of membership—is only part of the story. You need to also know the *next-best alternative.*

Are your benefits scarce, or are they widely available? Are there a limited number of alternatives, or none at all? If so, the value may be higher, and you can charge more to obtain it. If the next-best alternative is of equal value (or even slightly lower value), you may need to lower the *value* you assign to your organization's benefit as a key driver of membership.

If you work in a field that requires practitioners to obtain a certain number of hours of education in order to maintain a license, professional development may be one of your *primary benefits of membership*. But they are benefits, not drivers. These benefits are the so-called "golden handcuffs" used to create strong bonds between associations and their members. Some organizations compete with their chapters, state, or specialty associations. Others compete with the employers of their members. And some associations compete with for-profit companies that offer free continuing education to their clients or customers. Even if your professional development programs are highly rated by attendees, these may not be a high driver of membership for nonmembers who can easily access the same "benefit" from any one of many different sources.

Generational differences, advances in technology, and a downturn in the economy may have a great impact or very little impact on the decision to join. These factors, while important to acknowledge and consider because they may influence the decision to select an alternative offering, do not obviate the need to stay up-to-date, earn continuing education, and network with peers.

Action Steps

Conduct a Membership Value Study

A member value study goes beyond typical satisfaction surveys and will help you learn what is needed to retain members. A membership value study may be combined with a membership needs assessment, and it can also be conducted as a stand-alone survey. The goal of conducting this research is to measure the value of your benefits in terms of being a primary or secondary reason to belong to your association—or *not* a reason. Ideally, the benefits that are most important—your must-haves—are significantly better than the next-best alternative in the marketplace. Although

According to the Marketing General (MGI) Membership Marketing Benchmarking Report, the top reason members do not renew is *lack of value* (Marketing General Incorporated, 2012). If members believed the value they received outweighed the cost, they would find a way to maintain their membership even if they were experiencing a financial hardship or a lacked the financial support from their employer (see Table 1.4).

Table 1.4. Reasons for Not Renewing Membership

Budget cuts (lack of value)	17%
Lack of engagement (lack of value)	14%
Employer won't pay or stopped paying dues (lack of value)	12%
Could not justify membership costs with any significant ROI (lack of value)	11%
Lack of value	11%
Left the field	8%
Too expensive (lack of value)	5%
Forgot to renew	4%
Lack of relevance (lack of value)	3%

Source: Adapted from Marketing General Incorporated, 2012.

you may hope to learn what is unique and valuable about your organization, it is also helpful to learn what *isn't* working for your members. If you can identify the offerings that need to be changed or modified in order to provide true value, you may strengthen your relationships with existing members, in addition to recruiting many more new members.

Determine Willingness to Pay

One method for measuring value is by asking about a prospect's willingness to pay (WTP). WTP is the total amount people would pay to either obtain something they want or need or avoid something undesirable. This method is sometimes used for things that can't be valued in any other way, such as intangible benefits. Many believe that an individual's willingness to pay can vary based on a personal assessment of value. It can also be tied to branding and the perceptions of value that have been created by an organization that developed the brand.

As an analogy, think about the process of purchasing art. Imagine it is a warm summer day and you've made plans to attend a juried art fair. As you walk slowly through the aisles, one piece of art catches your eye. The artist has assembled just the right combination of colors and texture. You start to imagine the artwork on the wall above your fireplace. The artwork may have a price tag, but there isn't any way to compare the price or determine its tangible value. It is an original piece of art, and you haven't seen anything like it before. The value of the artwork is what you are willing to pay for it. Your willingness to pay is based on your perception of value and your financial ability to pay.

Now consider another example of willingness to pay. John and Sue buy apps for their iPads. John is willing to spend up to $.99 per app. He uses his iPad primarily for personal reasons and typically spends about one hour per day on it. Sue, on the other hand, uses her iPad for both professional and personal reasons. She relies heavily on her iPad to read books, make travel plans, track expenses, and play games. Sue is willing to pay up to $4.99 for a single app.

A disadvantage to asking open-ended questions regarding WTP is that you may wrongly assume people are willing to pay far more than they actually would if the situation becomes a reality. You must do the math: the total market demand is the sum of the quantities demanded by different individuals with different levels of willingness to pay.

Perform a Conjoint Analysis

When determining the value of the membership package, ask questions about whether the member or prospect values one item over another. For example, "Which is more important to you: (1) educational webinars or (2) local networking events?" Once this question is answered, the researcher asks a follow-up question, such as, "Would you be willing to pay $X for the option you chose?" This approach, referred to as a "conjoint analysis," is a technique some people use to measure how people value different features or benefits. The benefit of conducting a conjoint analysis is that you can understand which attributes are most influential in the decision to join, register, or make a purchase.

Taking it a step further, organizations can also ask current members how much they are willing to pay for an incremental reduction or increase in benefits. This type of trade-off study may help you understand the value and price sensitivity for many of the benefits you offer through membership. (Note: This technique is difficult to use when you wish to ask members or prospects to express a benefit's perceived value or their attitudes toward new programs, products, or features.)

Examine the competition. Look at your five highest-rated benefits in terms of value, then identify every possible competitor. If you have only three or four benefits that are truly unique and valuable, that's okay. In fact, it's more than okay! You don't need five or ten (or twenty-five) benefits to have a strong value proposition. Begin your competitive analysis as if you were a prospective customer. What would you find? What associations do you compete with for a share of your members' wallets and time? Can members and prospects find solutions through their employers or other companies that offer similar products and services—for free or at a lower cost? How does your combination of features and price compare to your competitors'? Do your members share some of the highly valued benefits of membership—namely, their copies of your journal or magazine, or the discounts they receive on programs and products—with their colleagues who are not members? Keep in mind that your competition doesn't include only other organizations that offer similar products and services; your organization may be competing with companies and entities that have never served your audience but could easily enter the marketplace.

A Real But Overlooked Threat

The history of modern enterprise is filled with stories of companies that were once leaders in their field and today no longer exist because they made two important mistakes. First, they did not completely understand what business they were in; second, they failed to consider all of the potential sources of competition. When Kodak filed for bankruptcy in February of 2012, some experts blamed its demise on management's inability to fully understand that it was in the storytelling business, not the production and selling of photographic equipment (Munir, 2012). Although the Kodak brand was built on the idea of helping consumers capture a *Kodak moment*, some people believe it lost sight of its mission and simply ignored technology innovations that dramatically changed how, when, and where people captured moments.

Additionally, according to Munir (2012), a teacher and reader in strategy and policy at Cambridge Judge Business School, University of Cambridge, "Kodak did not realize its own limitations, and consequently its strategy for revival never had much of a chance."

From well-established companies to young entrepreneurs, it is becoming easier than ever before to enter an established field and grab market share from well-respected brands. Competition has increased substantially because it is easy to conduct a search on the Internet for the best possible solution at the lowest possible price. Consider this: if I am looking for a book on market research, I have thousands of options. A quick search on Amazon for a *market research* book shows 411,150 results. I can purchase the book in paperback, hardcover, a Kindle edition, an audio edition, MP3 version, and in CD format. If I prefer to do my searching in person among physical books, I can visit my local bookstore or a library. College and university bookstores also offer a wide selection of books and periodicals on market research. Finally, I could turn to a number of associations, such as the American Marketing Association, the Marketing Research Association, and the Interactive Market Research Association, to name just a few. However, if I am interested in learning how professional associations use market research to examine the needs of their members, my options are considerably more limited. The value of a market research book published by ASAE: The Center for Association Leadership on this specific topic may be higher, because the information cannot be obtained from thousands of other sources. It's far more specific, and therefore very valuable.

Truly understanding the value of your benefits, the next-best alternative, and the needs of the marketplace will help your organization remain nimble and capable of adjusting to technology innovations and changes in the economy. The other side of the value coin is the scarcity or uniqueness of your benefit. Sometimes benefits are commodities; when that is the case, you need to create something truly unique if you wish to consider the benefit part of your value proposition.

Determine Value Before Bundling or Pricing a la Carte

Let's assume that some individuals who join your organization in order to help advance your cause or support your advocacy efforts will become members regardless of the benefits package you offer in exchange for membership dues. If you remove this group from the prospect pool, you are left with individuals who are weighing the tangible benefits of membership. Does membership in your organization provide enough perceived value to outweigh the cost?

Offering a la carte pricing instead of bundling benefits creates certain advantages. A la carte pricing allows prospects to select the items that hold the most relevant value to them as individuals. It also shows prospects the value assigned by the association to various products. Therefore, when bundling your benefits, you should consider offering a base membership with enough valuable benefits to outweigh the cost and offer other benefits on an a la carte basis.

Consider the Honda Pilot. This vehicle has a variety of features that come standard at its base price. You can purchase the entry-level Honda Pilot well equipped with everything from hands-free Bluetooth to safety features such as side curtain airbags and a rearview camera, without having to pay anything extra to receive these benefits. On the other hand, if you are looking to buy a new car and you know that you do not want, need, or wish to pay extra for features you will not use, the bundled base package of the Honda Pilot may be a deterrent.

Although bundling provides a financial benefit to associations, prospective members will also benefit from some bundles, if you position your bundle as a way to save money or provide specialized guidance. Individuals who are price sensitive and need to obtain the items you offer in a bundled membership in order to practice or maintain their license will appreciate a *good deal* if they see a considerable cost savings. Others may be looking for advice on what they need to advance to the next stage of their career.

Here is the reality check: if a prospective member can already access or obtain the information they need for free or at a low cost through another source, attend business networking events, and expand their network through LinkedIn or other sites, does membership provide enough unique and tangible value in return for the cost of joining?

Weigh the Risks Carefully Before Making Changes

Every action carries risk. The financial implications of changes to your benefits structure are just one thing to consider. The following are some of the risks associated with changing your benefits structure.

Risk #1: Membership Studies Tell You Only What Your Current Members Value, Not What Nonmembers Value

Why do some individuals join while others do not? It's a question that many organizations struggle with when trying to recruit nonmembers. Although a membership study can provide valuable insight into what motivates members to join and renew, it may not tell you why nonmembers have yet to sign up. In addition, levels of awareness may have a significant effect on the results of your membership study. Although I belong to many associations, my awareness of all of the programs, products, and services offered is very low in some cases. That is why I recommend a more robust approach to determining value. Each step identified in this chapter will provide you with a more complete picture of value based on membership status. In Chapter Two I go over the different types of member segments that should also be considered when determining the value of different benefits.

Risk #2: You Could Undermine Current Perceptions of Value

A la carte pricing can be perceived as: (1) flexible, because you give members and prospects the option of paying for only the products they use, or (2) stingy, because you've removed many of the perks included with membership. Consider the reaction of the traveling public when the airlines changed its pricing structure in 2008.

The airline industry reportedly made these changes in response to increasing fuel costs and declining revenues. Spirit's senior vice president, Barry Biffle, reported, "Instead of raising every fare in response to ever increasing fuel prices, our new luggage policy gives passengers the opportunity to control their cost of travel by packing lighter" (Stoller, 2008, para. 9). And in fact, according to Henrickson and Scott (2011), studies of this change revealed that airlines were able to keep prices low and compete with low-cost alternatives because of the revenue derived from the a la carte pricing structure.

To avoid being charged a checked baggage fee, however, an increasing number of passengers began carrying their bags to the gate. Business travelers became frustrated with the limited amount of space in the overhead storage bins and flights were delayed to accommodate the last-minute checking of bags. And according to a J.D. Power and Associates press release about their 2012 North America Airline Satisfaction Study, overall passenger satisfaction with traditional carriers has declined. So the jury is still out on whether this was the right move.

Risk #3: Changes to Your Benefits Package Could Have Major Financial Implications

If you change your membership model to one that asks members to pay for only what they use, you could risk losing financial support for programs that do not generate their own revenue. Therefore it is essential that you make financial projections based on a variety of scenarios of support. If some scenarios result in a significant reduction in income, you will need to identify other reliable sources—or reconsider that particular scenario.

Benefit Value Checklist

Use this checklist to determine how to price products or bundle benefits:

1. Is the program, product, or service a low, medium, or high driver of membership?
2. How many units were sold in the past year, and what was the weighted average price per unit?
3. Does the product meet a practice requirement (such as continuing education) or does it help with practice management (such as building or maintaining a practice)? Products that meet a practice requirement fulfill a need, whereas those that help with practice management are nice to have but not essential to earning a living.
4. Can members acquire the product from a competitor? If so, how do your features and costs compare?
5. If the product has been on the market for at least a year, what are the recent sales trends? Have sales of the product increased, decreased, or remained the same over the last three years?
6. Are there ways to enhance the product?
7. Are there opportunities to bundle the product and provide a discount for two products if purchased together?

Table 1.5. Asset Audit Template

Offering	Segment 1		Segment 2	
	Price	Value	Price	Value
Federal advocacy				
State advocacy				
Journal (print)				
Journal (online edition)				
Journal (mobile edition)				
Volunteer opportunities				
Standards and guidelines				
Certification program				
Closed social media community				
Discounts on educational programs				

Although these suggestions may seem counterintuitive, the ways in which people want to engage with an association vary. It's much like assembling ingredients in a stew: each individual ingredient doesn't have much impact by itself, but as they cook together, they blend to create the right balance.

2

Value Is in the Eye of the Beholder

I AM A MEMBER OF FOUR PROFESSIONAL ASSOCIATIONS. And I am not alone. According to the Pew Internet & American Life Project (Hampton, Goulet, Rainie, & Purcell, 2011), about three out of four Americans belong to at least one voluntary association; additionally, from the research I've conducted with more than thirty professional associations, I've discovered that most individuals belong to more than one association.

Like many of these members, I have limited availability to volunteer, contribute, speak, and participate in events. I am active in only two of the four associations I belong to. Although I realize there are many opportunities to increase my engagement by serving on a committee or attending a networking event, I just don't have the time. And sometimes I am simply not interested. I join some organizations to network, grow my business, and meet other individuals who share similar interests. I join other organizations because I want to receive their monthly magazine or access information on their website. I may not have the time or even be interested in volunteering or attending their networking events.

For each one of these organizations in which I'm actively engaged, the decision to renew is relatively easy. I typically respond to the first or second renewal notice. My lifetime value to the organization is high because I am a regular attendee at most meetings and I purchase many of their books and publications. It seems an obvious assumption that if the other two organizations could move me up the engagement ladder, there would be a greater likelihood that I will renew. In fact, this isn't just an assumption. I've conducted numerous membership research studies that showed the more a member is engaged, the greater the likelihood that he or she will renew.

There is only one problem. I am not interested in becoming a more engaged member in the other organizations, nor do I have the capacity to do so. I enjoy reading their publications and downloading articles or research papers to my laptop or tablet, but that is where my engagement ends—and I don't see that changing in the future.

When it comes time to renew, it's an easy decision. I simply ask myself, "Were my needs met over the past year?" Keep in mind that my needs differ based on the level of engagement I have with each group. As an active volunteer and participant in two of the organizations, I am looking for opportunities to network, share ideas, attend events, and contribute to the body of knowledge in the industry. For the other two organizations, I will be satisfied with my membership if it provides enough information or content in exchange for the cost of dues. It's really pretty simple.

There are two reasons I am sharing this story. First, not all members need to or want to move up an engagement ladder in order to be highly satisfied with their membership. Associations tend to focus on recruiting, retaining, and engaging members; they define engagement as volunteering, contributing, attending meetings and other events, or actively participating in the advancement of the field. What is more important than level of engagement, however, is the combination of cost, value, and satisfaction. In other words, members will happily pay the price of membership if the organization provides useful solutions to the problems they face.

Second (and this is a very large departure from the typical and traditional membership survey metrics!), demographics such as age, work setting, or title are not always the best predictor of whether someone will join an organization or the level to which that person will become engaged. Interests, needs, motivations, and attitudes should also be taken into consideration.

To support this theory, I examined the data collected from ten individual membership organizations in a variety of industries. In each membership needs assessment, we asked the following questions:

1. What is the primary reason you originally joined the association? (Select only one of the following reasons)
2. How would you rate your satisfaction with the association's ability to deliver what you need? (Scale of 1 to 5, with 5 = Very satisfied)
3. How likely are you to renew your membership next year?

Although the results were not surprising—the higher the respondent's satisfaction, the more likely they were to renew—I believe many organizations overlook the significance of this finding. There is a direct correlation between satisfaction and renewals, but members may be highly satisfied with their membership if the reason they joined (consequently, if the promise your organization makes) is fulfilled. On the other hand, if your research reveals that the members who are most likely to renew are those who are actively engaged, then the real issue that needs to be solved is identifying ways to deliver more value to unengaged members.

Two Similar Members; One Major Difference

To illustrate this point, I will share a story about Greg and Steve. In many ways, Greg and Steve are very similar. They were both born in the late 1960s—members of Generation X. They both work in the same city and are employed by organizations with similar size budgets and staff. Last year, both Steve and Greg became CEOs. So at this point, their demographics reveal they are of the same generation, have similar work settings, and have the same title.

Although both men are highly respected in the community, and they've provided leadership to their organizations during challenging economic times, Greg and Steve choose different routes to stay informed and up-to-date on changes in the industry. Greg is very active at the national level; he volunteers his time by serving on committees and speaking at industry events, and he makes it a priority to attend the annual conference each year. Steve, on the other hand, has attended only one national conference over the last five years. Although his level of engagement would be defined as low, he is completely satisfied with his membership because he finds value in the online resources and print publications. He feels very connected to his peers by engaging in the online private community, and he frequently purchases or downloads reports and publications.

In both cases, if the individual's perception of the value delivered by the organization were to diminish, he might eventually no longer maintain his membership. Yet for each, the needs are distinctly different. For Greg, if volunteer and networking opportunities were reduced, he might become less satisfied. For Steve, if the organization failed to deliver relevant content, he might reconsider his membership.

For individuals who wish to network with peers or give back to the community, an association can provide a unique outlet or opportunity. On the other hand, individuals who are seeking information or education are more likely to assess the return on the investment of their dues. They may consider other options for obtaining the information they need. If the value offered through membership is the combination of networking, volunteer opportunities, and access to information, and you are only interested in obtaining information, the price for admission may simply be too high to pay.

The key to achieving member loyalty and retention is synchronizing cost and value. If associations create a membership package that provides the most value to members who volunteer, participate, and engage, it's possible that they may not provide enough value at the lower levels of engagement. And these levels are critical to keeping the organization relevant.

Dig Deeper Than Demographics

Now, I want to paint a different scenario, one that allows Greg and Steve to select their dues and benefits based on their individual needs rather than their membership classifications. Classifying individuals based only on demographic factors such as birth year (generation), gender, work setting, or title may be of little use, because these groups sometimes have little more in common than those traditionally defined characteristics or traits.

At the same time, many associations classify members based on a number of other factors, such as the number of years they've been in practice or their position within their company. Then again, some organizations classify members by academic achievements or certifications, making them eligible for the most active level of membership in the organization. Few organizations, however, structure their benefits based on the needs and interests of the individual, regardless of their income, title, work setting, or years in practice.

This historical association membership model, interestingly enough, is rarely replicated in the for-profit world. Take Costco, for example. Costco boasts a membership of more than fifty million people. The company offers three types of membership: Executive, Business, and Gold Star. If an individual is interested in joining Costco, he or she may select the category of membership based on need, interest, and price rather than the individual's own title. The Executive Membership offers the same benefits as the Business Membership, with some additional perks for an extra fee. Designed to reward the business executive who purchases products for business and personal use, the Executive Membership offers 2 percent cash back on merchandise purchases. Costco doesn't ask for your title, how many years you've been in business, your age, and so on. (But note, Costco does offer a full money-back guarantee on membership dues if at any time you are not completely satisfied with your membership.)

Let's look at health clubs. Although health clubs are one of the fastest-growing industries in the United States, they have not been immune to the effects of the recent downturn in the economy. When the United States went into a recession and individuals began cutting back on discretionary spending, many fitness centers began to rethink their membership model. The result was the creation of alternatives to the prevailing high monthly membership fee with a year's commitment up front. For example, some gyms now offer month-to-month memberships or a low base price with additional charges based on, you guessed it, individual needs. If gym members wish to use the pool or tennis courts because that is what they enjoy doing, their price is adjusted based on what they value.

The Whitney Museum of American Art (the Whitney) is another example of a membership model that is built around allowing the individual to select what he or she wants based on interest and usage rather than traditional demographics. It is one of the very few nonprofit examples I could uncover that employs this model. But I'm convinced it has far-reaching merit and is something associations need to consider immediately.

Based in New York City, the Whitney Museum of American Art, known for its range of twentieth-century and contemporary American art, invites prospective members to custom design their membership through a "Curate Your Own Membership" program (Whitney Museum of American Art, 2013). The core benefits (and they do refer to them as "core") include unlimited admission, members-only viewing hours, a 20 percent discount on the museum store, and reciprocal admission to other art museums. The tagline alone says it all: "Customize your experience and maximize your benefits" (Whitney Museum of American Art, 2013, para. 1).

What is unique about this model is that the Whitney does not predefine members based on any one type of demographic. A social member could be a young professional, or she could be someone nearing retirement. And because benefits that are of high interest to one group may not be of interest to another, a member has the opportunity to customize or "curate" a membership to fit individual interests.

The Whitney offers five different types of membership modules based on interests: *Social, Insider, Learning, Family,* and *Philanthropy* (Whitney Museum of American Art, 2013). The fee for each module or series is $40, and members may select as many series as they desire.

Curate Your Membership

The *Social Membership* offers four passes to the summer cocktail reception to preview new exhibits, an invitation for two to the annual champagne reception for networking, ongoing invitations to cultural events through NYC— including receptions, gallery openings, and art fairs—and two guest passes to entertain friends or colleagues.

The *Insider Membership* provides an invitation for two to a behind-the-scenes tour of the museum including normally restricted areas, exclusive presentations by curatorial staff, and quarterly recommendations from curators and art insiders about other activities not to miss in NYC.

The *Learning Membership* offers invitations to lecture series that examine key issues in contemporary American art, invitations to gallery talks led by art historians, educational packets for major exhibitions to give special insight, and advance notice and preferred registration for all public programs.

The *Family Membership* focuses on benefits for children, including a Whitney Kids Passport, free admission to family programs, discounts on Stroller Tours when the museum is closed to the public, family guides for major exhibitions, complimentary guest passes for family caregivers, and advance notice for all family programs.

The *Philanthropy Membership* does not provide any additional benefits but offers members the opportunity to provide additional, tax-deductible support for the Museum.

In addition to the membership series, the Whitney offers patron groups designed to align members' interests with the museum's mission. These groups, which range in price from $2,500 to $25,000, offer individuals the opportunity to enjoy unique experiences (and clearly gives the museum a great opportunity to raise additional revenue). The Chairman's Council is considered the most prestigious patron group. It was designed to engage collectors and art patrons with exclusive programming and unparalleled access to emerging and master artists. Experiences include visits to artist studios, private art collections, travel opportunities, and behind-the-scenes activities. Other patron groups focus on education, preservation and documentation, young collectors, and early- to mid-twentieth-century American art.

When the museum began this program several years ago, it seemed to be the only museum to test-drive such a notion.

According to an artdaily.org article (Villarreal, 2010), the Whitney's director of membership and annual fund, Kristen Shepherd Denner, reported,

> To our knowledge, the Whitney is the first museum to offer its members a chance to personalize their way of belonging to the institution. . . . Museum memberships are generally centered on demographics. By tapping into each individual's core values and allowing them to customize their benefits, we hope to deliver a bespoke membership that is meaningful to them personally and responds directly to their interests and needs. Our goal is to give members a richer, more rewarding experience at the Whitney and communicate with them in a more relevant way. We want their relationship with us to grow [para. 2].

In a subsequent blog interview (Simon, 2010), Denner elaborated: "Some experiences completely cut across demographics. Some people like parties, some people want a solitary experience with art . . . and that solitary experience person might be 20 or they might be 80" (para. 4).

When a Member Says "No"

In their book *The Decision to Join*, authors James Dalton and Monica Dignam (2007) state, "A person's decision to join an individual membership organization is *not* a cost-benefit analysis" (p. 1).

According to the authors, the decision to join "involves a balancing act between a calculation of what's in it for me and for us" (p. 6). While there may be some truth in this finding when it comes to an association's loyal members, it does not necessarily hold true for individuals who have chosen not to join or who have let their membership lapse. Understanding why some individuals choose not to renew their membership is as important as understanding why individuals join. The obvious answer is that nonmembers—both those who have never been members as well as lapsed members—do not believe there is enough value.

To support this statement, consider one of the key findings from the 2012 Membership Marketing Benchmarking Report conducted by Marketing General Incorporated (MGI; 2012), considered by many to be the most exhaustive and comprehensive study in the industry. When more than 690 association executives were asked to cite the primary reason why former members choose to let their membership lapse, *lack of value* rose to the top of the list.

In addition to the findings from the MGI study, I examined research I've conducted over the last three years with lapsed members from five individual membership organizations. I began by reviewing the answers to two questions: "What is the primary reason you let your membership lapse?" and "To rejoin the association, I would primarily need . . ." The results supported the findings from the MGI study. More than half of the respondents in each study cited a reason consistent with the theory that lack of value was the primary cause for dropping the membership (Table 2.1). Furthermore, if the association were to provide additional resources of value, nearly half of the lapsed members would consider rejoining the organization (Table 2.2).

A Different Approach to Profiling

Real estate's mantra has long been *location, location, location*. For associations, it's *value, value, value*. I believe that if you want to attract nonmembers and retain existing members who are at risk of leaving, you need to understand the relevant value and deliver it for the right price. While my recommended approach isn't breaking news, it may be new for many. To create and deliver value, you need to consider the different reasons individuals join an organization.

Table 2.1. Reasons for Dropping Membership

What is the primary reason you let your membership lapse? (Data is aggregated)	
The cost of membership dues exceeded the value I received	27%
Lack of relevancy/Information too basic	15%
My company/organization will no longer pay my dues	12%
No time to participate	12%
No longer in the field	8%
Unemployed	3%
Other	23%

Source: Avenue M Group, LLC, 2010–2013.

Table 2.2. Getting Lapsed Members to Rejoin

Please complete the following sentence: To rejoin the association, I would primarily need . . . (select all that apply)	
Additional resources of value for my dues	44%
More relevant professional development opportunities	39%
More conferences held closer to where I work	30%
More resources available online	26%
Organizational funding	23%
Additional opportunities to interact with my peers	10%
More opportunities to volunteer and share my knowledge	5%
Other	24%

Source: Avenue M Group, LLC, 2010–2013.

As you reflect back on the story of Greg and Steve, two individuals who demographically appear similar in many ways but value different things, you'll see that your organization needs to provide real value at every level of engagement if you wish to attract and retain both types of members. Taking this one step further, consider another member of the professional community, Rachel.

Rachel is in her late twenties, a member of Generation Y. She is new to the association profession but has nearly five years of marketing experience from her previous position at a large consumer goods company. She's eager to learn about the industry and enjoys attending local events and educational conferences. Rachel and Greg appear very different in terms of their demographic profile. They are from different generations. Rachel is a woman; Greg is a man. They have vastly different resumes. Yet, Greg, as an active, involved member, has more in common with Rachel than he does with Steve, his fellow Gen X-er. If asked to rate the importance of staying up-to-date on changes in the industry, all three would rate this as very important. They all wish to succeed in their chosen field. All three value the work their association is doing to advance the profession. They simply want to interact with the association on their own terms, in ways that provide the most value to them as individuals.

Given the differences in how individuals wish to stay informed despite their common demographic traits, it makes sense to expand your definition of the types of members you wish to attract and retain at your organization. Instead of thinking of members in terms of experience, industry, title, or other obvious common factors, think of members in terms of their individual motivations, attitudes, and interests. The intersection of attitudes, needs, and importance may well be the best predictor of how individuals will respond to a call for action—to join, contribute, register, volunteer, or renew.

Why is it important to understand your members and prospects at a deeper level? From a predictability standpoint, creating member profiles will help an organization develop new membership categories that will allow individuals to select the benefits they value, want, and need. This will enable organizations to estimate their members' valuations and ultimately to create better marketing strategies. It should also help organizations retain members who are not actively engaged and have no plans to "move up the engagement ladder."

Now that I've established that not all members think the same based on common characteristics or demographics, I wish to introduce a different approach to creating membership categories. This approach is built around interest, need, motivation, and personal preference rather than position or title. It is designed from the members' perspective and can be priced based on value and offerings. Some of these categories may not apply to your organization; however, most associations will have some members that fall into many of these groups.

1. Information Seekers. Some individuals join to access information, opinions, or research. This may be the primary reason they join or a secondary reason. In both instances, they are *Information Seekers*. Although technology may change how information is delivered or accessed, these individuals' desire to stay up-to-date on industry practices and trends tends to remain constant. Because they are avid consumers of information, these individuals will value timely and useful information they can use in their professional lives. Depending on their technology usage and preferences, they may access information either digitally or through print subscriptions. Organizations with a high percentage of members who fall into this category must be prepared to deliver information based on the needs of these individuals today—as well as invest in technology and resources to ensure that they meet future needs.

An organization can offer varying levels of access based on interest and price. In addition, organizations can curate information on numerous topics and provide information seekers a bonus benefit that includes a "best of" series of articles.

One risk to creating a member segment focused on delivering value to information seekers is that it may be difficult to monitor or police access because *nonmembers* may use the membership account of a colleague in order to access information.

In addition, information seekers may find there are many other opportunities or resources to gain information. Associations often compete with companies or other nonprofits that offer the information for a lower price or at no charge. Therefore, associations will need to identify value-added opportunities to attract and retain members who are information seekers.

2. Lifelong Learners. Some individuals are drawn to their professional societies because they have a strong desire to pursue knowledge—even though it isn't required to maintain a license, practice, or position. Lifelong learners may have different motivations behind their pursuit of education. They may believe that it provides them with a competitive edge, or they may pursue it for personal and intellectual reasons. Lifelong learners attend conferences and read journals and books because they want to, not because it is required. Individuals who join an organization to fulfill the need to grow or actively contribute may seek a variety of benefits from their membership, including education, volunteer opportunities, and networking. With the advent of online learning, social media, and digital communication, lifelong learning is no longer restricted to those who wish to attend in-person events. With advances in technology that now provide convenient access to thought leaders, faculty, and instructors, associations have many opportunities to connect with members based on their interests and preferences.

3. Continuing Education (CE) Requirement Members. Many fields and industries require individuals to obtain continuing education in order to maintain their license. In years past, associations were often one of only a few providers of high-quality education that helped fulfill this requirement. Today, individuals can turn to their employer, other nonprofit organizations, and even supplier partners or vendors to obtain free or very low-cost CE. As such, individuals who may have joined an organization to maintain CE requirements may find that membership no longer carries the same level of importance or urgency. Some organizations have responded to the changes in the CE environment by including free CE as part of the membership package. While this tactic may provide additional value, it can also create a new segment of members who join and renew primarily to receive this benefit. In addition, individuals who can obtain free CE from their employer or other sources may no longer feel there is enough value in exchange for their membership dues.

4. Thought Leaders—Current and Aspiring. Forbes.com (2012) defines a thought leader as "an individual or firm that prospects, clients, referral sources, intermediaries and even competitors recognize as one of the foremost authorities in selected areas of specialization, resulting in its being the go-to individual or organization for said expertise."

Every organization has its thought leaders. Some are well established; others aspire to this role. They join the organization because they wish to share their knowledge, and they frequently seek recognition or acknowledgment for their expertise. These thought leaders may be very interested in serving on committees or working groups. Some individuals see this as an opportunity to raise their profile within the industry or community. They may contribute for different reasons at different times. If they are looking to advance within their company or obtain a new position that would be considered a promotion, they will find value in the opportunity to be published, speak at a conference, or be asked to serve on a prestigious committee or working group.

5. Rising Stars and Networkers. In the association world, networking has many definitions. It can help members build critical relationships that can result in new business opportunities and career advancement. Although there are many ways to gain a competitive edge or land a new position, some individuals turn to their professional association in order to expand their network. These individuals are the association's rising stars and networkers. In some instances, a rising star could be someone who is mid-career and finally has the time invest in their own career advancement. They want to grow professionally and increase their influence in the industry.

In recent years, networking has expanded from occurring primarily at in-person events and volunteer assignments to now include online networking and social platforms. Rising stars and networkers value exclusivity and opportunity. They are more likely to respond to calls for volunteers and encourage nonmembers to join and become active in the organization. Networkers and rising stars are often driven by a desire for success but also wish to give back and mentor others. Rising stars and networkers tend to be very loyal to an organization once they've made the commitment to join.

6. Mission Members believe very strongly in the purpose of the organization. They do not evaluate *what's in it for me?* because they join and renew to support the overall purpose and efforts of the organization. They are interested in advancing the field and may wish to participate in conversations focused on this topic. Mission members are often the most loyal members. They are also promoters of the organization and are likely to recommend membership to their friends and colleagues. You may see a lot of members who fit the profile of both a mission member and a thought leader.

7. Prestige Members. Some people view membership in a professional association as a way to add credibility and prestige to their resume or professional profile. These individuals may join because it will enhance their reputation among their peers, clients, customers, business partners, or patients. Organizations that require a rigorous application process that may include meeting certain qualifications or receiving an endorsement from another member could have a higher percentage of members who fall into this category. Associations with an international population may also have a number of members who join for prestige reasons. Exclusivity is important to these types of members, as they wish to differentiate themselves from nonmembers.

8. Uninvolved Members. Uninvolved members do not volunteer or attend in-person events or conferences. They do not engage in online or in-person networking events and often have limited interest in the educational opportunities offered by the association. Although uninvolved members come from all audience segments, it is helpful to identify any common traits for the uninvolved members within your organization. Retention rates for uninvolved members are typically lower than for the other member categories and will continue to be unless an organization can identify new opportunities to provide value—however, the value should not require them to become active members.

9. **Transactional Members.** Transactional members join organizations to save money. They are customers who become members because it makes financial sense. They may or may not care about your mission, vision, and core values. If they do care, it will not have an impact on their decision to join or renew. For these individuals, if the cost to join is less than the amount a nonmember must pay to attend a conference or purchase a product, the decision is easy. Organizations with a high percentage of

transactional members may experience high churn rates if they are unable to demonstrate an ongoing financial benefit of membership. Many organizations may claim to have few transactional members; they may point to their own member research that shows high levels of interest and satisfaction with their offerings. Yet these types of members exist in every organization. Identifying transactional members within your organization will enable you to market future offerings based on financial motivations.

In some situations, transactional members may actually cause more harm than good if the cost to acquire them as members is high and their retention rate, and subsequent lifetime value, are low. On the other hand, if a goal of your organization is to gain or maintain a high market share within your industry, you may want to design a new membership model that encourages transactional members to join and renew. The most common model used by associations to accomplish this goal is a group membership program with significant discounts and benefits for participating organizations.

Matching Benefits with Reasons to Join

Correlating the reasons a member joins to the individual needs and, therefore, the perceived value for each of those individuals is paramount to the next step. This is the point at which you must ask: What is the value of holding a membership card for our organization?

If you begin with a fee that allows any individual or company to join your organization, and that is based on the overall value of simply belonging to membership, then all other benefits can be offered a la carte based on individual interests and needs. Over time, interests and needs may change; however, you will be giving members the flexibility of selecting what they need when they need it, and ultimately increasing retention rates of at-risk members (those most likely to drop their membership because the value isn't the same).

With this "customized" model, an organization can offer a somewhat lower fee to join and create an affordable membership model that is inclusive. Before you begin to construct this model at your organization, you need to learn more about your members and prospects. Through market research and member profiling, you should identify the various types of members and their interests, attitudes, and values. Once you know your member base, you can create a base membership model and add-ons that deliver relevant value.

Most people are familiar with the most common individual membership model, which offers a few *benefits*, unique to members only, in exchange for a fee. This typically includes a subscription to a print and/or digital magazine or journal and access to information, articles, research, and other resources on the organization's website. In addition to the free benefits, many organizations offer members a discount on continuing education, books, and practice management resources. In some cases, the discount is designed to create a significant price difference between the member rate and the nonmember rate, because organizations wish to encourage nonmembers to join at the point of purchase. This membership model is currently in use by hundreds, if not thousands of individual membership organizations in the United States.

If your organization is struggling to attract new members, or even to retain current ones, this model may simply be out-of-date for your organization and your industry. Sometimes the needed change can be small—perhaps adding more relevant value to the overall membership package. In other cases, dramatic changes are necessary in order to reverse a downward trend in membership. The two membership models described in the following section take into consideration changes in the workforce, advances in technology, and the current economic climate.

Customized Membership Model

In this model, individuals are invited to join the organization for a very low fee, one that would not be a barrier for anyone regardless of household income. Once the member joins, they choose their level of engagement and the benefits they wish to access. The initial benefits may include discounts on programs, products, and services and a complimentary subscription to the organization's flagship publication. An example of a custom membership model is AARP. If you are over fifty years old, you may join the organization for $16 a year. In exchange for this fee, you will receive discounts on travel, insurance, health products, and other products as well as a monthly magazine. If a professional membership organization were to create a custom membership model in hopes of significantly increasing membership, they would need to drastically reduce membership dues and unbundle most of their benefits. Membership dues would simply give you access to special pricing on products and members-only events, opportunities, and resources.

Levels of Membership Based on What You Wish to Receive and How You Wish to Receive It

In this model, members choose the membership category based on the benefits they wish to receive rather than demographics such as position, title, experience, or career stage. For example, if continuing education is important—because it is either required or necessary—an organization could create one membership package that bundles education with dues. This may include unlimited access to continuing education webinars with the opportunity to add on in-person education as well. Another type of membership package is an electronic membership. This gives individuals the option of joining the organization and receiving only digital or electronic access to programs and products. A third type of membership package may offer networking or social events, including career-transitioning programs. As members move through their career lifecycle, they may select different levels of engagement or membership based on their needs at the time.

Case Study: AOTA and 136 Pieces of Data

When Chris Bluhm joined the American Occupational Therapy Association (AOTA) as its chief operating officer in 2005, membership was at one of the lowest points in recent history. In the late 1990s, AOTA's membership had dropped from fifty-five thousand to thirty-four thousand members. As members retired or let their membership lapse, the organization made little or no real effort to recruit new members.

This year, AOTA celebrated the eighth consecutive year of growth and counted nearly forty-nine thousand individuals as members. How did the organization achieve such an impressive turnaround within such a short period?

Bluhm explains,

> We went out in three fronts: First, we engaged the education community to get students in the door. Next, we sent out quarterly direct mail campaigns and tested different offers and messages. Finally, we invested our time and money into better understanding who are our members. We added to our existing AMS an additional 136 pieces of data on each of our members. We know, for example, our members' interests, household income, donation tendencies, and marital status.
>
> It's like running up a sand dune. You keep plugging away. It's still work. But instead of just trying random tactics, messages, and offers because we think, "Wouldn't it be nice if we offered this?" we look at data. Prior to having this data, we spent a lot of time trying different things, and many of them didn't work [personal communication, January 20, 2013].

Today, when AOTA needs to market its membership, programs, or products, the organization can send more targeted messages and offers to smaller groups rather than the same message to all members. Bluhm attributes some of the success they've experienced to his ability to access the data without needing to burden the IT department for every ad hoc report. Another change has been the implementation of a payment installment plan. AOTA offers members and prospects the choice of annual or monthly installments as well as automatic renewal. The next step will be to increase segmentation of messages to ensure they are creating value statements that resonate with all of the different audiences they serve. Bluhm also believes he can apply this data to efforts focused on retention and onboarding.

Bluhm firmly believes that "having hit such a low point in membership created a crisis, but real change comes from crisis. It gets people out of their comfort level. It's sometimes the only thing that gets people to change."

Action Steps

Different personal characteristics influence perceived value. To better understand how to reach members and prospects, organizations must change their approach to understanding these individuals on a personal level. This begins with the following steps:

1. Create better member profiles. Conduct a personal census of members and import the data into your database. You can enrich your information with third-party data. You can use Exhibit 2.1 to identify traits that will create a realistic portrait of your members.

2. Expand member research to include psychographic questions. Develop a process to regularly collect information about your members and prospects that is different from the information you've been collecting. Explore the values, interests, attitudes, and motivations of members. Ask members to agree or disagree with a list of interests, activities, and opinion statements (see Exhibit 2.2).

3. Apply marketing analytics and customize your messages. Create a ranking system of your members and prospects based on characteristics that have shown who is most likely to respond to different types of campaigns and calls to action. For example, let's say you are able to create a profile of members and prospects who are most likely to respond to promotions for a national conference. You can create highly targeted campaigns that will result in a greater return on your marketing investment. Put another way, you won't waste too many dollars on individuals who are extremely unlikely to respond. This should also free up resources to market other member benefits to individuals who may be interested in those benefits but not aware of their existence or usefulness.

4. Update records on a regular basis. Once you've created the member profiles, make a commitment to collect information and update member and prospect database files. This can be accomplished during the onboarding of new members or the renewal process with current members. You can also create campaigns with incentives for members to keep their profiles up to date. Although this effort may seem unrealistic, based on your existing resources and capabilities, it should be considered a top priority if you wish to fulfill your promise to deliver value, attract new members, and keep the ones who have joined.

As we've demonstrated, value is in the eye of the beholder, and if that is so, then you must sell what matters. As members of various member-based organizations, we have options—such as where we network, get industry information, and participate in professional education programs. Therefore, associations must be challenged to reconsider outdated membership models and breed new methods for packaging member benefits.

Exhibit 2.1. Member Profile Characteristics

- Personal demographics: age, gender, family size, birth date, household income, geography, ethnicity
- Professional demographics: education level, years in practice, work setting, size of practice, title, specialty area
- Lifestyle: hobbies, interests, and pursuits
- Life stage: Student, new to the profession, mid-careerist, seasoned professional, nearing retirement, semi-retired, retired
- Communities and socialization: online, in-person, types, frequency, purposes
- Technology: Adoption (early, mid, or late), device, frequency, usage, preferences, and behavior
- Personality traits:
  - Openness to experience: inventive and curious or consistent and cautious
  - Conscientiousness: organized and planned or spontaneous and carefree
  - Introvert or extravert: outgoing and energetic or solitary and reserved
- Donor type: frequency, type, amount, motivations:
  - Engage
  - Give back
  - Protect
  - Create a legacy
  - Educate

Exhibit 2.2. Sample Psychographic or Lifestyle Questions

Using a Likert scale, you can ask survey participants their level of agreement with the following statements.

Trends and Belief Statements
- I constantly seek new ideas, strategies, and approaches for the work I do.
- I work hard to stay-up-date on the latest trends and innovations in my industry.
- I am required to stay up-to-date on the latest trends and innovations in my industry as part of my job.

Leadership and Collaboration Belief Statements
- I enjoy building relationships with my colleagues and sharing ideas with them.
- I view myself as an influential leader among my colleagues.
- I like to be a mentor.
- I recommend books, videos, and other tools to colleagues to help them find new ideas.
- I aspire to leadership with my association.

Membership Belief Statements
- I belong to my association primarily for my professional development.
- I belong to my association primarily for making connections/networking opportunities.
- I like belonging to my association primarily because I support its mission.
- I belong to my association primarily for the fellowship with people with common interests.
- I belong to my association for the prestige of being a member.

Attitudes and Motives
- I enjoy meeting people in my profession.
- I enjoy learning about the industry beyond my specific job responsibilities.
- I like giving back to my community.
- Attending meetings and events is fun and enjoyable.
- I like traveling to meetings and events.

3

Sell What Matters

A FEW YEARS AGO, I decided to join a health club near my home. As an avid runner living in the challenging climate of the Chicago area, during the cold winter months my options for running outside are limited. On some days I either need to wear so many layers I look like the Michelin Man or have to skip my workout altogether. After two years of running outside during the brutal Chicago winters, I decided it was time for a change. Although I wasn't excited to move my workout from scenic trails to a treadmill, I was looking forward to the benefits of a well-lit and heated indoor gym.

As I began my search for a health club, I narrowed my list of requirements to the following items:

1. The health club needed to be within a ten-minute drive of my home.
2. On weekdays it must open its doors no later than 5:30 AM.
3. It was essential that there be plenty of treadmills in good working order.

I found two fitness centers that met my requirements.

The first fitness center answered the question "Why join?" with the following pitch: *Health club. Tennis club. Sports club. Social club. Whether you're playing doubles, lifting weights, working up a sweat, or having lunch with friends, you'll experience it all here.* The club offered indoor and outdoor tennis courts, a spa and salon, a pro shop, social events, and a full-service café that provided its members with healthy options for breakfast, lunch, and dinner. If you're searching for a wide variety of services, this club could easily meet your needs. Of course, there is a price you pay to have access to all of these benefits—and the price was nearly double the monthly fee to join the second fitness center I was considering. Focused on fitness, the second club offered far fewer amenities but still provided new equipment, a clean facility, and a friendly atmosphere.

In the end, it just didn't make sense for me to join an organization whose primary selling point was "We have it all!" I could afford to join either; price was a consideration only because I simply didn't want to pay for something (or many things) I wouldn't use.

I share this story because it illustrates an interesting point. To deliver real value and attract members, you don't need to offer the kitchen sink, the double oven, the floor-to-ceiling windows, and the surround-sound stereo system. You just need to provide members with products and services that benefit them but that they cannot obtain on their own or through another organization, and you need to do it for a fair price.

Conversely, you shouldn't arbitrarily limit your offerings. Many organizations effectively offer a robust portfolio of products and services that provide substantial financial support to the organization and diversify its revenues. Keep in mind that if your organization offers products or services that can easily be attained elsewhere or are being used by only a small percentage of your members, there is an opportunity cost as well as the potential for increasing your churn rate.

Understand Why They Join—And Why They Leave!

A report by the International Health, Racquet & Sportsclub Association (IHRSA), a trade association that serves more than ten thousand clubs in the health and fitness industry, sheds some light on why people join health clubs and why some let their membership lapse. According to IHRSA's website (2010), their IHRSA 2012 Trend Report revealed, "Approximately half (49%) [of health club members] join to lose weight" (para. 6). The rest join "to stay healthy and stay in shape" (IHRSA, 2010, para. 6). Additionally, "In quitting health clubs, the economic aspect plays a relevant role: 44% of former members think it is too expensive to keep training in health clubs" (IHRSA, 2010, para. 7). Reportedly, other factors that impact a member's decision to drop out of the club included lack of convenience, a drop in actual usage, and the availability of other alternatives, such as exercising elsewhere for free (IHRSA, 2010). When you consider that the top three reasons people join a fitness club (to lose weight, stay healthy, and stay in shape) and the three reasons they leave (lack of value for the cost, lack of engagement or usage, and a free next best alternative), you will notice a number of similarities to the association profession.

Over the past three years I've conducted lapsed member surveys with a wide variety of organizations, from small to large, local to national, and trade to professional. In reviewing this research, I was able to identify three primary reasons many individuals allow their membership to lapse:

1. Lack of relevant information
2. Cost exceeding the value
3. Satisfaction with alternative sources (there wasn't a compelling reason to belong, because the organization did not offer something unique that couldn't be obtained elsewhere)

How do you decide what services to offer and what products to sell? It begins with understanding your members and knowing their challenges better than anyone else. It involves digging deeply into their industry, practice area, specialty, or whatever type of membership you serve. Many associations ask their members to identify their greatest workplace challenges through a membership survey, yet fail to turn the knowledge they collect into tangible and meaningful benefits. Other organizations create educational programs, certifications, or publications, yet fail to connect these resources to the challenges their members face. They do the homework, but they don't apply that knowledge.

For instance, if an association believes a primary benefit of joining is the substantial discount that members will receive if they attend the national conference (where they'll receive valuable information), yet less than 50 percent of the members attend the conference, the math doesn't work. Convenience and usage may be two reasons there is a high turnover rate. If, on the other hand, the organization has identified ways for members to obtain the same information in a format that doesn't require them to travel to a national conference and assume the subsequent costs and time spent, the organization could provide more value and retain more members.

Legislative and professional advocacy is one way that associations promote the interests of their members. Yet we all know that nonmembers also benefit from the wide-reaching work of advocacy. So advocacy is not a benefit reserved exclusively for members. Therefore, can advocacy be eliminated as an exclusive benefit? There's no argument that it is a benefit, but is it *exclusive to members*? Do members join because of an association's advocacy efforts? For some organizations, advocacy is exactly why people join. Their members have very strong emotions about the subject or topic, and they are not looking for a tangible return on their investment. But this isn't the case for all organizations. On the other hand, developing best practices and benchmarking data and education are several primary methods by which associations can provide helpful solutions to members' problems. These can be customized, exclusive, and necessary.

Focus on Organizational Strengths

Many organizations find it difficult to evaluate their portfolio of products and services without first examining their internal weaknesses and external challenges and threats. (Does the time-honored SWOT analysis—Strengths, Weaknesses, Opportunities, and Threats—sound familiar here?) Although this may ensure that you've done your due diligence and have examined every possible outcome, it can also hold you back from developing new products that satisfy the unmet needs of your customers or members. In fact, many new products would probably never get launched if the companies that created them were afraid to take some risks and overcome seemingly large obstacles.

To sharpen your focus on the core benefits your organization is uniquely positioned to offer, I recommend taking an inventory of areas in which your organization excels. Table 3.1 lists a series of positive brand attributes. Go through the list and place a check in the Yes column for the ones that accurately describe your organization. Don't be alarmed if, upon completing this exercise, you find that your organization has just a few core strengths. In fact, there is an advantage to identifying only a few

Table 3.1.   Brand Attributes Survey

Brand Attributes	Yes
Awareness: High levels of brand awareness among nonmembers or customers	
Prestige: A high level of prestige associated with the brand	
Loyalty: High level of brand loyalty	
Trust: High level of brand trust or sincerity	
Quality: Reputation for delivering high-quality products or experiences	
Satisfaction: High levels of satisfaction with past purchases or experiences	
Knowledge: Knowledge and understanding of existing product lines	
Acquisition and profit: Competitive pricing structure	
Data: Ability to customize communications based on individual interests and needs	
Communications: Access to multiple communication channels (print, digital, mobile, online)	
Customer Service: Good customer or member service capabilities	
Reach: Broad geographic coverage of events	
Participation: Well-attended local networking events	
Product Line: High-quality face-to-face education programs	
Engagement: Active social media community (Facebook, LinkedIn, YouTube, private, or other)	
Retention: High retention of current members	
Loyalty: Strong word-of-mouth and referrals	
Market Dominance: High market share compared to competitors	

(Continued)

Table 3.1.   (Continued)

Brand Attributes	Yes
Uniqueness: Programs or products that are rare or hard to find	
Information: Access to market research regarding market needs	
Competitiveness: Programs or products that are difficult to imitate or copy	

very strong attributes. With limited resources of time, staff, and money, it's helpful to have a shorter list of strengths. If you're able to check off more than ten attributes of your organization, you may need to narrow your focus and concentrate on the attributes that pair up well with the creation of relevant new products or services.

If you do not have the information needed to assess your organization's strengths, you may need to conduct a branding survey before you take the actions recommended in this chapter. A typical branding survey includes questions that explore your brand's personality, prestige, trust, customer satisfaction, and loyalty from both the members' and nonmembers' perspectives.

Understanding the core strengths of your existing brand will help you differentiate your organization from its competitors and engender a greater sense of awareness and loyalty. The exercise in Exhibit 3.1 should give rise to a handful of strategic opportunities to expand your current products, programs, and/or services, while eliminating any that detract from your value proposition. In short, in addition to the "to-do" list that results from this process, there should be a parallel "stop doing" list!

Leverage Your Uniqueness

In 2005, Tom Morrison became the chief executive officer of the Metal Treating Institute (MTI), a non-profit trade association that represents the largest network of commercial heat treaters in the world. It was a pivotal moment in the company's history. After nearly a century of change, growth, decline, and reorganization,

MTI needed a strategy that would advance the profession and provide a worthwhile reason to join and renew. The industry was changing and, as Morrison told me, "Manufacturing just didn't seem very cool to the younger generation" (all Tom Morrison quotes from personal communication, January 10, 2013). At the same time, he didn't want to remove one of the key benefits the association provided to its members—that is, the chance to shake a hand and make a connection that could lead to new business opportunities. Although Morrison recognized that not all members desired the same form of interaction and engagement, the goals were the same: to save money, improve productivity, and increase profits. To grow the organization, Morrison understood that he needed to answer one very important question: "What can MTI do that our members cannot do, or cannot do for themselves, effectively?"

The answer, it turned out, was relatively simple: MTI could become a problem solver for members. Once MTI truly listened to its members discussing their major challenges and learned as much as it could about their businesses, the organization was able to identify five areas where it could provide benefits that would help members save money, improve productivity, and increase profits. How did they do that? They categorized every single challenge that a member voiced.

In the end, Morrison's criteria for creating a strong value proposition focused on just five core elements that he believed have always existed for associations, regardless of economic downturns, generational differences, or advances in technology. The five elements bring together individuals or companies with a common passion and purpose to help them:

1. Organize to better coordinate members' activities to achieve their goals
2. Lower individual costs by distributing expenses across a broader network
3. Access market intelligence, industry research, and best practices in training
4. Expand business opportunities through members-only networking opportunities
5. Stay up-to-date on industry news and information without dedicating too many resources (financial or human)

The result of these efforts was the creation of five primary benefits of membership:

1. Networking opportunities for business development at the local, state, national, and international level
2. Online and face-to-face training through regional and national meetings
3. Customized leadership development for top management in the industry
4. Financial benchmarking to help manage operations and purchasing decisions, including monthly sales statistics reports, monthly economic reports, and forecasts and quarterly outlooks
5. Industry news and information

Although many associations offer a similar list of benefits (networking, training, leadership development, data and information), what makes MTI's list of benefits so valuable is that the organization has invested its time and resources in creating best-in-class offerings in each category. In this instance, best-in-class refers to the highest-quality product or service that truly has no equal. Some vendors may provide similar services, but the general consensus is that their products are below the standards set by the organization offering a best-in-class product.

Take MTI's approach to financial benchmarking, which is a major benefit for its members. "We have financial data dating back to 1978," says Morrison. "We actually transferred that into an online system where our members log their numbers between two dates. They then go back out and file a report that gives them the trends on sales, monthly sales, and so on."

Thanks to this MTI effort, members can accurately compare themselves against the competition in the local market as well as the national market. "For instance, they can start to see that if your energy cost is going up [relative to the percentage of sales] and everybody else's is going down, you're losing business quotes," Morrison says.

Or consider what MTI does for its leadership. Although there are many sources for leadership training, MTI's programs are customized for its audience. MTI's products are created in multiple formats, including online programs, on-site training, videos, print publications, and in-person events. MTI does not replicate other programs and products that are easily accessible and readily available. It has created something unique for MTI members that is truly valuable to this audience, and this audience only.

Some associations offer marketing and practice management materials to help their members manage their businesses. Although their members may need these services, and members may even tell you through your market research that managing and growing their businesses are top priorities, your association may not be the best provider of solutions to these challenges.

Many organizations fall into a trap of trying to provide programs and products that address their members' most pressing issues, even when the organization does not have the expertise or resources to provide the best solutions. Just because you discover that your members struggle with work and life balance does not mean that your association should develop workshops, educational sessions, or books on this topic. This doesn't make the need irrelevant; it just means you may be able to help your members with work and life balance—but not necessarily develop full-blown products on the topic. For example, perhaps you can make their lives easier by providing them with industry data and research to help them make informed decisions faster.

This concept goes back to my belief that associations should focus their efforts on providing products, programs, and services that truly benefit the member by offering meaningful value *and* cannot be obtained from another source.

You won't attract and retain members with a "me too" list of programs and products that you've decided will benefit your members but that are readily available from other sources. One example may be a job board that is shared by many organizations. Another example? Discounts on car rentals, hotels, and technology. But your list may also include webinars, conferences, content, and networking. These are examples of "me too" products that may provide no value-add to your membership proposition.

That isn't to say that imitation is always bad or cannot be effective. You could offer similar products and services, but bundle them in such a way that you can capture a greater share of the market. In fact, if the result of imitation is a product that improves on the original concept and creates a unique offering for your association, imitation can be a smart business decision. The consumer world is filled with companies that many believe are innovators but are, in fact, copy cats of other products. From Visa to Disney to Zappos, businesses have been profiting from creating products or business models that improve on deficiencies or limitations of existing ones. Visa is one of the dominant players in the payment technology business in part because they enhanced an existing product (Diners Club) by enabling its bank customers to offer their customers more choices. Although Visa expanded its reach and its product lines, the company still focuses on delivering three things: choice, convenience, and security. Walt Disney did not invent animation; he simply developed and patented technology that significantly reduced the time needed to create movies. He also made dramatic improvements to the quality of animated movies. And Zappos was not the first online business to sell shoes, clothing, and other accessories. The products Zappos sells are not unique, and the prices are not lower than other online retailers'. It's been widely reported that the story behind Zappos' success—exceeding $1 billion in annual sales—was their creation of a dynamic and unique culture and their commitment to delivering the very best customer service. The difference is these companies do not imitate their competitors; they create unique experiences that differentiate them and provide more value.

Connect the Dots to Member Value

Unless you're the chief executive officer, you may have little control over eliminating a number of items from a long list of programs, products, and services your organization currently offers; however, you can change the promotion of these benefits. Rather than promote twenty benefits of membership, focus on the five items that your organization offers that are unique to your industry. Focus on what matters to your members.

What does your organization offer that cannot be obtained from any other company or association? If you work at a local, regional, or state association, and your education programs showcase some of the same speakers and content being offered through the national organization, you need to identify at least one or two features that differentiate your education. Do you offer the same education for a lower price? Do your members value the local networking? Will they save money and time because they do not have to pay any travel costs? If these factors differentiate your education, then include them in the promotion of that offering. The message may be inherent, but you need to make it transparent. Reinforce it at every opportunity. Your education must reflect positively on the organization and its brand. You may also need to seek new blood to supplement your existing expertise.

To achieve or sustain growth, associations must identify what will benefit the members, then deliver the products, programs, and services that can make a difference in the lives of their members and prospects. At the same time, the organization must be sure it is best positioned to offer those. Associations also need to consider how to package the benefits so that they are easy to access and consume. This also requires understanding the best way to get the message to all audience segments.

Looking back to MTI, once Morrison shifted his focus to ensuring that the organization provided its members with the products and services from which they benefit greatly, he quickly realized that it wasn't as simple as "build it and they will come." While that would be nice—a field of dreams, even—it just isn't realistic.

Morrison's next priority was to make sure his members knew about the benefits and, more important, how having access to the corresponding programs and services would significantly improve their personal and professional lives.

Morrison says, "I had to ask my staff: Are we helping people to 'connect the dots' in our association?" He explains that when an association connects the dots of information, programs, and ideas to the specific struggles of its members, then you can connect your members to your association in an emotional way that "leads them to be not just dues paying members, but believers in the organization."

For example, he tells the following story: "I was having dinner with a member and two of his key managers. As we talked about the standards and audits that they have to live by, it became very apparent there was a service that our association could provide that would be life-changing for their business; [it] could help them to improve their process and save them thousands of dollars in future audits. That is a dot that connects them emotionally to our association." Member value, according to Morrison, is driven by the *quality* of impact of programs, not by the *number* of them.

To get the word out about the benefits of belonging to MTI, Morrison and his staff used multiple channels, including face-to-face conferences, print and electronic newsletters, videos, Facebook, Twitter, and a blog. Although the industry leaders were men in their fifties and sixties, a new workforce made up of members from other generations needed to be engaged as well.

Over the course of seven years, during difficult economic times, Morrison has helped his association membership grow by 12 percent. Dues revenue has increased by 20 percent, and the net assets of the association grew 100 percent. In addition, the per-member revenue went up 28 percent and MTI's annual revenue other than dues rose by a whopping 400 percent.

"MTI ended another record year in revenue and net assets for 2012, further strengthening us to do some dynamic things for our members without charging extra dues," says Morrison. "Our incredible run over the last seven years has not been by luck, but by a systematic and strategic set of innovative measures to maximize membership value. To me, the statistics listed here are key to measuring member engagement. Are members spending more money with you on average year to year?"

His advice is simple: "The best way to help your members is to give them what they can't obtain on their own. And make it something they need to succeed in their industry. That's what we did at MTI."

When It Comes to Benefits, Less Is More

Creating a portfolio of products, programs, and services that yield meaningful benefits can be a challenge if your organization serves a multidisciplinary audience that includes both core and affiliate members. Over time, as more audience segments are added to your membership base, it is easy for your message to become diluted and your offerings to stray from your core mission. From travel discounts to financial services, offerings that do not provide real and unique value can damage your brand and dilute the perception that membership is essential. It's the double-edged sword of growth, which is why it's critical to keep an eye on the organization's mission and, at the same time, make sure what you're offering is truly unique—and you can prove it.

In 2012 I had a conversation with a membership director of a national organization that had experienced a decrease in its market share of its core audience. Although total organization membership had grown, the drop in market share reflected the U.S. Department of Labor projection that there would be tremendous growth in the industry over the next ten years. Recent efforts to recruit new members had shifted the focus away from its core audience. As a result, the largest area of growth was coming from affiliate members.

One of the organization's primary marketing messages to prospective members was: "Need a reason to join? How about seventy-five reasons?" Imagine asking a prospective member to sort through over six dozen products and services that the association offers as benefits. At first glance, this may seem like a good idea, as it "proves" how valuable the organization must be. Right? Look at everything it offers! Somewhere in that list, the organization hopes a prospective member will find a good reason to join. But it's more like walking into a bookstore only to find that there is no organization as to how the books are placed on the shelves. You can either spend a few hours searching for the book you wish to buy, or you can walk out of the store and try another bookseller where you find exactly what you need in a matter of minutes.

In addition, if you look at a list of seventy-five benefits (or seventy-five *anything*, for that matter) and decide that only five will truly benefit you, you'll say to yourself, "Why should I pay for seventy benefits that I don't want?" You'll recall that this is exactly the experience I had when choosing a health club. I resisted the idea of paying for services that I knew I was never going to use.

As we examined the organization's core offerings, we discovered that the real issue was not that they failed to offer enough value for the cost of membership. In reality, satisfaction among its core members was high; they found the education to be of high quality, and instructors were perceived to be knowledgeable and well prepared. The information the association shared through its publications and online resources was valued and frequently used by members. In fact, among their core audience usage of their products and services was very high. Finally, the most recent membership needs assessment revealed that a high percentage of members felt that the value they received was equal to or greater than the cost of dues.

The organization's primary challenge wasn't that it didn't provide enough value to its members; the biggest obstacle was how the offerings were packaged and promoted to prospective members. If the organization bundled those products, programs, or services into just five packages, then positioned them as *the* five reasons to join (that is, the core benefits), it could strengthen its brand and increase the likelihood of getting its message across.

Case Study: AAHPM Sells What Matters Most

Many organizations struggle to identify and deliver unique products. Others wrestle with how best to communicate value. But one organization we came across overcame these challenges with a small staff and limited resources. Here's their story:

The American Academy of Hospice and Palliative Medicine (AAHPM) is a professional membership society that includes five thousand physicians and other health care professionals committed to improving the care of patients with serious or life-threatening conditions. Members work in urban, rural, and suburban hospitals, hospices, managed-care facilities, and academic institutions. A majority of the Academy's physician members specialize in family and internal medicine and belong to more than one medical society. In fact, many Academy members hold memberships in other larger organizations, including the American College of Physicians (ACP), an organization with a membership of 133,000 internal medicine subspecialists, medical students, residents, and fellows.

Although the Academy serves a unique niche in health care, their members have numerous options when it comes to staying informed and learning from others within their field. The Academy neither wishes—nor has the budget or resources—to compete with ACP or any of the other medical societies or health care institutions that can easily provide education and resources to their members. Yet AAHPM has achieved consistent membership growth over the last few years.

How has it done this? The Academy knew it did not want to offer too many products. Additionally, it wanted to provide its audience with something they couldn't obtain elsewhere or do for themselves. Finally, the organization didn't believe it had to stick with the traditional set of products or programs it had always offered.

"We created, and updated every three to four years, our series of nine books that summarize the essential knowledge required to provide quality medical care to patients treated by our members," says Steve Smith, MS, CAE, executive director at the Academy. "A lot of people at the executive level think you need to forgo your products in one area to create new products in order to innovate or increase sales. They feel it's one or the other, but you've got to find the right balance" (all quotations from Steve Smith, personal communication, January 9, 2013).

What's impressive about AAHPM's book series, entitled UNIPAC, is that sales have generated as much as a million dollars in revenue in a single year—not a small amount for a relatively small association (annual budget: $5–6 million).

"We essentially have a half dozen products that work really well for us, and it's unusual for us to add a new product to our portfolio. We really try to keep our limited portfolio really current," Smith says. He explains that the Academy has a process by which all of their products are reviewed and assessed every three years. Based on reviews, they decide to either continue to invest and update the product, divest or discontinue the product, or allow the product to exist for another cycle before being reevaluated again.

"Most of the time, we're reviewing products and decide to update the content. But on occasion, we decide to pull a product off the shelf and say, 'We're not going to do that anymore,'" Smith explains. Sometimes the Academy revises or extends the product model. Every time a new edition comes out, it sells, because people want the latest version of that essential tool that is used to teach and serves as an important reference.

As technology advances and preferences for obtaining information change, the Academy has observed and adjusted. They have also created a variety of options and price points from which members can choose. They offer the books in a series or individually. Members and customers can buy just the books, or they can opt to also purchase the corresponding online learning modules. Flexibility is built into the product. It was customized based on the varying and changing needs of the members. What also helps sell the books is that they are frequently updated.

Smith subscribes to a new product development analogy common in the consumer product world: "When something's new, consumers want it. If Tide and Tide Plus are sitting next to each other on the shelf, most will want to purchase Tide Plus. It's been really interesting to see this play out in our Academy product offerings as well. We actually sold a lot of the product this year because many of our members were preparing for their certification exam."

So what has Smith learned from this incredible success that other associations can study and emulate?

1. Do a few things really well.
2. Identify what you're providing that's unique to what your customers or members want or need from you.
3. Continue to ensure that the quality of that product or that program is exceptional, through market research, evaluation and redesign, or updating of products, so that your marketplace knows that you're constantly enhancing and innovating.
4. Resell that same product to many or more people as you continue to refurbish it.
5. Look for product extensions. If you have a product that does really well for your program, add to it and extend that brand.

The Academy's essential book series has been around for more than ten years; it's now in its fourth edition. "We don't have to create the next big thing; we already have one that's works really well," Smith reiterates. Now, he says, it's about expansion. The Academy has extended the product into the e-learning environment. It's not a new product that would essentially compete with the original one, and it will not take sales away. Next there will be an ebook, in response to member demand. "Members wish they had our books available at the bedside, which means adapting it for a tablet and smartphone, and we're ready to do that now," Smith maintains.

Again, it comes down to finding out what matters to your members and then selling that. So a successful product solves a problem, addresses a need, and makes membership in your association valuable because it offers what a member cannot get elsewhere. As Steve Smith says, your customers often become your members: "I don't think that associations can flourish without a portfolio of desirable products, or at least a few really successful ones. Membership alone isn't going to keep you going or growing, and neither is your conference or course . . . Education products, and just products in general, are more accessible to customers and consumers versus just members. I believe in the model where people begin as customers and evolve to members. I think you're better creating a product that meets the needs of a broader customer base that can include your members, but isn't limited to your members."

Action Steps

1. Complete the brand attribute quiz to create a list of existing areas in which your organization excels. From there, determine at least one thing your organization does better than anyone else. If you work at a local or state association, and the one thing you do better than others is help members connect locally with others, expand these opportunities. If your organization has access to, or can easily provide, specific benchmarking data on best practices that will help members improve their efficiency and profits, develop products or services in these areas. Both of these offerings support an organization's efforts to achieve its mission and serve members.

2. Determine the unique selling position for each of your products, or at least your primary products. List the features and compare your products to your competitors'.

   a. What sets your organization apart? Write down up to three challenges your members and prospects face. Next to each item, identify a unique service of your organization that can be leveraged and promoted.

   b. If you do have a competitor, what is the one area they cannot imitate? Think back to the Zappos example. When the company first opened, they couldn't compete on selection, and they didn't want to compete on price. Instead, they differentiated themselves by providing unparalleled customer service. If you purchase an item from Zappos, they give you 365 days to return the item. Plus, they offer free shipping both ways. An organization may not choose to compete on price or selection but could, for example, provide unique access to industry thought leaders.

3. Conduct a brand survey to measure member and nonmember perceptions. Ask study participants to identify the challenges they face and their perception of your organization as a solution provider (see Exhibit 3.1). Do they hold a similar view of your organization, compared to the self-assessment you conducted? Does your organization have strengths that you were unaware of? Did you overestimate some of the areas in which your organization excels?

4. Categorize your programs, products, services, and other offerings into two columns: those that translate into benefits that support your brand promise and those that are tangentially related to your mission.

5. Finally, don't sell everything; just sell what matters. Review your marketing and communications to ensure that your messaging reflects the relevant and meaningful benefits, based on various audience segments. A list of items to review include: organization website; social media sites; blogs; membership recruitment materials, including emails, electronic and print brochures, and renewal notices; publications; annual reports; media/PR communications; and any other vehicles being used to communicate or reinforce the benefits of membership.

Exhibit 3.1. Sample Questions for a Brand Assessment Survey

(Note: In this type of survey, be sure to include demographic questions to determine brand perceptions based on different audience segments.)

1. What are the three most pressing challenges you face today in your industry?
2. What do you think is the purpose of [name of organization]?
3. Compared to other organizations in the industry, what are some advantages of belonging to this organization?

(Continued)

Exhibit 3.1. (Continued)

4. How did you first learn about this organization?
5. How likely are you to recommend this organization to friends or colleagues? Please explain.
6. What is your level of agreement with the following statements about this organization? Choose from the following: 1 (strongly disagree), 2 (disagree somewhat), 3 (neutral), 4 (agree somewhat), 5 (strongly agree).

Customer Service
- Responds promptly to requests.
- Always provides satisfactory responses to inquiries.

Quality
- Provides real-world solutions.
- Offers best-in-class solutions.
- Delivers programs or products that are superior in quality.

Pricing
- Prices programs or products competitively.
- Provides value that exceeds the cost.

7. Which of the following attributes do you associate with this organization?
- Credible
- Creative
- Influential
- Effective
- Scholarly
- Innovative
- Sensible
- Helpful
- Trustworthy
- Political
- Social
- Analytical
- Organized
- Advanced
- Serious

- Balanced
- Logical
- Sophisticated
- Purposeful
- Visionary
- Selective
- Practical
- Prestigious
- Responsive

What other words would you use to describe this organization?

Focusing on just a few things instead of everything will help improve the value of the association's offerings—and, in turn, the value of membership. With laser-focused marketing, you create an environment that allows for more flexible pricing strategies and clearer revenue streams.

Although most associations have a set pricing structure in place, the small adjustments suggested in the next chapter can have a large impact on the bottom line. Therefore, we will delve into pricing modules that have worked to significantly increase an association's revenue.

4

Charge More or Less—And Other Alternative Pricing Strategies

"HOW MUCH IS YOUR MEMBERSHIP IN ASAE and the Center for Association Leadership?" This is the question I asked a group of senior staff from the American Urological Association (AUA). Staff from every department in the organization were sitting around the table, waiting for our meeting to begin. The purpose of our meeting was to discuss a potential increase in membership fees as well as a change in how benefits would be bundled with dues. Before we began our discussion, I went around the room and asked everyone who was a member of ASAE to tell me how much they paid to belong to the organization. Only one person in the room could accurately tell me how much she had paid the previous year. What was even more interesting was the range of fees suggested by the individuals in the room. One individual could have sworn she paid about $275; another one thought it was closer to $600.

We went through this exercise because I wanted to demonstrate that, for many of the items we buy, we do not have an actual sense of what we pay or even how much the product, program, or even membership in a professional organization should cost. There may be a gut feeling that something is too expensive or something else is priced too low, and therefore we may question the quality and value of the item. However, studies have shown that very few people can accurately quote the price of many of the items they buy. The exercise I conducted with the AUA staff in the conference room on that day served to reinforce that finding.

Of course, there are a few exceptions to this rule, specifically when it comes to frequency or loyalty to a brand. For example, you probably know exactly how much you pay for items bought on a regular basis, such as your morning cup of Starbucks coffee, a song downloaded from iTunes, or a can of Diet Coke purchased from the vending machine in your office building. Yet even if you know exactly what you pay for these items, you may be willing to pay more for them than the next best alternative because of a perception of unique value and quality.

Price, and the perception of value and quality, are intertwined more than most people might think when they, as association professionals, consider how much to charge for membership, programs, products, or services.

In the early 1950s, Pillsbury learned an interesting lesson when it raised the price per package for its original cake mix from 10 cents to 25 cents. At 10 cents, sales were dismal. When Pillsbury raised the price to 25 cents, sales skyrocketed. After the initial product launch, Pillsbury quickly realized that a negative perception had been formed because consumers believed quality was directly related to price. Lower price was equivalent to lower quality, not to a great value (Berry, 2008).

In some instances, if a product is priced too low, people will question its value. This concept holds true for many luxury brands, including Nordstrom and Coach, North Face and Cartier. For these companies, price is an important part of their value proposition. They sell prestige, exclusivity, and quality, elements frequently associated with—and expected from—a higher price tag.

Although raising the price proved to be a good move for Pillsbury, determining the right price for association membership, programs, and products isn't always so simple. According to Nagel, Hogan, and Zale (2010), authors of *The Strategy and Tactics of Pricing*, "The purpose of strategic pricing is to price more profitably by capturing more value, not necessarily by making more sales. When marketers confuse the first objective with the second, they fall into the trap of pricing at whatever buyers are willing to pay, rather than at what the product is really worth" (p. 319). Here we are reminded of the principle of willingness to pay [WTP], introduced in Chapter One.

Consider Small Change for a Large Impact

To bring this concept back to the association industry, let me return to the AUA conference room, but rewind it just a few years. In 2010, the organization found itself at an interesting crossroads. Although expenses had gone up, it had been nearly ten years since the organization had implemented a dues increase. Patricia Banks, AUA's director of marketing and communications, explains the situation:

> Ironically, our research revealed that our members felt they were getting good value for the money. We also couldn't make any changes without going to the board for approval. Nobody really wanted to do that. So that created another layer, or barrier, if you will. Ultimately, we realized we had to make some changes because we could see that industry dollars would soon be going away. One of the basic values of the organization is financial stability, and we were a financially strong association. It was essential that we adjust our pricing if we were going to maintain this stability and continue to thrive during these changes [personal communication, January 11, 2013].

However, before AUA could implement any changes, it needed to learn and understand the answers to the following questions:

1. How should AUA bundle (or unbundle) its current offerings to create a membership package that was valuable and relevant to members yet offered new or increased revenue streams for the organization?
2. What would be the operational and financial implications of any changes to the current structure?
3. What were the pros and cons of various pricing strategies as viewed from other departments within the AUA?
4. How would a new pricing strategy impact member recruitment, engagement, and retention?
5. How would a new pricing strategy affect attendance at AUA meetings?
6. How would changes to the current pricing structure enhance AUA's ability to expand internationally or into new audience segments?
7. What restrictions, constraints, challenges, and barriers would need to be overcome in order to successfully implement changes to the pricing structure?

8. How should AUA communicate changes, if there were any, to its members and prospects?

To find the answers to these questions, we looked at how other health care organizations that were similar in size and scope, but served other specialties, priced membership dues and bundled their benefits. The study we conducted with other health care organizations revealed:

- Associations with dues revenue accounting for 50 percent of their total annual revenue had very little opportunity for major changes to their dues structure because of the high level of risk involved.
- An association pricing strategy must be flexible enough to allow the organization to offer mission-critical products, such as practice guidelines or research, for a nominal fee or for free.
- Many organizations charge nonmembers a higher price for programs, products, and services as an incentive to join the organization. Yet some organizations find that some individuals join to receive the discount but don't need to purchase the product on an annual basis; retention rates for this type of member are low.

Next, we examined AUA's membership drivers. Before we added or removed any benefits, we needed to take an honest look at interest in and usage of the benefits that were already being offered to members via membership dues. Finally, we reviewed the economics of the organization to accurately predict the financial implications of any changes that may occur as a result of our recommendations.

Once we had our recommendations, we interviewed current members to gain feedback on the new pricing structure. This gave us additional confidence that the new approach to pricing would be embraced by the membership. We also felt it might uncover any unforeseen issues that we were unable to predict.

In the end, the AUA made two important changes. First, after more than ten years of keeping the dues at the same rate, the organization implemented a new policy that would increase dues every year by a very small percentage rather than a large increase every seven to ten years. Our market testing of this idea showed that not only were the members in favor of this approach, but some assumed this was already occurring and were surprised to learn that dues hadn't been raised in years. In addition, when AUA announced the change to the membership of more than eighteen thousand members, the organization received only one letter of disapproval.

The second change the association made was to unbundle the annual meeting registration from membership dues. This change impacted only one category of membership that had previously been given the opportunity to register for the meeting at no charge through early-bird registration. The new early-bird registration fee would be $75, hardly a barrier to attending a large national multi-day medical meeting. Market testing revealed that members supported this action. A few doctors we interviewed acknowledged that expenses related to travel and the challenges of being out of the office were greater barriers for them than the dollar figure of $75. In addition, although the annual meeting attracts thousands of attendees each year, only one-third of AUA's active members took advantage of the early-bird registration. Some paid the regular registration rate; others attended in alternate years. As such, both attendees and nonattendees believed it was important to pay their fair share rather than expect all members to pay for a benefit some would not use.

Benefits of AUA's Action

- Even after the increase, membership dues were still priced competitively.
- Small annual increases would be nearly invisible to members.
- A policy to increase dues every year eliminated the need to address the issue every few years.
- The small change in price resulted in a cumulative increase in revenue.
- By charging members a fee to attend the annual conference, AUA expected to see a lower no-show rate, because members had to make a financial commitment to coming to the meeting.
- Only members who actually took advantage of the benefit (annual meeting attendance) would be required to pay for it.
- Increased revenue from registration fees offset a drop in industry funding.

Consider another example of a major retailer trying to sell products based on their value. In January 2012, J.C. Penney announced new "Fair and Square" pricing. The idea behind this strategy was that customers today are more informed than ever about how much something should cost. They can walk around a store, find a shirt or sweater they are interested in buying, use their smartphones to check the price of comparable products from other retailers, and make a purchase. According to Alexander Chernev, professor of marketing, Kellogg School of Management, Northwestern University (Forbes, 2012), J.C. Penney vowed to price its merchandise so that "customers will not pay literally a penny more than the true value of the product" (para. 4). Accordingly, J.C. Penney reduced the price on all items by about 40 percent.

The concept didn't work. Within several months of launching the new campaign, store traffic had declined by 10 percent and sales were down by more than 20 percent (Chernev, 2012). Why did this happen? Some speculate it was because value is subjective and relative. However, I believe that if the customer can compare the regular price to a sales price or an alternative price, there is a greater sense of value as well as urgency to make the purchase. Twelve months later, J.C. Penney changed its advertising campaigns, with a new tagline: "How do we compare?" The new campaign offered a different approach to "Fair and Square" pricing. Advertisements now stated: "We don't mark it up just to mark it down. Our prices are unbelievably low every day and that's why we want you to see the difference for yourself. We're making it easier for you to see the value of jcp by comparing our prices and styles to those found *elsewhere* so you can look better and live better—all without the specialty store price."

With this new approach, Penney compared the manufacturer's suggested retail price or a competitor's price to Penney's "everyday" price. The reason? Shoppers need a reference point in order to consider and appreciate the value.

Look Toward Viable, Valuable, and Strategic Pricing

How do the approaches taken by the AUA and J.C. Penney apply to associations? Does your organization use cost-plus pricing, or are you strategic in your approach? That is, do you look at last year's prices and the item's cost and add a slight margin for profit, or have you considered your overall objectives before establishing the price? Cost-plus pricing is generally implemented because it's easy to calculate and requires little information. However, one downside is that it simply is not strategic, nor is it usually in an association's best interest.

Results from a recent benchmarking study conducted with seventeen individual membership organizations found that the driving factor for many organizations when determining the price of dues or products is a focus on "providing the lowest possible cost to the member." Sound familiar? Although this approach may seem appropriate at first glance, considering the nature of mission-based organizations, it can backfire when economic or legislative forces impact the buying decisions of members, prospects, customers, and partners. Organizations can still be focused on their cause and remain mission-driven yet price their programs, products, and services with an eye toward making a profit.

Nagel et al. (2010) believe that "cost-plus pricing leads to over-pricing in weak markets and underpricing in strong ones—exactly the opposite direction of a prudent strategy."

Even if members and prospects cannot recall what they last paid last year for their membership or to attend the annual meeting, there still may be some sensitivity to price. Because members and prospects vary in their price sensitivity and preferences, organizations should consider a variety of pricing strategies to enhance their marketing efforts to sell membership, programs, and products. The following are some reasons to considering implementing a strategic approach to pricing:

• **Increase demand for a product.** Some products, such as webinars or digital publications, lend themselves to creative pricing strategies because there isn't an incremental cost to selling more seats or publications. Whether a webinar attracts twenty registrants or two hundred registrants, the cost to produce the program does not change. The same is true for digital publications, such as your journal, magazine, reports, or e-books. If you wish to increase demand for a product, you can lower the price; however, before you move down this path, you must consider the size of your potential audience. Lowering the price or offering a discount may not drive enough revenue to the organization if the target audience is too small. If you lower the asking price to attract more purchasers, be sure to show the full price before the discount. This will give the potential buyer that nice feeling of receiving a "good deal" and additional value at a lower cost.

• **Increase response rates during a shorter period of time.** Many organizations offer a lower rate to register for a conference if the attendee registers by a certain date, also known as "early-bird registration." Some organizations offer an initial lower membership price to attract new members to their organization. However, I believe the days of early-bird registration and lengthy lead times to respond to campaigns are behind us. Six weeks is too long a time frame for people to act. If you want to increase response rates to a campaign for membership or registrations for a program or event, you need to create a greater sense of urgency. Here are some ideas:

  • Offer a tiered pricing structure based on the number of seats or memberships sold during a specific period of time. For example, the first one hundred seats or new members who join can receive a 50 percent discount, the second hundred will receive a 25 percent discount, and the remainder who register or join by a certain date will receive a 10 percent discount.

  • Offer a discount code that must be used within twenty-four hours. For example, every Thursday an organization could promote—via social media, their website, and email—a special discount code that expires at midnight.

  • Create a pricing structure that offers the largest discount four weeks before a program. Each week, the price may increase by 5 or 10 percent.

• **Penetrate new markets.** For some organizations with a high market share of their core audience, the only opportunity for growth comes from expanding into new markets. This may include international markets or affiliate markets in their industry. When you move into a new market that may be unfamiliar with your organization—and with the strength of your brand promise—you may initially find that prospective members have a lower perception of the value of membership. Therefore you may need to make a price adjustment during the initial launch in a new market. And before setting a price, it's essential that you understand the perceived value, the next best alternative to your offering, and the pricing sensitivity of the new audience segment.

The American Bar Association takes its price testing one step further by conducting pricing pilots in which a select group of members or prospects are offered membership at different dues rates for the test. Part of the benefit of pricing tests is that actual behavior is observed rather than relying on survey responses. Additionally, the pricing or program requirements can be adjusted as more is learned about the audience or opportunity. Pilot testing can be extremely useful prior to launching major strategic initiatives like flat-rate group pricing or bundled membership packages.

• **Meet strategic goals and subsidize other benefits.** Unlike for-profit companies, most associations provide benefits such as advocacy, practice guidelines, or research to their members either at no additional cost or for a very low fee. These activities are designed to meet strategic or mission-based goals. As such, other programs, products, services, or even membership fees often need to be priced so that they can help subsidize the expenses of nonrevenue-generating programs or membership categories. This may also include student, international, or other "protected classes" of membership.

• **Gain a competitive edge.** When organizations—both for-profits and nonprofits—wish to gain a competitive edge, they offer something extra without "charging" more. For example, online retailers may offer free shipping. This gives the online retailer a competitive edge over a traditional brick-and-mortar store. Not charging for a product or service is a pricing strategy that could also be used by associations. From career coaching to free shipping of publications or products, associations can gain a competitive edge by offering something for free as an incentive to complete a transaction.

In addition, organizations should consider the following issues around price sensitivity:

- Do members need-to-have or wanna-have the product? This is Economics 101; is your association employing this argument?
- Is it difficult to compare the new product or program to other programs or products?

- Is there prestige associated with joining your organization or attending your annual conference? Just being a member of an organization may confer prestige on a member. On the other hand, achieving an advanced level of membership, such as becoming a Fellow or a Diplomat may bestow added value and prestige. If this is the case, an organization may be able to charge more in exchange for the distinction bestowed on the member.

Cost-Plus Pricing Alternatives

The following six pricing strategies offer viable and valuable alternatives to cost-plus pricing, as well as ways an association could potentially implement them.

• **VIP pricing.** For years, associations have structured their annual meeting or program pricing based on deadlines and/or membership categories. With VIP pricing, an organization can add a new layer to its pricing by providing value-added benefits to individuals willing or interested in paying for additional privileges. The VIP pricing category may be offered to anyone regardless of their status, title, or category of membership. VIP pricing gives organizations the opportunity to charge more money for value-added services. The same way airlines charge more for first class or business class seats. Examples of added benefits offered by organizations include autographed copies of bestselling books from keynote speakers, invite-only cocktail receptions, VIP registrations, and reserved premium seating.

Don't Leave Money on the Table

The Walt Disney World Marathon partners with *Runners World* to give interested runners a race experience unlike any other. Called the *Runner's World* Challenge, the program offers customized training plans, connections to experts, and VIP treatment during the race weekend. Runners also receive a private packet pick-up, exclusive prerace walkout to the race start corrals, books and publications, and an invitation to the VIP access to a post-race celebration. Only a limited number of spaces are available, and even though runners must pay an additional $300, the program quickly sells out each year (Disney, 2013).

A look at the American Academy of Hospice and Palliative Medicine (AAHPM) shows how VIP pricing works in the association world. AAHPM took a new approach to pricing a highly valued and often sold-out course that prepares individuals for the hospice and palliative medicine board certification exam. Similar to the approach taken by the airline industry, AAHPM staff created a pricing structure that offered practitioners seeking a solid review of hospice and palliative medicine competencies the opportunity to attend the intensive board review course at a budget-friendly price (coach class) or with additional benefits (first class).

As part of the process, AAHPM staff identified a list of benefits that would provide additional value to attendees and a revenue boost for the organization. In addition to offering member and nonmember prices to attend, AAHPM offered a limited number of premium seats for an additional $250. Participants who paid the extra fee received:

- Reserved seating in the preferred section (the first five rows of the middle section of the room)
- A special express registration line and entrance into the lecture hall
- A wine and cheese reception with course faculty
- A special gift from AAHPM, including two popular AAHPM books (*Primer of Palliative Care* and the accompanying workbook), an AAHPM pen, mints, and a Starbucks gift card

The result: AAHPM sold 120 of 126 premium seats prior to the course, generating an additional $25,000 in net revenue. On site, staff sold the last four seats and raffled two remaining seats to other attendees.

"It gave us an opportunity to talk one-on-one with attendees and make a large course [1,250 total attendees] feel more personal" says AAHPM's marketing and membership director, Laura Davis (personal communication, January 9, 2013). "A staff member greeted them each morning and helped 'police' the section so they knew others couldn't get into the space. This ensured attendees had a reserved space in the auditorium each day." And it made them feel special, like a VIP—as it should. They had paid for it.

The pricing strategy exceeded expectations in every way. "There is no downside to offering it," Davis says. "You really have nothing to lose. You don't have to buy the items or plan the reception until you have sold some of the packages."

• **Urgency pricing.** Urgency pricing is a strategy that combines a monetary incentive and a tight deadline. Groupon perfected this approach with its daily deals, limited quantities, and twenty-four- to forty-eight-hour deadlines. As Groupon-style offers became more mainstream, early-bird pricing strategies that offer four to six weeks to respond no longer inspire people to act. Four to six weeks is not urgent, but twenty-four hours is. Organizations that wish to increase attendance for an event or even sell memberships during a specified campaign period should offer a financial incentive for responding within a very short period of time—such as within the next twelve hours. Without the sense of urgency, there is a greater likelihood that a potential member or attendee will forget to respond to the offer.

The American Academy of Pediatrics implemented such a strategy to increase online education sales. I developed a program for the organization called "Thrifty Thursdays," intended to create a sense of urgency and increase demand. Through this program, potential attendees have the opportunity to register for a webinar at a significant discount. To take advantage of the offer, individuals must register by 11:59 PM on the day the offer is made. They can register for the course after the deadline; however, they won't receive the discount. The result? Registrations for some courses increased by more than 1,700 percent.

Value Plus Pricing Example

If you wish to subscribe to the *Harvard Business Review*, you have two options. You can receive ten print issues and unlimited archive access to HBR.org for $89, which includes a full year and over twenty-five years of past issues, including more than four thousand free articles, case studies, and more. Or you can purchase the all-access subscription for $99. With this option, you receive the same benefits you would for the Print + Online membership, but you also receive access to the tablet versions of HBR so that you can read them on your PC, Mac, tablet, smartphone, and other mobile device. The difference in price is just $10, less than the cost to download just one issue of the *Harvard Business Review* on your tablet.

• **Monthly versus annual dues billing.** Many organizations offer annual or multiyear memberships. This structure, created decades ago, gives little flexibility to individuals who wish to pay smaller amounts more frequently. For example, an association could offer an annual membership for $199 or a monthly membership for $20. This option provides flexibility while at the same time generating additional revenue for the organization. Young professionals who are watching their budget or are unsure about making a long-term commitment may be more responsive to such a structure. The benefits of offering a monthly payment option include the following:

- Poses less risk for the potential member, which could translate into higher response rates
- Provides an alternative to a money-back guarantee
- Eliminates an economic barrier

Although this model is not commonly used in the association community, a few organizations now offer an installment plan for membership dues. Time will be the ultimate judge of this strategy's success. But one example worthy of consideration is the approach of the American Nurses Association (ANA). Simplifying its members' payments through auto-pay via credit cards or a direct withdrawal from a checking account has helped the ANA increase its renewal rate. The ANA also allows members to pay on a monthly basis, rather than pay a one-time annual fee. As part of its promotion for this option, the ANA states, "Our payment plans are easy and affordable. Select your membership and get involved today for only $15.75 per month."

• **Loss leaders.** Each Thanksgiving, many grocery stores sell turkeys at a price below the actual cost. For this big-ticket holiday item, shoppers compare prices before selecting the store they will use for the rest of their groceries. In response, stores discount turkey prices and increase margins on other items. The turkey is a "loss leader" that will generate bigger sales of other items.

An example of a loss leader for an association is student membership. Many organizations offer free or very-low-cost membership to students as a way to encourage them to become active in the organization, attend programs, and ultimately move up to a regular, full-priced membership upon graduation. Another example of a loss leader is a new member orientation event or cocktail reception. These events are designed to encourage new members to become more involved and spend more money with the organization.

By using the loss leader pricing strategy, your organization could potentially attract a different set of customers or members, as they may be coming to you for one thing and end up purchasing or being attracted to something quite different. Basically, this strategy aims to eliminate competition so that you gain an advantage in the market and perhaps strengthen your organization's brand. This strategy also lends itself quite well to word-of-mouth marketing.

Using this principle, you can conduct an inventory of your association's offerings to determine whether there are any loss leaders that could drive sales of other products, publications, or programs. Another approach is to subsidize the price of your annual meeting by 90 percent and create an a la carte menu of the other events and activities associated with the conference.

• **Supply-and-demand pricing.** A supply-and-demand pricing strategy provides monetary incentives for individuals or companies to act quickly if they wish to receive the greatest overall savings or discount. For example, the first day that tickets go on sale for a concert or show, consumers may choose from multiple price points if they wish to attend. As the supply of available tickets decreases, prices frequently go up. An association could apply this strategy in two ways. First, it could increase prices slightly every week by small increments. For example, during the first week of promotion, conference registration could be offered at $99. The organization could raise the price by $20 each week for eight weeks or until it is sold out. Another approach to supply-and-demand pricing is to offer the first one hundred seats at a low starting price and increase the price as supply dwindles. Although this pricing strategy has been used for product or program pricing, it could also be applied toward a membership campaign focused on recruiting affiliate members or industry partners.

• **One hundred percent participation/Multiyear commitment.** A new twist on group billing is 100 percent participation. The premise behind this pricing structure is offering a significant savings or value-added offering to organizations that commit to

100 percent participation of eligible employees. This concept combines individual membership sales with group billing and provides companies and organizations with an incentive to enroll all of their employees as members of the association.

The Virginia Society of Certified Public Accountants (VSCPA) offers CPA firms or companies the opportunity to enroll all of its CPAs in the Society in exchange for a variety of benefits—including recognition of participation, a unique logo to signify their commitment, and a 25 percent discount on VSCPA courses. Other organizations offer a significant membership dues discount in exchange for 100 percent participation.

• **Good-Better-Best Pricing.** Most organizations offer prospective members one price based on their qualifications or demographics. For example, an organization may offer a student membership fee, an early careerist fee, and a full membership

Membership as a Business Operation

Associations do not need to change their dues structure to rethink their pricing strategies that focus on groups. Based on research, gap analysis, and individual communications with members through think tanks, the American Medical Association (AMA) created a special pricing structure for physicians in group practices: commit to AMA membership for three years and be eligible to join the AMA at a discounted price. AMA Vice President of Membership Colleen Lawler says this change was necessary because of the changing demographics of AMA's membership. "Even though currently a large percentage of physicians practice in solo and small groups, the trend in physician employment is moving toward group practices," says Lawler (personal communication, August 3, 2012).

"It is important for organizations to view membership as a business operation," she continues. "Continuous review and analysis of protocols, processes, and performance results can lead to new insights that can produce positive results. You can never lose focus on the importance of quality improvement and providing a strong value proposition for members." There are some clear and significant benefits for organizations that implement group membership pricing options. As Lawler states, it's about offering the very best value for a large number of people, leading to a wider net of satisfied customers.

fee, but this pricing structure is based on employment or experience status. It doesn't provide the fully employed and experienced member with any options. If they wish to join the organization, they must pay the full price. Having a variety of price points—from low to high—gives individuals (prospects and returning members) additional flexibility. It allows them to choose the price that best meets their interests and needs. The *Good* price may provide a very basic membership with a few benefits, such as access to the website and a digital copy of the organization's journal or publication. The *Better* price may include a copy of the print publication and special discounts to popular programs or events. The *Best* price may include free registration or free products. With the Good-Better-Best pricing option, many members are likely to choose the *better* or *best* pricing option.

What Is Your Pricing Goal?

Before you determine the price for membership, programs, products, or services, you must establish a pricing goal. Is it to increase membership within a target audience? Increase attendance to an event? Meet a strategic or mission-related goal? The following worksheets (see Tables 4.1 and 4.2 and Figure 4.1) will help

Table 4.1. What Is the *Next Best Alternative* (NBA) to Your Product?

Company/ Organization	Product Features/ Benefits	Positive/ Negative Differences	Value	Price

Company/Organization = Any competitor, including employers, associations, companies.
Value = Low, medium, high based on must have or nice to have.
Price = Actual or lower or higher than your organization.

Table 4.2.   Pricing Worksheet

What is the base price (cost) per unit (production and shipping)?			$___
Are there competitors?	If yes, complete the NBA. If no, move on.	Positive or no competition: Add 10–30 percent Negative subtract 10–30 percent	$___
Are there complimentary products? Can it be sold in bulk?	If yes, bundle products and offer discounts. If sold in bulk, offer an incentive.	Bundle and offer a 10 percent, 15 percent, or 20 percent discount on complimentary products.	$___
What are the sales trends, if applicable? (Increase, decrease, no change, no data)	Have sales increased, decreased, or stayed the same?	Increased—no change. If sales have decreased, is the market large enough to sustain a discount? If yes, apply a discount.	$___
What is the value of the product?	Is it unique? Does it help meet a requirement? Is it delivered digitally? Is it sold to international audiences?	Offer varying prices based on packaging.	$___

Figure 4.1. Pricing Decision Tree

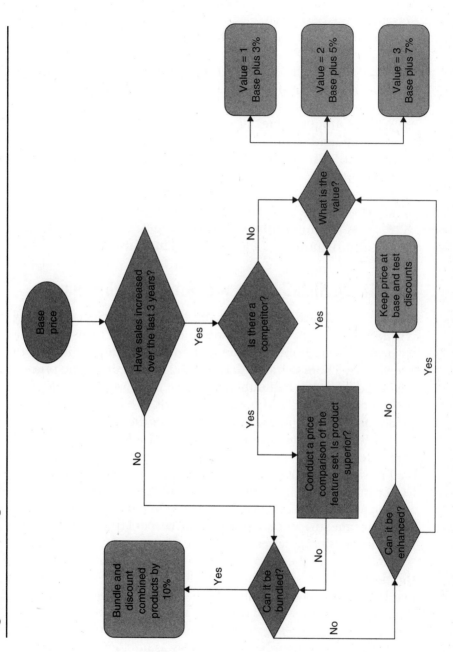

you define your audience, identify the next best alternatives, and determine the best price.

Describe the product, including features and the current price:

1. Can the product be bundled with complimentary products?
2. Who is the competition? List organizations, companies, employers, publications.
3. What is unique value? First, best, only, required, availability, in-depth, and so on.
4. Who do you serve? How do you define your audience segments?
   - List demographics (title, position, work setting, age or career stage, specialty, and so on)
   - List psychographics (value, budget, image or prestige, information-only, social, networking, advocate, and so on)

Case Study: HIMSS Grows with Group Membership

In 2011, Healthcare Information and Management Systems Society (HIMSS), a cause-based, not-for-profit organization focused on better health through information technology, celebrated its fiftieth anniversary. There was a lot to celebrate. Each year for the preceding decade, HIMSS had published more than two hundred member-centric resources and hosted hundreds of education programs locally, nationally, globally, and virtually over the Internet.

Under the leadership of H. Stephen Lieber, president and chief executive officer, the organization has more than quadrupled in size in just over ten years and is now accepted as a global leader in the field of health care technology. Although this may appear to be a success story built on being at the right place at the right time, the story behind the success at HIMSS shows it was more the result of a series of strategic moves.

In 2007, membership in HIMSS totaled just over seventeen thousand. In the six years that followed, membership grew to nearly fifty thousand, including 570 corporate members and more than 225 not-for-profit partner organizations. Although health care and technology are two of the hottest issues being discussed today, the current membership model was not designed to attract the entire population of prospective members who would help the organization achieve its mission.

"My members work for somebody else most of the time; they work for the CLO, the CEO in hospitals, and large group practices or they work for companies," Lieber told me (all H. Stephen Lieber quotes are from personal communication, February 2, 2013). "I realized that we had to extend our reach beyond members because we are trying to achieve a mission beyond the members' control. They don't solely control the achievement of that mission. Therefore, we're very interested in various ways in which we can (1) expand the definition of membership, and (2) engage in a lot of activities trying to reach people other than members."

All for One and One for All

Lieber and the team at HIMSS developed a membership model that offered membership to everyone at a hospital, regardless of his or her position. Although each person might not be part of the group the organization was trying to reach, it didn't matter, because, according Lieber, "It won't cost you a dime more to add those people. So I wanted to take away the economic diffusion as a member." HIMSS was able to offer the group membership to everyone because of advances in technology and the way HIMSS distributed its content and information. Rather than see advances in technology as a disruptor to the legacy membership model, Lieber took advantage of the new opportunities.

"This is something that was possible only because of change in the way our world works as we were able to move away from print and mail to electronic," Lieber explained. "That freed me up to do this, because I have virtually no cost associated with adding an additional member. Because I'm not sending them anything in the mail, I'm not printing something for every one of them. Once I'm producing these things electronically, adding one more email address doesn't really have a cost associated with it."

The program was designed to attract governmental agencies and not-for-profit organizations. "I didn't want the CIO to have to go to the hospital CEO or CFO and ask if the hospital could join.

That would only introduce another person in the decision making process," Lieber said.

> The nontechnology people in a health care setting are the CEO, a CFO, the chief medical officer, chief nursing officer. They are folks whose responsibilities extend way outside of IT, but they run units or departments or institutions that are very technology dependent. I want them to hear it from us. I want them to hear what we're thinking, what we're developing; I want them to see the comparison with people like them, but it's not an ordinance where you normally would pay attention to things. With the organizational membership program, the CIO says to the executive team, "Hey, I signed all of you up to be member of HIMSS because each and every one of you at some time was in my office or I'm in your office, and we're talking about technology and options and issues. These are things that I think you ought to hear."

In the preceding year, HIMSS had reached a point where the association had as many individual members in its affiliate program as were coming into the organization one at a time, or even more. In fact, Lieber maintains that prior to this program, the organization's average penetration in a hospital was two to four people. The last time he checked the numbers, it was somewhere north of a hundred people.

Lieber did have one concern. Before the program was launched, would current members move from one category to another, which could potentially result in only modest growth? His concern turned out to be unfounded; HIMSS actually saw both vertical growth and horizontal growth in the member organizations.

"The CIO can add everyone from his or her department, and we were able to attract individual members from across other departments," Lieber said.

Financially, HIMSS was able to create this type of group membership program because membership revenue represents only 12 percent of the total budget. With a larger audience, HIMSS is able to grow its conferences and sell more products, thus increasing revenue in these other areas as well.

"There's a huge strategic connection among all of these activities, and each of them feeds the other," Lieber explained. And that strategic connection results in a win-win-win—the association grows its membership, sales of products, and conference attendance, and members are even more satisfied with the organization.

HIMSS Membership Structure

Tables 4.3 and 4.4 show the structure that HIMSS employs for its group membership model. The organization's website (http://www.himss.org/membership/) explains how it works: "HIMSS Organizational Affiliate program is an enterprise-wide opportunity

Table 4.3. HIMSS Organizational Affiliate Membership

	Associate	**Pioneer**	**Principal**	**Executive**
Dues	$3,175	$5,275	$8,975	$13,675
Education	Two comp registrations to annual conference	Four comp registrations to annual conference	Eight comp registrations to annual conference	Twelve comp registrations to annual conference
	Unlimited registrations to virtual conference	Unlimited registrations to virtual conference	Unlimited registrations to virtual conference	Unlimited registrations to virtual conference
	Ten seats to eLearning Academy	Fifteen seats to eLearning Academy	Thirty seats to eLearning Academy	Forty-five seats to eLearning Academy
Membership	Unlimited individual membership and chapter membership			
Discounts on JobMine and CPHIMS exams	10–20 percent			
HIMSS Analytics Product Discounts	3 percent	3 percent	5 percent	7 percent

Table 4.4.   HIMSS Individual Membership Program

	Online Only	Chapter Only	Regular (includes one chapter)	Student
	$30	$30	$160	$30
Chapter events, website, news		X	X	X
Volunteering		Chapter only	X	X
Discounts to educational events		Chapter only	X	X
Discounts on JobMine and CPHIMS exams			X	X
Publications and industry news	X	Chapter affiliated resources only	X	X
Tools and resources	X	Chapter affiliated resources only	X	X

for every staff member—from clinicians to business personnel—to have access to the most exclusive and highest quality health care IT education, advanced professional development resources and select health IT networking opportunities.

"This comprehensive benefits package empowers entire health care organizations, reaching beyond IT: expanding the limits of employee awareness and knowledge and enhancing interdepartmental collaboration around initiatives to boost productivity, advance strategy, and more efficiently plan and manage systems in the pursuit of improved patient care."

Corporate membership is based on annual revenue:

- Diamond ($25,000)
- Platinum ($14,000 for companies with annual revenues > $10 million)
- Platinum ($8,500 for companies with annual revenues < $10 million)
- Gold ($8,000 for companies with annual revenues > $10 million)
- Gold ($3,500 for companies with annual revenues < $10 million)

Action Steps

Before you can implement a new group pricing structure, you will need to complete the following steps:

1. Define the goals and outcomes or the benefits of having a group membership program for the organization. If your goal is to significantly increase market penetration, your approach to developing a group membership program will be significantly different than if your overall goal is to increase revenue. Defining the goal of this initiative at the very beginning of the project is imperative. It will lead many future decisions as you go through the process. Next, you will want to build internal consensus for the program from every department in the organization. Examine the financial and operational implications of bundling various benefits with membership. Ask each department to express their goals of the program and their concerns regarding any challenges needed to implement it.

2. Identify three to five primary needs of the target audiences. Most organizations have primary and secondary audiences. Your primary audience includes your regular full or active members. It may also include students or young professionals. For the purposes of a group membership program, secondary audiences typically include individuals from other departments in the company or support staff. In this step, you need to understand their motivations and needs and what types of bundled packages might appeal to them in their role.

3. Identify the logistical benefits of a group membership.
Group membership programs work best when there is an administrator who will serve as the primary point person for the account. During this stage, you should conduct telephone interviews and/ or deploy an electronic survey to identify challenges and, ultimately, overcome any objections. Program administrators are busy people, and a common challenge is lack of time and resources to implement a group membership program. The key to making this type of program work is to design a program that is easy to implement, access, and use without requiring too much of the primary point person.

4. Develop up to three membership models that could realistically be implemented. During this stage, you will look at the financial implications of a new membership model. You will need to take into consideration past purchases and your existing market penetration. Look at the financial data from the past three years to determine how much each individual spent with your organization. Creating pivot tables in a spreadsheet program will help you summarize a lot of data by organization. By mining the data that already exists in your AMS system and developing potential membership models aimed at capturing a greater market share, you should be able to predict potential outcomes of each new model.

5. Test the ideas in the marketplace. Once you've selected the membership model that provides you with the greatest opportunity to meet your goals, it is important to test the idea in the marketplace. In my experience, you can gain valuable feedback from telephone interviews with decision makers and account contacts. This may highlight unforeseen logistical issues and challenges. It should also give you a sense of which organizations will be most likely to participate or respond to an invitation to join the program. They will be the low-hanging fruit. Be prepared to make some modifications to the program based on feedback.

6. Align staff responsibilities with program implementation.
Before launching the new group membership program, you will need to either add responsibilities for an existing staff person or hire new employees to manage the program. If your goal is to significantly increase market share, and if the program is successful, you should plan to add staff members who can provide high-touch customer service and program management to ensure

high retention rates. A dedicated sales and account team can be proactive in engaging new members to take advantage of the benefits of the program. People on that team should also serve as a liaison to other departments to ensure that the program is functioning at the highest level and everyone is meeting their goals.

7. Create a proactive engagement plan. Organizations will sign up to participate in a group membership model if it saves them time and money and provides solutions to their challenges. They will renew if these goals are met. Before you launch a group membership program, ensure that the benefits package provides savings to the bottom line for the organization. By that I mean that savings that can be tracked and reported on during the renewal process. I recommend creating a twelve-month engagement plan for organizations that participate in the program. Each month should include reminders of special benefits and offers. The focus of the twelve-month plan is to achieve high engagement rates for participating organizations.

8. Establish program goals. To clearly define the goals for each department, and to create a sense of accountability, it's helpful to set some performance metrics. The key metrics include the number of individuals who participate in the program, participation or registration in events and programs, and sales revenue from products and programs. A secondary set of metrics should include data from a member satisfaction survey and the financial return on the marketing investment.

9. Pilot the program before launching it to the entire membership. Once you create the new group membership program, you may be eager to conduct an industry-wide launch. Although you've tested the idea in the marketplace and fine-tuned the program based on feedback and an internal assessment, a soft launch is recommended. Begin by identifying ten to fifteen organizations that either have expressed interest in this type of opportunity or have a history of being strongly committed to the organization. Invite them to participate in the pilot program, and let them know that you want their feedback during the program.

Removing the barriers to joining your organization should result in either growth or higher retention rates, yet it most likely will not convert all prospects or customers into members. And, as you will read in the next chapter, that is OK. Market positioning is the art of sacrifice. You must give up on attracting the wrong types of members to attract the right ones to your association. This can be done in a measureable way that ignites the membership marketing team and provides them with a sensible target prospect.

PART TWO

WHO ARE YOUR MEMBERS?

Members or Customers? Developing the Most Qualified Prospect List

I HAVE A CONFESSION TO MAKE: I own a marketing agency, but I do not belong to an association that focuses exclusively on marketing. Although I am aware of a few such associations that provide information, education, and networking opportunities—benefits that I value—I am a customer for those groups. I am not a member.

A few years ago I reviewed these associations' websites and considered joining, but I soon realized they had overlap value with two of the societies to which I already belong. I attended one association's conferences, however, to try it on for size. While I found it helpful to hear a different perspective and approach to nonprofit marketing, the sessions were not nearly as relevant as the ones offered by my primary association. Even so, there were some things I might have found valuable. So why haven't I joined these organizations?

There are two primary reasons. First, I can obtain much of the information I need through various other resources that are priced competitively and are available to everyone. Second, I'm not interested in the intangible benefits these organizations offer, such as leadership, networking, or volunteer opportunities. Let me explain.

When I think about obtaining information on the latest trends in my industry, I have many sources to which I can turn. With a few clicks of the mouse or a touch on my iPad, I can purchase and download the latest business books from my Amazon Prime account. And before I buy, I can read the reviews and even take a "look inside" to see if the book is written in a style I find easy to read and understand.

Ask your association: Do we publish unique and highly relevant information that can be accessed or conveniently downloaded by members? If so, are there some good alternatives to our products, ones that are nearly identical in quality and/or price?

I also subscribe to the print and digital editions of the *Harvard Business Review* (*HBR*). Over the last few years, an increasing number of colleges are beginning their conversations with, "Did you read the article in the *Harvard Business Review* last month on . . . ?" From leadership to management to strategy, I have found many thoughtful case studies and articles on topics that are relevant to the association industry.

Ask your association: What other sources of information do our members turn to when they are seeking information on the latest trends in our industry? What journals, magazines, and websites do they reference in their conversations at our meetings and events? What articles do they share with each other in our private or social media communities or our discussion groups?

Finally, one of my favorite sources of information on best practices, trends, and news is SmartBrief (*www.smartbrief.com*), a media company that provides electronic newsletters to more than one hundred professional and trade associations including the American Association of Advertising Agencies, the Mobile Marketing Association, the Word of Mouth Marketing Association, and National Retail Association, among others. The SmartBrief on Social Media newsletter helps me stay on top of social media trends in the consumer world—many of which are relevant in the B2B world.

Ask your association: Are we repurposing information that is currently being offered by other organizations, or do we identify topics and issues and create our own content? Do we allow nonmembers to subscribe to our newsletter/magazine or is it for members only?

The bottom line is that when I need association-specific information, networking, or opportunities to give back to the profession, I turn to ASAE: The Center for Association Leadership or the Association Forum of Chicagoland. I also belong to a few other associations because membership in those groups provides me with helpful information I need, for a price that is considerably lower than if I were to remain a customer rather than a member.

How do you encourage individuals like me to join your organization? The surprising answer is: you don't. And the reason is simple, yet hard to conceptualize when you're working hard for every dollar of dues: *Not every person should be a member.* Some individuals should remain customers.

Once you've clearly identified your value proposition—based on what you offer, the needs of the marketplace, the emotional connections you create, and the price—you've completed only half the steps needed to grow or sustain membership in your organization. You also need to understand *who* will value what your organization offers through membership and *who* may prefer to remain a customer.

I've spent the early part of this chapter focusing on why some individuals don't join an association. We will spend the better part of the second half discussing how to: (1) determine which prospects are most likely to join, and (2) decide on the most effective strategies and tactics for converting prospects into members.

Who's Qualified?

Scoring "leads" (in association speak: prospective members) is a common practice used by for-profit sales departments to rank the likelihood that a prospect will convert into a customer. Many companies assign a score to the leads they receive, because they do not want to spend valuable time or money pursuing individuals who are not qualified to make a decision or purchase a product. While there are numerous ways to identify the top prospects within your association's database, I will go over the steps you should take to help your organization save considerable money and time. More important, this will help you recruit more members.

Now I realize that many organizations will read the preceding paragraph and immediately think, "We don't have enough information on our prospects to assign them a score." Some individuals may avoid this step because they have too many prospects or leads in their database and therefore it is just too big a project to undertake. And some may think it will be too expensive or too time-consuming. But consider this: successful membership recruitment campaigns happen when organizations are able to capture the prospect's attention and make an offer he or she can't refuse. And both of these tactics rely on an organization's ability to market to a highly qualified list of prospective members.

Whether you have $10,000, $100,000, or $1 million to spend on your next recruitment campaign, your efforts should result in either a break-even scenario—recruiting enough new members to offset the cost of the campaign—or a small profit. This will occur only if you market your organization to a qualified list of prospects.

Lead Scoring Basics

The closer the prospective member is to your organization's existing core members, the better the fit with your other programs and products. Why is this important? If you create a recruitment campaign that successfully attracts a thousand new members, yet most of these individuals do not reflect your core audience, it may be nearly impossible to attract them to your programs and events. Therefore, although you've successfully sold membership, you will probably fail to sell much else. This audience may also be significantly less interested than core members are in your magazine or journal content or the information and resources on your website. As such, when it comes time for these members to renew, they may not. Consequently, you are more likely to experience a low retention rate. If your organization struggles to retain first-year members, it is highly probable that you are working with a prospect list that is not an ideal match for your organization.

When it comes to scoring leads, organizations should consider three kinds of information: demographics, activity level, and recency (see Exhibit 5.1).

Exhibit 5.1. Sample Attributes to Consider

Demographics of the Individual
- Age
- Recent graduate or student
- Degrees received
- Years in practice
- Title
- Role

- Level of manager
- Specialty
- Membership status—former member or never a member

Demographics of the Prospect's Employer
- Type (private, public, government, nonprofit)
- Number of employees
- Geographic location
- Annual budget
- Number of current members employed by the organization

Activity Level
- No activity
- Requested membership information
- Joined LinkedIn group
- Viewed a video
- E-newsletter subscriber
- Journal/magazine subscriber
- Downloaded a report or white paper
- Purchased a product or publication
- Attended a free event
- Attended a paid event or program
- Contributor or program facilitator
- Former volunteer

Recency: Length of Time in the Database
- New
- Less than one year
- One year
- Two years
- Three or more years

Optional: Lead Source
- Member referral
- Rented/purchased list from licensing board
- Rented/purchased list from state association
- Rented/purchased list from list broker

Demographics is the most obvious place to start, in part because most organizations collect at least some of this information through the application process. To begin the process of assigning a score to prospective members, you must first understand the demographic profile of your current members. You'll want to know the composition of your membership in terms of age, gender, title, practice area, work setting, and educational background or degrees earned. (See Exhibit 5.1 for a more complete list of demographic factors.) If this data isn't readily available from your association management system (AMS), you may need to conduct a census of your members. I recommend including questions that identify both demographic information and psychographic data. This information will create a more complete profile of your members—their interests and their motivations. Conducting a census or updating the records every two years is a good practice as well.

The second area of measurement when assigning a score to a prospective member is their *activity level*. Has the prospect ever attended an event or conference? Does he or she attend paid events or free events? Has the prospect downloaded a free white-paper report and purchased a publication? Does he or she subscribe to your newsletter, comment on blog posts, or has he or she submitted an article for publication or presented at an industry conference? Based on the prospect's level of activity, you may choose to assign a lower or higher point number.

The third area to consider, and often one of the most underrated metrics, is the *recency* of their interaction with your organization. Recency may be calculated by looking at the time between their last purchase and the present, or it could be examined by the length of time they've been customers and not members. In this exercise, it is more important to consider the number of years a person has been a customer. A long-time customer is often less likely to join your organization than a newer one.

There are, of course, exceptions to this rule. For example, if it has been a few years since you've asked your customers to join the organization, long-time customers may still be a good fit for your organization simply because they haven't been asked until recently.

These three factors (demographics, activity level, and recency) can be assigned point values. Although you can assign any point value, I recommend a tiered point scale for each category. You then define how important each attribute is in relation to another. Let's look at an example.

If you work at a large national health care organization, you may already know that your best prospects are individuals who are currently in school or are recent graduates. In this situation, you would assign a higher point value to these two audience segments; you would lower the point value based on the number of years in practice.

Student = 25 points

Graduated less than one year ago = 20 points

One to two years ago = 15 points

Three to four years = 10 points

Five to seven years = 5 points

More than seven years = –5 points

If you have limited time and resources, I recommend selecting two or three items from each area in Exhibit 5.1.

Assigning Points: A Range of Methods

Once you've compiled your list of attributes from each of the categories detailed in Exhibit 5.1, there are two approaches to assigning a score to prospective members. The first is fairly easy; it can be used by any organization, regardless of size, resources, or availability of data. The second approach requires a significant commitment to acquiring and using explicit and implicit data.

Simple Approach

1. Create a profile of the ideal member (or members, if you have multiple membership categories). Look at your current membership. Are there certain groups in the industry that are over- or underrepresented in your membership? If you work for a medical society or a scientific organization, you may attract more academics than practitioners. If you work for a financial or legal association, your organization may attract more individuals from larger firms than smaller practices. Note that at this point we are not focusing on how to diversify your membership or attract new members from underserved audience segments; that will be addressed in Part Three. In this chapter, we are mostly concerned with creating a list of prospective members who are highly or moderately likely to join your organization, because they will be interested in and satisfied with the programs, products, and services you currently offer.

To achieve this, you need to create a prospect list that matches your "best" members. In other words, you want a list of prospects who, once converted to members, will remain members for the long haul. The real value, in terms of actual dollars, can be determined by a simple equation called the "lifetime value" (LTV) of a member. Calculating this will also help you justify your investment in prospecting in the way this chapter suggests. (See Table 5.2, at the end of this chapter, for an illustration of how to calculate the LTV of a member. Regardless of whether you decide to move forward with the prospecting methods laid out in this chapter, understanding how to determine the LTV is worthwhile.)

There are three metrics to consider when determining your best prospects: tenure, demographics, and behavior. In terms of tenure, I recommend creating a list of all the members who have been with your organization for no fewer than three years. What do these individuals have in common? Look at their profiles to determine any common characteristics, such as industry, employer type, employer size, title or position, years in practice (graduation date), specialty area of practice, or other factors. You may also wish to add geographical information, if that is something your organization captures and is typically used for marketing to your audience.

Next, narrow down the list to individuals who have had some level of interaction with your organization, beyond just paying their dues every year. Activities may include attending an in-person event or webinar, purchasing a product or publication, speaking or writing for a publication, serving on a committee, or referring a colleague for membership. This is not a complete list; use it as a starting point for your own list.

Finally, create profiles of the *ideal* member or members. These individuals will have the greatest likelihood of joining your association and, more important, renewing their membership after the first year.

2. Assign values based on criteria used in the profiles. Create three groups within each profile based on the number of factors they have in common: low (1), medium (2), and high (3). Individuals who meet nearly all of the criteria receive a three; some of the criteria, a two; and none of the criteria, a one.

3. Assign values to prospects. Sort your prospect list based on how individuals match up with your "best" members. Prospects that meet most or all of the criteria, yet have been customers for more than three years, should be removed from the high prospect list. Although these individuals match key metrics, their tenure as customers reduces their value—unless, as stated earlier, you have not recently asked them to actually join the membership (see Table 5.1).

Table 5.1. Scoring Model

Attribute	Value	Score
Title	Partner	+15
	General counsel	+10
	Associate	+5
	Office manager	−5
Organization Size	500+ employees	−5
	250–499 employees	+5
	100–249 employees	+10
	Less than 100 employees	+15
Organization Type	Private practice	+15
	Company	+5
	Government	−10
Activity	Magazine subscriber	+5
	LinkedIn member	+5
	Attended paid local event	+10
	Attended paid national event	+15

(*Continued*)

Table 5.1.   (Continued)

Attribute	Value	Score
	Attended free local event	+5
	Purchased one product	–5
	Purchased multiple products	15
	No activity	0
Recency	New	20
	Less than one year	15
	One year	10
	Two years	5
	Three or more years	–10
Source	Member referral	20
	Recent attendee	15

Category	Points
Demographic profile	25
Activity level	25
Length of time	15
Lead source	15
Total points	80

Advanced Approach

Many organizations maintain a database that houses demographic information such as age, size of company or budget, or historical behavior such as past meeting attendees or recently licensed professionals. This is obviously important information to capture and store, but using it in your marketing won't necessarily result in a successful conversion to membership. Some of these individuals will require more effort in enticing them to join than just an appealing piece based on typical demographic or behavioral information. These prospects need to be prompted in the right way.

The good news is that you should be able to differentiate between potential members and nonjoining customers, but it is going to require some time and attention. It begins with collecting some different, yet very key, demographic facts about your prospects. Do you know the answers to the following questions about the prospects in your database?

- What year did they graduate from undergrad, graduate school, or a residency program?
- What year did they enter the workforce?
- How many years have they been in practice or working in the field?
- What type of organization do they work for (a private or public company, government entity or nonprofit)?
- How many products have they purchased from your organization over the past three years?

What is their membership status—that is, are they lapsed members or have they never been members?Although additional information, such as household income, interests, and other activities, is extremely helpful, most nonprofit organizations are unable to collect this type of data or have not yet done so.

One of the most relevant pieces of information you can collect on prospective members is the number of years they've been in practice. Sometimes this can be determined by their title or graduation date. Although you may not have collected this information in the past, it is a vital bit of data to acquire from customers or prospective members. The reason? The research I've conducted with individual membership organizations has shown that individuals are twice as likely to join an organization during the early stages of their career than in the later stages. Plus, you have a greater likelihood of keeping them as members. It makes sense, if you think about it. These individuals often have the greatest need to obtain specialized information, advance their careers, and expand their networks. They need to belong to an association! If this is true for your organization, then prospective members who are in the early stages of their career, therefore, will receive a higher score or rating than those who are in the middle or later stages.

For example, many health care organizations have increased efforts to attract students and recent graduates to their organization through preferred pricing programs and academic partnerships or referral programs. Scharan Johnson, the director of membership development at the American Physical Therapy Association (APTA) I introduced in Chapter One, is a firm believer in focusing her recruitment efforts on students and recent graduates. "The fastest-growing segment of APTA's membership is students, a category that's more than doubled since 2003. On average, between 2007 and 2012, 88 percent of new APTA members annually joined as students," Johnson told me (personal communication, January 10, 2013). "Generally, when we increase our focus on students and new professionals, these efforts pay dividends for associations whose members' professions require a specialized degree, certification, and/or licensure to practice. For us, it's arithmetic. At APTA, effective strategies that demonstrate value and inspire students to belong and participate are yielding big results."

The return on the marketing investment may also be significantly higher if the organization is able to retain them as members over a longer period of time. Although this isn't true for all industries or all individuals, we have seen a trend in this direction for many groups.

The criteria used by the APTA to measure the likelihood of a prospect joining the organization may be different from what's used by your organization. What is most important is to determine what factors increase the likelihood that a prospect will join your organization.

Scoring Model for Legal Association

For some of the attributes listed in Table 5.1, you should assign a positive point value; others should receive a negative point value. You may decide to assign a negative point value if the person has been a customer for a long time or had only one transaction with your organization a few years ago but never joined despite being asked.

If the ideal prospect is a partner at a small law firm who also attended an event within the last year, then a combination of the attributes should equal or exceed the threshold to be considered a very good prospect for your organization. On the other hand, if the prospect works for the government or a large law firm and has attended a few events over the last three years, the likelihood that this person will join your organization may be low.

As you complete this exercise, I recommend assigning points based on a variety of factors, because most individuals will have characteristics that overlap with other factors you are considering when scoring your prospective members. For example, if the average member joining your organization has been out of college for ten years and is established in a management position, those meeting these criteria may appear to fit the profile for a good lead for your next marketing campaign. However, if the prospect has been a customer or an "active participant" with your organization for more than three years but has never joined, the score should be lowered.

Once you've assigned points to various attributes, you can set a profile rating based on a scale. For example, you may determine that anyone who receives 75 points or more is an A; 50–74 points, a B; 25–49 points, a C; less than 25 points, a D. Once you have determined the scores and mapped it to a rating, you can determine follow-up steps.

A = Priority—call prospect

B = Good fit—continue to include in recruitment efforts

C = May not be ideal—highlight the difference between the member and the nonmember price

D = No interest—no longer include in recruitment mailings

Although this is not a foolproof way to ensure that your marketing dollars are well spent, it should increase the likelihood of achieving higher response rates to your campaigns. It should also provide you with a clearer picture of which types of prospects have a low, medium, or high potential for joining the organization.

If the marketing associations I first referred to in this chapter applied this approach to my file in their database, they would quickly realize that I do not match most of the demographics of their *ideal* member.

Ultimately, the value of developing a scoring program for your prospects is to save your organization money by increasing the return on your marketing investment.

Determining Lifetime Value

To determine the lifetime value of your members (see Table 5.2), you will need to know the following:

- Average length of time your members belong to your organization. If you have different membership categories, you may wish to determine this number for each category.
- Average yearly membership dues.
- Total non-dues revenue earned by the organization. This figure should include advertising dollars, subscriptions, publications sales, sponsorships, registrations, and anything else that involves revenue related to a membership offering.
- The cost of servicing a member over the lifetime of the membership (multiply the cost of servicing a member by the average number of years a membership lasts). This figure should include all expenses including overhead, administration, and direct expenses incurred while servicing members.

The following is an example of how to calculate the lifetime value of a member with the following assumptions:

- The total number of members equals 2,782.
- The total membership expenses for one year is $1,371,222.
- The lifetime value of a member is $1,519.

Table 5.2. Calculating the Lifetime Value of a Member

1. Calculate the average length of time a member belongs to the organization.	Six years	
2. Calculate the average yearly dues that a member pays.	$207	
3. Multiply the average length of time a member belongs to the organization by the yearly dues. (Step 1 × Step 2)	$1,242	Lifetime Dues Value of Member
4. Calculate the total revenue earned from member purchases of products and services during the previous year.	$1.5 Million	

5. Calculate the value of a member's non-dues purchases for the year by dividing the total revenue earned from all purchases of products and services during the previous year by the number of organizational members (Step 4/total number of members).	$539	
6. Multiply the results of Step 5 by the average length of time a member belongs to the organization (Step 5 × Step 1).	$3,234	Lifetime Non-Dues Value of a Member
7. Add the lifetime dues value of a member and the lifetime non-dues value of a member together (Step 3 + Step 6).	$4,476	
8. Cost of servicing a member over the lifetime of their membership.	$2,957	
9. Subtract the cost of servicing a member from the lifetime value (Step 7 – Step 8).	$1,519	Lifetime Value of a Member

Case Study: The ABA's Approach to Grabbing Low-Hanging Fruit

Most organizations have a list of prospects made up of individuals who just need a little more prodding to get them join. This audience segment is already aware of your organization and ideally has had a positive experience in the past. Therefore they should not require a lot of effort to get them to join, thus they represent low-hanging fruit as far as membership goes. While scoring the prospects in your database is one approach to gain this segment, it isn't the only one. Another approach is to take advantage of your member sales force.

The American Bar Association (ABA), one of the largest associations in the country, learned that this type of approach worked very well for recruiting lawyers to the organization. Again, the idea behind most member referral campaigns is that your members should be the best sales team available to get others to join. They are more likely to recruit like-minded members and to have considerable influence. Although the ABA uses a variety of different approaches, one of the most successful campaigns was its member-get-a-member program (see Figure 5.1). In this case, success is defined as a program that helps the organization grow by recruiting new members with the greatest likelihood of staying with the organization. The ABA does use other tactics to increase membership, yet retention rates for members who come in through other channels are lower.

Initially, the member referral program was offered to only a select group of individuals whom the organization believed would be most interested in participating in the program—and whom they felt would provide the greatest return on the marketing investment for the program. The first year the program was launched, the ABA printed and mailed holiday cards with coupons that the select group of members could pass along to friends and colleagues who may be interested in trying out membership in the ABA. The coupons were free gifts of membership, good for a limited time, thus creating a sense of urgency. The program achieved the modest goals established by the organization. Members embraced the opportunity to help the organization grow and had the tools to invite their colleagues to join.

During the second year of the program, the ABA expanded the audience to include volunteer leadership at all levels and members from a key market segment. Within the target segment, ABA tested the member referral program with members who had recently joined as well as long-standing members, and the organization found that newer members were surprisingly good at recruiting members.

Kevin Henderson, director of membership at the ABA, said, "In the first two years we learned a lot about what we could do to improve the program and increase the number of referrals. Participants told us that they would pass along additional free

Figure 5.1. ABA Member Referral Program Promotion

membership cards if they had the opportunity. They also told us that 'it would be great to send invites to join the ABA electronically' and through social media" (personal communication, February 15, 2013). Members also told the ABA that they wanted to keep track of their efforts and compare themselves to their colleagues. Henderson added that he looked at other member referral programs in both the nonprofit and for-profit communities for ideas.

Listen, Tweak, and Improve

In the third year of the program, the ABA created an online portal that allowed members to track how many people they had recruited and how many were recruited overall. "We made it easier for them to share the message during the third year," said Kirsten Rider, manager of membership at the ABA, one of the primary staff members responsible for implementing the program (personal communication, February 15, 2013). "It was very turnkey. We created opportunities for members to share messages on LinkedIn, Facebook, and Twitter. We also created a sample email they could edit and send to their contacts in their address books." In addition, the ABA created digital coupons that could be downloaded and printed so that members were no longer limited in the number of members they could refer for membership. They still mailed the initial package with twenty-five cards to their best prospects, but with the digital component of the program they were able to expand their efforts to a broader audience.

The ABA also made some additional changes and expanded the program to all ABA members. Paula Cleave, ABA division director, membership, who led the staff on this initiative, said, "We created a very successful campaign called *Rewards for Referrals,* by offering a tier-based reward system where members could earn certain prizes such as iPods and iPads. The campaign included direct mail, email, and a web-based portal to check their status and share the membership offer [that] they knew through email and social media" (all Paula Cleave quotes are from personal communication, February 15, 2013). Cleave also leveraged an active LinkedIn community to promote the program: "We tried to make it easier for members to get the word out to people. In the past we printed small cards. This year we went electronic, utilizing social media, to share that offer."

Within three years, the ABA had recruited more than 7,500 members through this channel. What makes this approach an even greater success was that these members have a much higher likelihood of renewing their membership—which ultimately means a greater lifetime value.

Cleave had found that after doing the campaign year after year, there was campaign fatigue—specifically throughout the association's leadership. So they decided to take a break, coming back with a new angle that focuses on testimonials. This approach, according to Cleave, is a natural extension of the member referral program and still fits in with the strategy of leveraging existing member support to help grow the organization.

Keep It Fresh

What differentiates the approach taken by the ABA from business as usual is that it used tactics to market the program based on the scope and size of the audience. When the organization developed the first campaign, it focused on tapping a small group of ABA leaders to recruit friends and colleagues. Staff invested in a print campaign with a special offer. Because the campaign was small and targeted, they were able to keep costs low and monitor the results. And ABA's president at the time, Carolyn Lamm, was highly engaged in the program.

"We included a select group of members in this effort and that did very well. We created a nice buzz among the leadership," said Paula Cleave. "Most of the folks doing the recruiting were volunteer leaders, including from every section and division within the organization." The ABA found the feedback to be very positive; the idea of a competition among the leadership was appealing. The board stepped up, then, and essentially gave the message that there was no reason a leader within the organization couldn't get at least one member to join. "I believe it was very helpful to have this message come from our leadership," said Cleave.

In the third year, the focus of the program was changed to cast a wider net and leverage the goodwill and interest of the broader membership.

> In past years, only a select group received the communication. This year we made it available through our website. Any member could participate in the campaign. We also put stickers on the cover of the *ABA Journal*. We ran advertisements in our publications, and mentioned it in our e-newsletters, and included the offer in outreach done to other associations. We encouraged members to post it on their law firm intranets and heard of people putting it on their blogs. Staff were allowed to participate. There are a couple hundred lawyers on the ABA staff, and they were some of the best ambassadors. They were allowed to win prizes, and why not? That campaign did really well for us [Paula Cleave, personal communication, February 15, 2013].

To encourage staff participation, the ABA's executive director gave detailed updates at staff meetings and awarded prizes to top recruiters on the staff. Prizes included a full comp day or a half comp day to the top recruiter.

In the end, the ABA gave away fifty-nine iPods and forty-eight iPads. To earn an iPod, an individual needed to recruit between ten and twenty-four new members. To receive an iPad, they had to recruit at least twenty-five new members. If an individual recruited more than one new member, they received an entry into a drawing for airline gift cards.

This program was successful on a variety of levels. First, the volunteer leadership and senior staff threw their support behind the program. Second, the program was integrated into events and meetings, the website, and ABA's social media presence. Finally, they tracked the progress and sent members status updates.

To begin this process for your association, start asking all members, on a scale of 0 to 10, *how likely are you to recommend membership to a colleague or friend?* Create a profile of the members who responded with a 9 or 10. If your survey reveals that individuals who have, for example, at least ten years of experience are the most likely group to recruit their friends and peers, you can create a campaign designed specifically for this group. Alternatively, the survey may reveal that newer, younger members are more likely to recommend membership because they have a greater need for some of the offerings provided by your association that are beneficial to them, or they have a need for the cost savings provided to members. With a higher level of customization, the program will have a greater chance for success.

Understanding who is likely to promote membership, if given the opportunity and prompted by the organization, is very important. Additionally, this approach also tells you what types of members fall into this category.

The VIP Sure Thing

Once you've identified who *should be a member* of your organization, *give* (not *offer*) these members a six-month free trial membership. By this I mean *sign them up*—not invite them to take action themselves to sign up for it. With this approach, you create a list of individuals who are similar to your current members but have not yet joined. You may have a list of one hundred or one thousand names. If you've gone through the steps described earlier in this chapter, you should be able to identify and build a prospect list of VIPs. Enroll them as full members and provide them with all of the benefits of membership. Let them know that they were selected for this program because it is important to the community that they are a part of your organization.

The six-month membership should expire when all of the members in your organization are asked to renew. For example, if your membership year is July 1 through June 30, you would enroll them January 1, and at the end of June they would receive a simple invoice asking them to renew. If they ignore the invoice, they should be dropped from the membership rolls. As unusual as this approach sounds, my experience has been that organizations can have as high as an 80 percent retention rate if they target the right group: the VIPs who *should be a member* of the organization. And the best part is, the only cost is the incremental cost of sending the new member the various onboarding materials, such as a new member packet and magazine or journal.

Action Steps to Create the Right List

1. Develop and implement a consistent scoring system for prospects and customers. Although it will take time to establish criteria and assign points to prospects, it will pay off in the long run. In fact, some people say if you improve the quality of your leads by 10 percent you can experience a 40 percent increase in response rates.
2. Examine demographic, behavioral, and recency data to determine a prospect's score. Look at prospects that reflect your best members. Examine the characteristics of long-time customers who have never joined.
3. Remove long-time customers from your prospect list. Continue to market programs and products, but not with the same messages or calls-to-action.
4. Develop and implement marketing strategies and tactics that are customized based on demographics and behavior.

Action Steps to Apply the Right Marketing

If you want to increase both response rates to your marketing campaigns and renewals of first-year members, it's essential that you build a database of qualified prospects. You can develop a very creative or even disruptive marketing campaign that nevertheless fails, simply because you are speaking to the wrong audience. Once you have used one of the approaches I describe earlier in this chapter to determine who are your best prospects and who should remain customers (and have taken the first set of action steps to create the right list), it's time to consider what marketing tactics make the most sense for your organization. Although there are many strategies and tactics you should test and incorporate into your recruitment strategy, the following suggestions should be considered by all size and types of organizations.

1. Segment your marketing efforts. When you begin segmenting your marketing efforts, you need to consider the following elements:
- Tone: Should the tone you use be formal, conversational, or humorous? Even the most conservative organization should consider different tones for different audience segments.

- Message: The headline is one of the most important elements of the campaign. That one line will either entice the recipient to read more or get your appeal tossed into the recycle bin. The message must be relevant to the audience segment.
- Benefits: What are the one or two key benefits of joining your organization, based on the audience segment? You don't need to list every benefit, just the ones that matter the most to this group.
- Features: What are the tangible things they will receive with membership that connect to the benefits? What are the outcomes of using the features?
- Calls-to-action and incentives: Different audiences may respond differently to calls-to-action and incentives. A call-to-action may be *Download the report* or *Join by 11:59 on March 14.*
- Timing: What day of the week or time of the day works best for each audience segment? Some groups may be more likely to respond to an appeal sent over the weekend or in the evening.

2. Differentiate and humanize your organization. *Networking, information,* and *education* are three of the most overused words in association marketing. When an organization uses stale, familiar words such as these, their statements become invisible. By incorporating stories and a conversational tone into your marketing collateral, you become more human and less institutional. Although it is important to maintain your reputation for high-quality education, information, and resources, it is also essential that you appear approachable.

3. Increase the frequency of appeals. For some prospects, it may take up to twenty exposures via email, direct mail, social media, and phone calls before they join the organization. Although that number may sound both excessive and expensive, a 2010 study conducted by the *Journal of Marketing* showed that most organizations successfully gained new customers if they exposed them to nine or ten mailings, three or four emails, and three phone calls over a period of three months. This study focused on business-to-consumer selling; however, our experience with associations has yielded similar results. Using fewer touch points to reach prospects may result in both lower overall response rates and lower returns on marketing investments.

4. Create strong calls-to-action (CTAs). Some prospects believe they should join but just haven't completed the application form yet. Others may be thinking about joining but have not heard a compelling reason to act today. Strong CTAs include creating a sense of urgency, with a reason or incentive to respond immediately. Audit your marketing materials to ensure that every email, letter, postcard, brochure, or digital marketing piece includes a strong call-to-action.

5. Leverage content to acquire new members. Ready for a complete departure from the typical ways to market your organization and its programs, products, and services? Develop a content marketing program. With this approach, you identify topics of high interest or concern within your community and then connect the topics to your organization and its offerings. Instead of marketing events and conferences, member benefits and knowledge resources, promote a topic that is covered by these offerings and connect the topic to your resources. For example, if obesity is a hot topic of discussion among your members and their patients, incorporate some of the content on this topic from a report or publication into a newsletter and then promote any magazine articles, upcoming webinars, books, and other products related to the topic. Another way to leverage your content is to create and promote a promotional white paper based on a collection of articles or research on a hot topic. You can offer the report to prospects in exchange for their contact information. This will provide you with potential leads that have a good likelihood of being interested in the information and education you provide to members. The key to content marketing is connecting relevant and interesting content to your organization's offerings.

6. Activate your referral program. Many organizations offer some form of member-get-a-member or referral program that includes incentives for encouraging nonmembers to join. If your program isn't resulting in a high number of referrals, consider the following tactics:

- Develop different referral programs for different audience segments (like the ABA case study).
- Turn up the volume on your referral program by offering unique incentives at different levels. Reward members who participate by providing the names of prospects as well as those who are successful at recruiting new members. Promote your program in a fun and engaging way on your website and through various social media platforms.

Create a VIP—Sure Thing Program. Automatically enroll your VIP prospects in a six-month trial membership program that expires during the regular renewal period. Once the membership expires, send a membership renewal invoice (no letter). If you've targeted the right audience and demonstrated the value of membership during the six-month timeframe, you should have a high retention rate for this group.

■ ■ ■

A highly targeted marketing program is more likely to provide you with the results you desire. It requires a greater dedication of time and resources, but the payoff makes it worth the effort. However, this approach is not foolproof. In Chapter Six, we will demonstrate how one more piece of data can dramatically improve the results of your campaign.

6

Behavior and Preference Are Very Different Things

THE OTHER DAY, I was having coffee with a friend of mine who has three school-aged children and who enjoys shopping, working out, reading, and going to movies. She also loves a bargain—and, consequently, Groupon. She has the app on her iPhone and receives emails from Groupon alerting her about daily deals in her area.

This particular morning, however, she was irritated with the company. The day before we met, she had planned to take her children out for lunch at a new restaurant that she heard was supposed to be kid-friendly and fun. The friend who recommended the restaurant had sent her a text that morning: "Check Groupon. I just received a $20 for $10 deal yesterday." My friend immediately hit the app on her phone, but the deal did not pop up. She searched and searched, but still the deal was not being offered to her. In the end, she Googled the name of the restaurant and the word "Groupon" and was able to purchase the Groupon. (Did I mention that she is also determined?)

"At first, I was surprised—and annoyed—that the restaurant deal was not offered to me," she said to me. "I mean, my friend and I live in the same vicinity, we like the same things, we both have kids. Why did I have to search for that deal and she knew about it?"

Setting our coffee aside for a moment, we logged onto Groupon to try to figure out what had gone wrong. We turned to her profile, and it immediately became apparent. My friend's selected preferences (or, as Groupon calls them, "Favorite Deal

Types") consisted of Bookworm, Good for Kids, Healthy Living, Movie Buff, Pampered, and Well-Groomed. What she had not checked off, from the list of 50+ areas of interest, was "Foodie" or "Quick Bites" or "Let's Do Brunch." The list is nearly exhaustive— from "Adrenaline" to "World Music"—indeed, it's overwhelming.

"I picked what I thought I really needed at that time and what I felt I would buy," she explained. "But obviously I need to eat. Now that I think about it, I've bought more Groupons from restaurants than any other area of interest. Why didn't they look at my past purchases?"

"In other words," I said, "your behavior would have told them a lot about what deals to send to you." So we went back to the app and found that, in fact, her previous purchases were recorded and easily accessible to her; Groupon labels them "Expired and Used" deals. I pointed out, "You're interested in more than just your selected preferences, based on examining your past purchases. They are different things."

This example shows that asking your target audience about their preferences alone may not provide you with accurate information. You need to look at an individual's behavior as well. Indeed, this was recognized by anthropologist Margaret Mead, who observed, "What people say, what people do, and what they say they do are entirely different things."

Dig Below the Obvious to Make Decisions

Much has been researched and written about the motivations, needs, and interests of adult learners. And with the book *The Decision to Learn* by Lillie R. Albert and Monica Dignam (2010), the association industry can examine this issue on a much deeper level than ever before. In this chapter, I will apply the key findings from the ASAE Foundation's benchmarking research studies called the *Decision to . . .* series, and my own research with numerous associations to provide insight and recommendations on how to incorporate data into making decisions that will ultimately impact membership recruitment and retention.

In *The Decision to Learn*, the authors noticed a trend similar to what I have observed in much of my own work with associations. They examined how 7,848 individuals who were members of at least one of the twelve participating associations use the various sources of professional education to advance their professional goals. Among the authors' conclusions: "Association learners strongly prefer in-person programs but will participate in distance learning. Across all demographic segments, respondents reported a strong preference for in-person education programs over distance formats. In fact, the distance formats consistently fell at the bottom of the list in terms of preference ranking. Actual participation, however, tells a different story. The majority of respondents participated in some form of distance learning in the past year" (p. 2).

Albert and Dignam further suggest that the reason for the contradiction between preference and behavior "may lie in the perceived barriers." Although I believe this could have a significant impact on the decision to participate in a professional development program, other factors may be at work as well.

As we all know, market research can be, and is, used to help organizations identify needs, interests, and preferences of members and prospective members. It's also helpful if you want to evaluate the effectiveness of your programs and measure satisfaction with past experiences. And you can use research to identify both the challenges that your members are experiencing and where they (as well as prospects) currently turn for solutions to their most pressing issues.

Good research will dig below the obvious. It will deepen your understanding of the competitive advantages you have in the marketplace, if you ask the right questions. Most important, however, good research will uncover how your organization can meet the following three needs: affiliation, aspiration, and identity. Yet it also requires a disciplined approach to synthesizing the data in order to apply the findings to realistic and actionable steps, given the organization's culture and economic realities.

There are limitations, however, to what market research can offer when developing new products or programs. Carolyn Marvin, Professor of Communication at the University of Pennsylvania's Annenberg School and author of the book *When Old Technologies Were New* (1990), writes that throughout history, individuals view new technologies only as "a fancier version of the present" (p. 190).

In other words, our ability to rate interest in a new program or product is limited by existing knowledge of what is available today. Your members may be willing to share the problems or challenges they face and their views of existing programs and products, but it is difficult to accurately predict reactions to new programs or products based on market research. Your organization needs to be an expert on the topic and, more important, be *perceived* as an expert on the topic. Your organization needs to understand the marketplace, pricing thresholds, and alternative solutions to the problem. Your organization must be creative in its thinking and its approach to the "problem." And you need to examine past behavior, not just responses to a survey. In your next membership survey, if you ask participants to rank or identify their preferred style of learning, you should follow up by asking: In the last twelve months, have you participated in any of the following professional development activities? (This would be followed by a list.)

Additionally, when your association is identifying topics of high importance, further exploration may be needed to determine if your organization would be perceived as the best provider of information on that particular topic. Or even the natural provider. Even the most creative marketing professional cannot save a product or program that isn't well suited for the marketplace.

People Don't Know What They Don't Know

For years, a myth has been perpetuated that Apple does not listen to their customers. It turns out that they do listen to customers on a daily basis by asking one single question: How likely is it, on a 0–10 scale, that you will recommend this product or service to a friend or colleague? As a result, the average net promoter score (NPS) for Apple stores in 2011 was 72 percent, with the best stores achieving a 90 percent NPS (Reichheld & Markey, 2011). Apple listens to its customers, according to the book, for the purpose of creating positive experiences at the store. They do not rely on their customers to answer the question, "What can we create for you that doesn't exist today?"

In a 1998 interview with *Business Week* correspondent Andy Reinhardt, Steve Jobs said, "We have a lot of customers, and we have a lot of research into our installed base. We also watch industry trends pretty carefully. But in the end, for something this complicated, it's really hard to design products by focus groups. A lot of times, people don't know what they want until you show it to them" (Reinhardt, 1998).

A second, fascinating example of this was explained by author Malcolm Gladwell. It's about spaghetti sauce. Gladwell, in his book *The Tipping Point* (2002), tells the story of a psychophysicist from New York named Howard Moskowitz. In 1986 Moskowitz got a call from the Campbell's Soup Company, which makes Prego. Prego was directly competing with Ragú and was coming up short. The fact was, Prego had diced tomatoes, which made it thicker than Ragú, and Campbell's felt this was more ideal, as it would stick to the pasta better. Still, Prego was not winning the sauce wars. Hence Campbell's was desperate for new ideas.

What most companies do, as Jobs mentions as well, is conduct focus groups and ask consumers what they want. However, Moskowitz strongly felt that people do not know what they desire if what they desire does not yet exist.

Instead, working with the Campbell's kitchens, he came up with forty-five varieties of spaghetti sauce. These were designed to differ in every conceivable way: spiciness, sweetness, tartness, saltiness, thickness, aroma, mouth feel, cost of ingredients, and so forth. He had a trained panel of food tasters analyze each of those varieties in depth. Then he took the prototypes on the road—to New York, Chicago, Los Angeles, and Jacksonville—and asked people in groups of twenty-five to eat between eight and ten small bowls of different spaghetti sauces over two hours and rate them on a scale of one to a hundred. When Moskowitz charted the results, he saw that everyone had a slightly different definition of what a perfect spaghetti sauce tasted like. If you sifted carefully through the data, though, you could find patterns, and Moskowitz learned that most people's preferences fell into one of three broad groups—plain, spicy, and extra-chunky—and of those three, the last was the most important. Why? Because at the time there was no extra-chunky spaghetti sauce in the supermarket.

In 1989, Campbell's launched an extra-chunky Prego sauce and, within ten years, made hundreds of millions of dollars on it.

An even older version of the truism voiced by Jobs and Moskowitz exists in the form of a simple quote by Henry

Ford: "If I'd asked customers what they wanted, they would have said 'a faster horse.'"

Although I am a firm believer that associations should make a commitment to collecting and analyzing data, I do believe that membership surveys have limitations, and the results can be misleading—to which Jobs, Moskowitz, and Henry Ford all have attested. Research data must be paired with other key data points that track past behavior, an examination of environmental trends and conditions, and a creative team that is not limited in their thinking about what can exist tomorrow that may not exist today.

Market Research Findings and Debunking Assumptions

Understanding how members perceive your association and its role in their professional lives is very important to keep in mind when considering both your value proposition and new opportunities to expand your portfolio of programs and products. In other words, members may not perceive your organization to be a solution provider to the top challenges and issues within the profession.

Individuals frequently perceive the primary role of a professional organization as being something other than a go-to source to help solve the top challenges they face on a personal level.

In one of the studies described in *The Decision to Join* (Dalton & Dignam, 2012), when respondents were asked to identify their professional challenges or concerns, public awareness was identified as the top issue. Yet this did not become a primary factor that influenced their decision to join their professional association. In fact, respondents ranked this activity far lower on a list of factors that influenced their decision to join.

Another example that shows the difference between top issues or challenges faced by the profession and perceptions of the organization and their role in addressing these issues can be found in a membership study I conducted with librarians. In this study, nearly half (49 percent) of respondents identified *collaboration* as the top workplace issue. Yet less than one-fourth (23 percent) of these individuals saw the association of which they were a member as a solution provider in this area. Although there may be many factors that affect this perception, the solution isn't necessarily that the association should start to offer new programs to help solve workplace issues or challenges.

Many associations use the net promoter score metric developed by Satmetrix, Bain & Company, and Reichheld (2010) to measure the loyalty of their members and customers. The NPS metric asks: On a scale of 0 to 10, how likely are you to refer a friend or colleague? According to the authors of the book, individuals who select a 9 or 10 are considered *promoters*, while those who select 0–6 are *detractors*. *Passive* members will answer the question by selecting a 7 or 8. There is an assumption that promoters are extremely satisfied members and are actively recommending membership—and are active participants in association activities.

However, net promoter scores, as seen in the Apple example earlier in this chapter, can be misleading. They may not be a true indicator of an organization's opportunity to grow membership through referrals. If an organization has a formal incentive-based referral program that uses frequent reminders and strong calls-to-action and requires its leadership to actively recruit members, there is a greater chance the organization will grow through referrals regardless of their NPS.

According to research conducted by ASAE: The Center for Association Leadership in its *Decision to* series, there is a direct correlation between level of involvement and promotion of the organization (see Table 6.1).

Although some volunteers are sometimes twice as likely to select 9 or 10 and be labeled as promoters, when compared to less active members, the research I've conducted with numerous

Table 6.1.   Member Involvement and Promotion

Involvement level	Promoters 2011 study
Governance	69%
Committee	60%
Ad hoc	44%
No involvement	38%

Source: ASAE Foundation.

membership associations has revealed the following interesting findings (based on aggregating the data from these studies: Avenue M Group, 2010–2012; SmithBucklin & the William E. Smith Institute for Association Research; Roper Center for Public Opinion Research, 2006; and Aguaro Seminar at Harvard University's Kennedy School of Government):

- Both promoters and detractors come from all demographic audience segments, including those grouped by age, gender, work setting, job function, career stage, and volunteer status.
- When promoters were asked if they had recommended membership in the organization over the last twelve months, on average, less than one-third responded yes.
- Environmental conditions—such as the economy, politics, workplace trends, and culture—may have a greater impact on the likelihood to recommend membership than will overall satisfaction.
- Awareness of an association's offerings and how these items can benefit a member based on individual needs may affect the net promoter score more than satisfaction.
- Even organizations with a low NPS (below 20) may still experience high retention and high participation rates if they actively market their offerings or deliver a must-have benefit.
- Organizations with a low NPS score may have a high number of new members who join through referrals, because they have an active member-get-a-member program in place.

Advances in and the adoption of technology have created an opportunity for organizations to reach new audiences. Individuals who in the past may have been unable to engage with the organization dues to certain barriers now can take advantage of some of the unique offerings created by their professional association. There is an opportunity for associations to rethink their pricing structure by creating opportunities for prospective members to engage in meaningful ways at a low incremental cost to the association.

This has come about because although individuals still prefer to network and learn through in-person events rather than online activities, barriers such as lack of time, lack of money, or an undesirable location may prevent them from participating in such association-sponsored events. When you combine this finding with the trend data on adult internet usage provided by Pew Research Center's Internet & American Life Project (Duggan & Brenner, 2013), you will begin to understand the primary reasons why preferences and behavior are often at odds. First, it's easier than ever before to access information and network with peers. Second, the investment—of both time and money—needed to achieve your goals is low. Finally, there is a higher degree of control over your time when you choose to use your smartphone, tablet, or laptop to access information, education, or network with peers.

- Eighty-one percent of all adults use the Internet.
- Forty-five percent of American adults are smartphone owners.
- Slightly more than one-fourth (26 percent) of American adults own an e-book reader, and 31 percent own a tablet computer.
- Most adults (91 percent) use a search engine to find information; 78 percent look for information online about a service or product they are thinking of buying; 71 percent buy products online, and 51 percent do some form of online research for their job.

Source: Duggan and Brenner, 2013.

One of the main factors that may influence an individual's decision to join an association is career stage, so it stands to reason that organizations helping members advance or succeed in their careers have a very good opportunity to connect with the next generation of members. It may just occur at a later age than with previous generations. Individuals are most apt to join and become engaged with your association when they cross the threshold between having a job and having a career. In some industries, such as health care, engineering, finance, or law, this may come during their mid- to late twenties. While this is good news, it does not guarantee that this group will join your organization. They must believe that the value they will receive will outweigh the cost. They must see your organization as considerably better than the next best alternative. They must believe there is a direct connection between membership and career advancement or success.

The truth is, differences in generational needs are exaggerated and sometimes even inaccurate. Generation X and Y may be slower to join an association because their entry into their professional careers may be delayed due to a variety of personal decisions and economic realities. Yet research shows that fears regarding their lack of interest may be unfounded. In the book *10 Lessons for Cultivating Member Commitment*, Dalton and Dignam (2012) examined the results from a study commissioned by SmithBucklin in 2006 and conducted by the William E. Smith Institute for Association Research, as well as the results from the *Decision to Join* studies. Their findings "not only negate the assumption that inherent differences would incline younger generations to take a pass on association membership, it clearly documents the premise that entry-level age groups are simply slow to join" (Dalton & Dignam, 2012). The studies further revealed that while individuals in their twenties may be less inclined to join their professional association, this changes dramatically once they move into their thirties.

Ask the Right Questions

Here are examples of questions that will help you uncover more information about preferences, motivations, and behaviors.

1. What motivates you to participate in a professional development program?
2. In the last twelve months, have you participated in any of the following professional development activities?
   - In person, led by an instructor
   - Offered as part of a conference
   - In conjunction with a regularly scheduled meeting
   - Offered by your employer in-house, facilitated by an outside consultant or trainer
   - On-the-job demonstrations of equipment, techniques, or procedures offered by a supervisor or coworker
   - Self-paced study using books, manuals, CDs, DVDs, or other offline media
   - Offered by your employer in-house, facilitated by staff
   - Brown-bag or information presentation

- Distance learning, with an instructor in real time
- Distance learning, with an instructor at your own pace
- Distance learning blended: some portions without an instructor, other portions with an instructor in real time
- Distance learning without an instructor

3. Which of these are your preferred forms of professional development?
4. What learning style works best for you?
   a. Logical: You prefer using logic, reasoning, and systems.
   b. Verbal: You prefer using words, in both speech and writing.
   c. Social: You prefer to learn in groups or with other people face-to-face.
   d. Social: You prefer to learn in groups or with other people online.
   e. Solitary: You prefer to work alone and use self-study.
5. How much of a barrier to participation are the following?
   a. Employer does not encourage professional development.
   b. I am unable to use time during work hours.
   c. Lack of comfort with technology required for learning.
   d. Lack of financial support from employer.
   e. Lack of personal disposable income to devote to professional development.
   f. Lack of time to devote to study.
   g. Inconvenient location.
   h. Time conflicts with other commitments.
   i. Unable to travel long distance (or out of state).

Source: Albert and Dignam, 2010.

McDonald's Adult Burger Doesn't Cut the Mustard

The story of McDonald's Arch Deluxe is a good case study of how preferences shared through market research may not reflect future behavior or outcomes.

The Arch Deluxe story actually begins years before its launch. Although McDonald's was the largest restaurant chain in the United States during the 1980s and 90s, increased competition from Burger King and Wendy's and a lack of new product innovation were reported as two of the reasons the company decided to create a new burger as an alternative to the current product line. (Competition and the need for innovation are common drivers behind many organizations' entry into new program or product lines.)

The first two attempted alternatives to McDonald's traditional hamburger—called the McDLT and the McLean Deluxe—did not meet sales expectations and were discontinued shortly after their launch.

A few years later, McDonald's began testing the Arch Deluxe. The May 1998 edition of *Mac Today* revealed internal research showing that while 72 percent of consumers believed the chain made good burgers for children, only 18 percent agreed they made good burgers for adults. *Mac Today* also stated that eight out of ten adults who tried the Arch Deluxe during early market testing said they would buy it again.

Promoted as the "burger with the grown-up taste," the Arch Deluxe was marketed as a burger that kids would hate and grown-ups would love. With an estimated $150 to $200 million advertising budget, the problem wasn't lack of awareness or visibility. People simply didn't think of McDonald's as a place to meet the demands of a sophisticated palate. People expected McDonald's to deliver convenience at a low price.

Why did McDonald's create the Arch Deluxe in the first place? Some speculate it was in response to a demographic trend pointing to a growing adult population. Many articles that evaluated the launch of the Arch Deluxe (as well as the ultimate discontinuation of the entire Deluxe product line) noted that the product "was well researched" and that "people would love to eat a burger designed specifically for adults." Ultimately, the biggest mistake was that McDonald's lost sight of what they were known as: a kid-friendly restaurant with budget-friendly food.

Case Study: Association Forum of Chicagoland Fails . . . Or Do They?

About eight years ago, when I was working for the Association Forum of Chicagoland (the Forum), a colleague in another department asked me to help market a new event: a half-day workshop that addressed one of the major issues our members faced on a daily basis. She was excited about the concept because it would be the first time our association would offer a session on the topic. A recent survey of our members had revealed that the issue was one of their top challenges, and it seemed that the session would be highly valuable and well attended.

My colleague was also interested in expanding our education curriculum and potentially attracting a wider audience. Our research had revealed that although our members were satisfied with the educational programs we were currently providing, some of our programs did not address their most pressing needs. Plus, we had recently seen an increase in competition from other organizations interested in expanding into our market. We strongly believed we needed to engage our members by developing and offering new programming, and now we had some data on the content they said they needed most. Another element we considered was that our association was local, serving individuals in the Chicagoland area only, not people who were based all over the country (or world). We were similar to a regional organization or a chapter in that our members did not need to travel far to come to our events.

Unfortunately, on the day of the Forum's program, the room was only half-filled with attendees. Of course, you can point to a number of factors that may have had an impact on registration and attendance, and we discussed these issues during our debriefing after the meeting. We felt certain the topic was still of high interest to our members, so we made the decision to host another session on the topic. We changed the location. We tried other marketing tactics to promote the program. Yet the results were similar to the first event's. What had happened? Was the topic no longer relevant? Were we no longer viewed as a provider of high-quality education? Did we use the wrong marketing tactics? Was the program priced too high?

Our research, which was conducted by an external marketing research firm, asked members to rank the top challenges they faced in their professional lives. They were also asked to list other sources, besides the Forum, that they turned to for information and education. And they were asked to rank their preferences for attending continuing education sessions: webinars, on-demand webinars, or in-person events. The results were not surprising. Our members preferred in-person events over webinars because in-person events offered opportunities to learn from both the session facilitator and one another.

We were puzzled: why, then, did the new in-person program fail to attract the attendees we expected? We were doing research, listening to members, and making data-driven decisions. What went wrong? Looking back, I realize that we relied too heavily on our market research and did not consider other factors that could impact our ability to sell the program. Upon completion of the second program, I examined attendance records for the in-person events and compared them to registrations from the previous three years. Although we were not in the midst of the recession, I learned that attendance was down at all half-day events. On the flip side, events with the highest participation rates were those held first thing in the morning or programs that lasted for a full day. Even though we had asked members in the market research study to select their preference for the length of time to attend an educational program, their responses did not reflect their behavior. There were exceptions, of course, yet the data was clear: half-day courses were not very appealing to our members.

Next, I examined the type of events that had the highest attendance records. They all had one thing in common—they offered practical, hands-on information. Our members wanted to learn "how to" so that they could make immediate changes in their own organizations. These types of programs were also easier to justify if they needed a supervisor's approval to attend. If the program had been designed for a more experienced audience, this might have not been an issue. However, we had targeted the program for entry-level and middle management.

Ultimately, I learned that preferences expressed in an electronic survey are not always a good predictor of behavior, which is why my friend's Groupon dilemma sounded so familiar to me. While individuals may prefer to attend an in-person educational event, faced with other constraints, such as timing and budget, they may look to online resources or webinars for solutions to some of their challenges.

So, although we had asked members how they prefer to learn, we hadn't dug deeper—into their actual behavior—by asking them what types of educational programs they had attended in the last twelve months.

Not a Failure But a Lesson Learned

As it turns out, the Association Forum wasn't the only organization to launch a new program (or product) that failed. Not surprising, but sometimes a hard notion to swallow for associations with limited budgets and demanding boards. The fact is, well-known and well-loved brands have made similar mistakes with the development of new products. Netflix's disastrous launch of Qwikster lasted only twenty-three days. New Coke was abandoned within weeks of its launch. Products fail for many different reasons. However, there are a few lessons we can learn from these epic failures:

• You cannot predict member response to future actions by just asking about their preferences, interests, and challenges. You must also ask members about their past participation and perceived barriers.

• If you spend many years building your association's brand around a specific promise and then make a change that, in the minds of your audience, alters the very essence of who you are and what you represent, there is a good chance you will feel a backlash from your most loyal members. This may happen even though you've conducted an independent research study testing a new product, program, or offering and received very positive feedback.

• Price always plays a role in the decision to join, register, or make a purchase. In some situations, the issue really isn't affordability; rather, members question whether there is enough perceived value for the cost. Alternatively, people may be willing to purchase an inferior product, or attend a competitor's educational program, if the price is lower and the difference between the two is minor.

• Timing can play a key role in the success or failure of a product launch. You may be too far ahead of your members—or too far behind. In either case, a good idea can fail simply because it was launched at the wrong time.

• A topic, program, or product may rate high in terms of interest but low on demand. There may be many topics your audience will find interesting, but are they demanding products and services to fulfill a need? Can members choose among many solution providers in the marketplace?

• A great program or product can fail if it is offered to the wrong target audience. Use your market research efforts to understand, on a deeper level, your target market. And don't ignore the size of the target market either. An ideal product designed for a target market can fail because the audience is simply too small.

Action Steps

1. To ensure that you understand your organization's strengths and weaknesses, conduct a membership needs assessment. To clearly define your organization's brand as members and prospects currently perceive it, conduct market research. But if you want to create new programs and products that will be embraced by members today and in the future, expand your research efforts to include an assessment of past behavior and an environmental scan of the marketplace. Engage stakeholders in the process, yet expand the group to include individuals who are not too close to your brand and will bring a more critical perspective to the assessment of new product development.

2. Toss aside assumptions you may have made about differences in generational needs, member loyalty, and the value of your current offerings. Consider, for a moment, whether there are other factors that may be influencing the decision to join, participate, volunteer, purchase, renew, and recommend membership to others. Create a list of items you can change or create that could reverse existing trends.

3. Examine and address, at a deeper level, all of the barriers to success. Some of the best new products can fail if the need to overcome certain barriers—be they timing, technology, culture, or price—is too great. Begin this process by assuming you can overcome barriers, but then examine what will be required to succeed in your efforts.

4. When recruiting younger members, it's all about show and tell. Consider promoting the benefits of membership based on how each offering will help them advance and succeed in their careers. Share stories and examples that demonstrate the outcomes of taking advantage of membership in your organization. Create profiles that showcase different career paths, and emphasize how taking an active role (volunteering, participating, or using your association's resources) helps members advance in their careers.

5. Keep in mind that behavior is very different from preference. Even if your members are twice as likely to prefer face-to-face meetings to webinars or virtual conferences, a better predictor for success is how they've behaved over the past twelve months. This isn't to say that you should eliminate offerings based on past behavior, or that you shouldn't try new ideas. I am simply recommending that you weigh past performance in addition to needs and interests when creating new programs or products.

6. Create and nurture a culture that embraces flexibility and speed when building new programs and products. Some of the best new products fail because it took too long to get the program or product through the development process. Although your organization may adhere to a rigorous quality assurance process before launching any new program or product, this may not be necessary for everything you offer. Streamlining the process for product development will increase the likelihood that your organization provides relevant resources in a timely manner. One of the best ways to ensure that your organization has access to the latest data, so that you do not need to wait until information is collected before you can make decisions, is to increase your commitment to the collection and use of all types of research.

7. Understand that success can come from failure. The experience of creating a program based on market research with members, testing various marketing tactics, and still coming up short of your goals can be, ultimately, a successful failure. We all have these, and if we are smart we will take the time to assess what went wrong in order to learn from our mistakes. In the Association Forum case study in this chapter, this mistake could easily have been repeated had we not taken the time to examine the entire process. To ensure that we didn't make the same mistake twice, our CEO asked each director to evaluate the program based on our various responsibilities.

In the end, we came up with a new plan for developing new programs or products. We identified a list of research that should be reviewed prior to launching a new program. We considered the size of the marketplace and the potential interest in the topic. And we created a list of criteria to see if the new program or product fit into our brand. Once we created this process, we decided that we should allow for some flexibility to ensure that we could still be innovative in our efforts to create new products. As a result, we created a sounding board to help us identify any potential pitfalls or obstacles that had not been revealed through our own vetting process. A new process doesn't guarantee success, but it can give your association better guidelines for how to allocate your time and resources.

8. When you create a new program or product, one that is completely different from the other offerings in your portfolio, you need to spend money and time educating your members about its value and use. Innovation has its risks and its rewards. And associations must be willing to try new ideas if they are to remain relevant and continue to attract new members. Once you've made the decision to venture into a new area, you need to create a plan to inform, educate, and sell the product. If every communication effort is focused on selling the offering, you may find that interest and sales fall below expectations and goals.

9. Take advantage of social media communities and engage members in the efforts to educate others about the offering. Develop a strategy that leverages the content being shared in the new offering in a way that will pique the interest of potential customers. If you're lucky, you will hear from early adopters about the benefits of using your product. You may also learn about some of the weaknesses in your product. As part of your communications strategy, build in some time to collect, assess, and apply the feedback you receive. You may need to change the way you position the offering and its benefits.

10. Consider eliminating some of your offerings. Retailers use loyalty cards to determine what consumers want, with the goal of reducing their unwanted inventory and increasing sales. If less is more in the retail world, the same may hold true for associations. Adding new programs or products may not increase your value proposition if the message is cluttered with too many offerings.

■ ■ ■

When it comes to predicting how an individual will respond to a call to action, behavior trumps preference. But if you want to remain relevant long into the future, you should not limit your focus to the past. In the next chapter, I will describe how your organization can balance its efforts by creating a culture that encourages risk taking and forward thinking.

Look at Where Your Members Are Going

Skate to where the puck is going to be, not to where it's been.
—WALTER GRETZKY, father of Wayne Gretzky (former professional hockey player, head coach, and leading point-scorer in NHL history)

ONE OF MY FAVORITE WAYS OF THINKING about the business of associations is through sports. Maybe it's because I feel that being part of a team is extremely valuable in dealing with a variety of personalities—as association professionals must do day in and day out—and feeling that sense of responsibility. Or perhaps it's because, while sports is about wins and losses, it's also about how you conduct yourself in positive and negative situations. It could just be that I love watching people working their hardest to be the best at whatever it is they are doing—whether it's playing baseball or running an association.

From provocative analogies to inspirational quotes from legends themselves, there is so much to learn from the sporting arena. One of my favorite stories about an athlete's rise to stardom has to do with a player who was arguably the National Hockey League's greatest player of all time: Wayne Gretzky.

When Gretzky entered the NHL in 1979, his critics believed he was too small and too slow to succeed. Over the years, he grew slightly in size but still finished last in stamina, strength, flexibility, and vision tests conducted by his team on an annual basis. How then did Wayne Gretzky go on to break more records than any other NHL player? Some people point to his ability to consistently anticipate where the puck was going to be and respond in a timely manner. Hall of Famer Bobby Orr said, "He passes better than anybody I've ever seen. And he thinks so far ahead" (Swift, 1982, para. 9). Others thought he had a "sixth sense." Gretzky himself attributed his abilities to the coaching he received from his father early on in his career, as well as his dedication to studying the game and logging many hours on the ice. Wayne Gretzky beat the odds and became one of the best hockey players in history because he was able to anticipate what would happen rather than just react after the fact. He developed this faculty by analyzing the game and honing his skills.

Gretzky, famous for the quotation that provides this chapter's epigraph, thought about where the puck is going, not where it had already been. He used a systematic approach to determine how to stay one step ahead of other players. He understood that the most reliable and predictable way to anticipate what *will* happen is to study the actions of players based on specific situations, all the while keeping an eye on the ultimate goal: scoring. He studied the game, the players, and the plays.

In the association world, nothing is more important than understanding, at a very deep level, what your members need and want in the context of their existing challenges and the solutions that your organization currently offers. By understanding their needs and emotional connections, you can better identify motivations and anticipate future events. In an effort to imagine and create new products and services that may provide value to your members, a common route taken by many organizations is to ask members what you should offer that doesn't exist today. I've never seen this question provide meaningful data that can help organizations add more value or create new products. Understanding what solutions currently exist, however, will provide the necessary context for anticipating future needs. In some cases, the alternative solutions may be inferior or may not meet their needs. In other situations, there may not be an affordable or relevant solution to their challenges.

Additionally, in sports, success on the field isn't the result of talent or strength alone; rather, it comes from being able to pick up on visual cues, combined with the knowledge and experience to anticipate what will happen next. Top athletes like Gretzky don't actually have better peripheral vision than their peers. They just know what needs to be done with the information they receive, and they are able to respond quickly. They are able to focus on the situation and remain calm in most situations.

What else do elite athletes and anticipatory organizations have in common? According to Kramer (2012), Olympic Games winners "understand that competition is the ultimate form of cooperation" because it forces them to push past limitations. They also know that perceptions begin with how they see themselves.

Consider the following examples (*not* from the sports world) of how individuals and organizations have overcome the odds to become leaders in their fields, largely by anticipating the future.

It Sure Pays to Be Online

Although it may feel like we've always used smartphones, tablets, and computers to bank online, make travel arrangements, and purchase everything from cars to shoes, less than ten years ago most of these activities were still conducted offline. Facebook was launched in 2004, and the first iPhone was sold in 2007. According to the Pew Research Center, in March 2000 only 17 percent of internet users were banking online (Fox, 2002, para. 2). During the early days of the Internet, most people used it to conduct searches for information, get sports scores, or communicate with one another via email. Many of the dot-com companies that were formed during the late 1990s strove for growth over profits, and as a result, they burned through a lot of cash and closed their doors. When the dot-com bubble burst in March 2000, many companies with multimillion-dollar budgets, as well as backing from well-established companies, declared bankruptcy and either packed up altogether or were absorbed into larger organizations.

For all of these reasons, and probably more, one could easily make the argument that the year 2000 may not have been a good time to launch an online payroll company aimed at small businesses. Although internet usage was undoubtedly increasing, U.S. consumers were not actively using the Internet for financial transactions (Fox, 2002). Many small business owners connected to the Internet by way of a slow dial-up service. In 2002 only 21 percent of all internet users had high-speed connections at home (Horrigan & Rainie, 2002). Of the small number who even used a broadband connection, only 22 percent used it for financial transactions such as banking or to pay a bill.

Another factor that could have strongly discouraged a new company from entering this space was the dominance of four major payroll companies in the field. When a small business owner thought of payroll, they typically turned to their CPA, used Intuit's QuickBooks, or the services of ADP, Paychex, or Ceridian. These companies had brand awareness and trust. They also had the bandwidth and the resources to invest in an alternative method for providing payroll and related tax-filing solutions. On the surface, the challenges were enormous and the chances for a new entry to succeed appeared low.

Eyes Wide Open (and Looking Forward)

Despite all these challenges, in 1999 the founders of start-up SurePayroll, Troy Henikoff and Scott Wald, thought they had a winning proposition. The management team recognized that small business owners needed an affordable, convenient, and easy way to process payroll. Existing solutions did not offer the combination of all three qualities. Processing of payroll was time-consuming and prone to errors. Second, the new company was not tied to a legacy system that would make it difficult, from a financial and operational standpoint, to create an alternative product that could be both affordable for small business owners and profitable for the company. The major payroll companies had built a business model on an infrastructure that included dozens if not hundreds of processing centers, large staffs, printed checks, and delivery people and their vehicles—all of which are cost centers that need to be factored into the price they must charge in order to be profitable. Finally, SurePayroll created a business based on a software-as-a-service (SaaS) solution that essentially allowed them to more easily implement enhancements and keep up with the demands of their customers.

One trend that SurePayroll was able to leverage was the growing need for convenient solutions. In 1998, founder Scott Wald realized that the Internet was very good at delivering information or services for a low cost to people and businesses that were widely dispersed. Looking at the rise in popularity of online banking from 2000 to 2002, it was clear that three factors were driving consumers to online solutions: convenience, time savings, and control. Additionally, consumers were switching to online banking because it saved them money (Fox, 2002). SurePayroll succeeded where others failed because they not only anticipated the needs of their audience but also created a product that could easily change or adapt to advances in technology and greater use of the Internet.

Would You Bet Your Job?

In subsequent years, SurePayroll's management team, led by its president, Michael Alter, viewed the changing landscape as an opportunity rather than a threat. He talks about it in my kind of terms!

"If you think about baseball players who bat just .300, the negative is that they strike out seven times out of ten. In fact, [their results are] negative more times than they are positive," Alter says. "But, they make lots of money! And we make them heroes. In business, people try to do something different; they try to get higher results. But why would your odds be better than the top baseball players'?"

Alter goes on to discuss how organizations continually try to reach that one great idea. However, that is extremely difficult if the likelihood of failure is great, because so many cultures punish failure. SurePayroll, he explains, does the opposite.

"We reward risks," Alter says. "We talk about them, and what employees learned from the mistakes. We try things, and sometimes they don't work; we then ask questions like 'How can we do this better?'" He feels this is even more critical as a business ages.

"I have made some mistakes," he continues. And Alter says this without regret or remorse. Rather, he states it rather proudly. And hastens to add: "But you don't bet the company. There is a saying in business that a great CEO never bets the business, but every couple of years he bets his job. And I think that's true." Because the world is changing faster than we are used to, Alter says, you've "got to go to where the world is going, not to where it is today—it's classic Wayne Gretzky."

And the company put its money where its mouth is by coming up with an award that truly encourages staff to take risks. Modeled after the People's Choice Awards, the program is called the SureChoice Awards. For most of the awards that have to do with traditional business excellence—customer service, collaboration, and so on—peers are required to nominate another individual. However, there is also a "Best New Mistake" category, and for this particular award, a person nominates him- or herself. There are prizes for first, second, and third place, and a monetary award for each. There clearly is an incentive to take pride in a mistake you've made, because you have to actually nominate yourself. You are willing to share this mistake with others so that they can learn from it as well. The point is that people are more than happy to share their successes, so why not failures, when a failure usually leads to a learning experience?

"We are trying to encourage an environment where you try new things," Alter says. "As a business grows, there is a tendency for incremental change. A lot of times, incentives and a company's culture protect what they know, so they do what works. The problem is, if you always do what's always worked, someone will do it better. You need to evolve and grow your business. We created the Best New Mistake so that employees would try something different, and if you're wrong, you learn from it."

And it's paid off. Over the last few years, SurePayroll has earned numerous innovation awards, including *PC Magazine*'s Editors' Choice winner, CompTIA's Most Innovative Small and Mid-Sized Infrastructure, and one of the "Top 75" Most Innovative Companies in Chicago.

Case Study: HIMSS Proactively Makes Progress

By now, we hope it goes without saying that there is no silver bullet for membership; nothing will absolutely guarantee an influx of members nor a 100 percent retention rate. If that were the case, this book would be irrelevant and associations would be up to their eyeballs in dues revenue. The Healthcare Information and Management Systems Society (HIMSS), which I talked about in Chapter Four, is a perfect example of this.

You'll recall that I discussed the association's group membership program and how it was wildly successful with respect to dollars and number of members. However, that alone is not enough to sustain growth for any organization regardless of size. And some people do believe that the size of an organization or the industry it serves matters when it comes to surviving (and thriving) in today's ever-changing world. I would disagree with that, and so would HIMSS.

Technology has played a major role in the advancement of health care for decades, but when you walk into a hospital today you'll be truly amazed by technology's enormous impact on patient outcomes. From the ability to create a complete record of a patient visit and follow-up treatment to incorporating evidence-based information and quality management, health care IT has transformed the way medicine is practiced in the United States and around the world. Even though a recession gripped most of the world during the latter part of the previous decade, employment and funding in health care technology is actually predicted "to grow by 18 percent between 2013 and 2016, according to data from the Bureau of Labor Statistics" (Taylor, 2013). Very good news for HIMSS.

Again, HIMSS is a cause-based, not-for-profit organization exclusively focused on providing global leadership for the optimal use of information technology (IT) and management systems for the betterment of health care. HIMSS pursues its mission because the leadership, staff, and membership believe that lives can be saved, outcomes of care improved, and costs reduced by transforming the health care system through the best use of IT and management systems. Leading this charge on behalf of the organization is H. Stephen Lieber, president and chief executive officer of HIMSS. To accomplish these lofty goals, Lieber firmly believes his organization must be proactive rather than reactive to a rapidly changing environment.

There are a few factors in the health care technology industry that HIMSS cannot control. HIMSS does not play a role in the development of health care IT or management solutions. Nor does HIMSS control demand for new technology. In fact, most people would agree that health care and technology are changing and advancing at such a rapid pace that there is increasing uncertainty about what might lie ahead just six months from now. Faced with this much ambiguity, it would seem to be much easier to be responsive to clearly stated industry needs rather than anticipate new ones.

That isn't how HIMSS operates. The management team at HIMSS has an unstated, yet universally held belief that the organization must do more than just react to trends and advancements in health care IT. To successfully advance the industry and achieve their goals, HIMSS must stay one step ahead by knowing the industry and the "business" of health care IT better than anyone else—including its members.

In fact, this belief has transformed HIMSS over the years and helped it grow more than 1,000 percent over the past decade. Over a period of eleven years, Lieber has helped HIMSS grow from a membership of just under 12,000 individuals to a membership of 50,000 individuals, 570 corporate members, and 225 not-for-profit partner organizations.

Know the Industry, Make It Count

"Years ago, HIMSS knew who our members were, but we didn't really know their business," said Lieber (personal communication, February 2, 2013). "Because you get so focused on the micro details of the individual, you forget about learning more about the environment members work in. As an association, we ought to be impacting the environment as well as the individual."

As Lieber transitioned HIMSS from an organization that understood its members but not their environment, to one that understood every aspect of the profession and industry, he remained focused on the fact that there are limits imposed on associations and how they earn non-dues revenue.

"You need to identify programs or products that are consistent with their mission and appropriate for the industry," Lieber told me. "In our case, we realized there was a big need for IT market intelligence and foresight so that members could be better prepared for what's next in health care IT. The problem was that we were existing in an environment where the industry had none of that information."

HIMSS decided to collect this information through the use of two important questions: (1) How could HIMSS know the industry better than anyone? and (2) What did the industry need that currently did not exist? This led to the creation of a new product called HIMSS Analytics. The tagline, "It's How You Know What's Next," accurately describes the benefits of the product. The mission of this division of HIMSS is to provide the highest-quality data and analytical expertise to support improved decision making for health care providers, health care IT companies, and health care consulting firms. To ensure that the product was relevant and valued among all audiences, HIMSS set out to create a resource that offered independent, objective analysis and insight and accurate, reliable data, information, and knowledge; and that leveraged industry experts skilled in health care IT, market research, analysis, and strategy. As a result, HIMSS Analytics was able to offer value-based solutions that could help members lower cost, increase revenue, and improve operational and market performance.

Fill the Gap, Become Essential

Although HIMSS Analytics provides significant revenue for the organization—and helps it fill an unmet need in the industry—it also provides the organization with concrete data that it can use to use to stay one step ahead of its members, which is critical, according to Lieber (and Alter, at SurePayroll, and the Great One, Wayne Gretzky).

"We use the data for our public policy and advocacy initiatives because we know what's going on. It very much serves that need to know and then allow others to act on that information," says Lieber. He adds that because no one was specifically requesting this information, there was some risk in undertaking the business venture. However, once HIMSS analyzed the situation, evaluated the needs and gaps in available information, and vetted the idea internally, Lieber realized that the risk of doing nothing at all was even greater. Similar to Steve Jobs, Lieber understands that growth and sustainability depend on the ability to anticipate needs rather than just react or duplicate existing products. (Remember Malcolm Gladwell's Prego spaghetti sauce story, discussed in Chapter Six? People commonly don't know what they need if what they need doesn't already exist.) Today, HIMSS Analytics helps the organization anticipate the needs of members and the industry, plus it helps members gain insight by spotting trends and pinpointing new business opportunities.

Lieber's advice to organizations is to identify the one or two things that your organization should provide that will help better serve your members, serve common interests across society, and provide a better business model than what exists today. He also recommends taking a disciplined approach that incorporates data-driven decision making.

"To be relevant and grow as an organization you need to anticipate and, sometimes, even build the demand," Lieber says. Although you may not be able to predict the future, you can have a hand in creating it.

What's the Big Deal About Big Data?

"Big data" is the catchy buzz phrase being tossed around the enterprise-sized organizations and discussed in business magazines. A search of the *Harvard Business Review* website revealed nearly three hundred articles on the topic of big data. Not surprisingly, many people believe big data will be one of the top disruptive trend in 2013. Although much has been written on the topic of data and innovation, most of it has ignored small businesses and nonprofit organizations. McKinsey Global Institute calls big data "the next frontier for innovation, competition and productivity" (Manyika et al., 2011).

Yet advances in technology have created opportunities for any size organization to make a commitment to mining their existing data to help grow their organization. In the book *7 Measures of Success*, ASAE: The Center for Association Leadership (2006) state, "Remarkable associations gather information, analyze it, and use it to become even better."

Furthermore, "'data-driven strategies' refer to a continuous loop where they track members' needs and issues as well as the wider environment, then incorporate the findings into strategic and operational planning and program delivery" (Collins, 2006, p. 2). Although the organizations profiled in the book demonstrate their commitment to data by relying on concrete research data to make decisions, I believe this should be extended to how organizations approach building a prospect list that will be the foundation of their future recruitment efforts.

Encyclopaedia Britannica Reinvents Itself

It may seem a little unusual to include Encyclopaedia Britannica in a chapter about anticipating needs, essentially being proactive, and not reacting situations that arise. Just mentioning "Encyclopaedia Britannica" likely conjures a few memories in your mind (if you are thirty-five or older). You may remember the iconic library bound set proudly displayed on a shelf in your childhood home. Or you may think of Encyclopaedia Britannica as the company that was replaced by Wikipedia. Some individuals may even remember when Microsoft bundled a CD-ROM encyclopedia named Encarta with its computers; they thought this would surely kill the brand that had been around since 1768.

After a peak in sales in 1990, the venerable brand began to collapse. The prestige of ownership disappeared when families no longer displayed the books on their shelves and as alternative sources for information that was free and easy to access became available. A CD-ROM version was too expensive, and the traditional sales model of "door-to-door" sales became obsolete.

So how did Encyclopaedia Britannica avoid extinction? First, they focused on what differentiated them in the marketplace—unmatched editorial quality. Second, they anticipated that new opportunities would open up as access to the Internet expanded. The organization, with its reputation for quality and broad name recognition, reestablished relationships with consumers through a new digital subscription model.

Make All the Difference

In the March 2013 issue of *Harvard Business Review* (*HBR*), Encyclopaedia Britannica's president Jorge Cauz (2013) shares the story behind the transformation of the company and the day they announced they would no longer produce bound volumes of information. Contrary to what many may think, the staff celebrated the occasion with cake, balloons, and a toast to "the departure of an old friend" (para. 2).

After a few failed attempts at a new business model that would leverage the high-quality content in a profitable way, Encyclopaedia Britannica landed on an idea that would ultimately bring together its mission of being a global educational publisher with its customers' need for a timely, relevant, and trustworthy source for information and instruction. Rather than trying to compete with Wikipedia, the management team focused on editorial quality and reliability, two areas in which Wikipedia appeared to fall short, according to Cauz (2013). The two areas Britannica would focus on held great appeal to educators, which helped boost sales.

Change wasn't easy, as it generally never is regardless of circumstances or industry. It used to take years, then weeks, then hours to update content. Today, content is updated every twenty minutes. Britannica also changed their business model so that they were no longer just an encyclopedia-only company. Sales have increased over the last five years, and renewal rates on subscriptions hover around 98 percent.

Not Making a Change Is as Risky as Changing

Why have I included Encyclopaedia Britannica's turnaround story in this chapter of the book? The company shares a number of similar traits with the association community. Although other companies competed with them by publishing volumes of reference materials indexed in a similar format, the quality of the information from Encyclopaedia Britannica was widely considered superior to other brands. They had also built a business model around selling and delivering their value through print editions that were saved and displayed on a shelf. This is remarkably similar to the prestigious journals, magazines, and other publications created by associations. Their purpose was to inform, educate, and provide a point of reference that was highly reliable—yet another trait shared with many associations. And Britannica was slow to leverage its strengths, including brand awareness, quality, and content, because it had built a business around a process that included a sales staff and a printed product. It took many years for the organization to rethink its business model, yet once it did, the company looked ahead rather than responding to existing market forces.

Britannica could have closed its doors forever had the company not examined the problems with existing solutions and anticipated the need for objective, transparent information written by qualified experts. Once the need was identified, the company determined the best channel for making the information accessible to, and easy to use by students, teachers, parents, and others.

I believe the Encyclopaedia Britannica model provides a very good example of how it is never too late for an organization (or person, for that matter) to change or to get on the path that leads forward, rather than one that follows where others have gone before. (This, of course, hearkens back to the wisdom of Robert Frost nearly one hundred years ago: "Two roads diverged in a wood, and I / I took the one less traveled by / And that has made all the difference.")

Consider the next case study, which returns us to the health care arena.

Case Study: Massachusetts Medical Society Models for the Future

Sometimes, even though change is generally uncomfortable and often avoided, when it actually does happen, it feels as if the changes happen overnight. But rarely is this the case. It is usually the convergence of a number of factors, over a period of years, that creates seismic changes in a field.

In the health care industry, there have been numerous indicators that the practice of medicine is undergoing a major change. First, although many people can still remember a time when their doctor worked in a small private practice, the number of physician owners or partners who have become employees has grown dramatically over the last six years. In fact, a recent workforce study conducted by Merritt Hawkins in 2011 revealed that there has been an increasing trend toward physicians becoming employees of hospitals rather than hanging out their own shingle or joining a group practice (Massachusetts Medical Society, 2012).

Another factor affecting the physician workforce is a shortage of full-time physicians. According to the Association of American Medical Colleges (2012), by 2025 the United States will experience a shortage of 124,000 full-time physicians. Of course, health care reform has undoubtedly had an impact on the practice of medicine and the employment of physicians in various workplace settings. In addition to these challenges, advancements in technology, shrinking budgets, and other financial constraints all pose threats to the current membership model used by medical societies.

Even as many medical societies struggled to grow—or even simply maintain—their current market share, one organization proudly can claim it achieved a nearly 20 percent increase in its market share in less than three years. The Massachusetts Medical Society (MMS) not only was able to build a sustainable membership model that would allow physicians to join the organization through a group membership program but also considered alternative ways to deliver products, programs, and services that would benefit the membership.

"Our current membership model was not designed to meet the needs of the new generation of physician employees," said Stephen Phelan, director of membership at the MMS (personal communication, February 13, 2013). "We realized that we needed to develop a new program that provided specific benefits to employees but would not cannibalize our current revenue structure. Just like the practice of medicine is changing, our model needed to change. We can't wait for these changes to take place before we make changes to our organization. What works today may not work tomorrow." MMS implemented an operational approach to change by creating a group enrollment program to encourage medium and large health care institutions to enroll most, if not all, of their physicians in the Society (see Exhibit 7.1). To participate in the program, groups must have five or more physicians on staff. Since the program's inception, the number of members in the group enrollment program has increased by 100 percent and the organization has saved $10,000 in renewal expenses.

Phelan told me that he and his team looked at how things were done, then imagined how they could be done differently in the future. "We want our members to feel proud of the organization," Phelan stated. "We are the oldest medical society in the country, and we have the [New England] Journal [of Medicine]. But we cannot rest on history." The MMS, like so many associations, was also seeing a decrease in demand for the printed version of their publication. However, the New England Journal of Medicine

Exhibit 7.1. Massachusetts Medical Society Group Membership Program Copy

An ever-increasing percentage of members are part of physician groups that join the Society to take advantage of our group enrollment options. Along with savings of up to 30 percent off regular state dues, our group enrollment program also offers convenience.

Groups of five or more physicians are eligible to receive the following discounts:

- 100% participation, 30% discount
- 90% participation, 20% discount
- 80% participation, 10% discount
- 75% participation, 5% discount

Save Money, Simplify Enrollment, and Reduce Hassles

In addition to the savings, group enrollment offers significant practice management benefits:

- Simplified billing with one dues invoice for your entire physician group
- Accurate membership information with group rosters
- Reduced practice administrative hassles for physicians
- Valuable practice benefit to new-hire prospects by offering free MMS membership

had always been one of the key offerings provided with membership. The association struggled with a decision.

"We had students and residents say to us 'We prefer to get the information online,'" said Phelan. "The young physicians wouldn't throw out the printed *Journal*, but they would stack up, and they wouldn't read them." So the association examined costs; they looked at exactly how much it cost to print one copy of the *Journal*. Then they looked at the cost of moving to an online version and, more important, the value of the publication's content—whether online or in print.

"If we gave the *Journal* to members online only, the intrinsic value was still there," said Phelan. They offered residency programs free membership and, at the same time, would offer free access to the online journal to that group. The results spoke for themselves. "We were able to double our residency membership," he noted, "and we saved a couple of hundred thousand dollars a year [in printing costs]."

Phelan's words bear repeating, as they ring true for most associations: "We don't want to rest on history. We needed to show that we are forward-thinking."

You Don't Need a Crystal Ball, Just Crystal Clarity

Obviously, you cannot predict the future or the future needs of your membership (current and future), but there are a variety of things you can do to ensure that your association is positioned to take advantage of changes in the environment. Once you've taken the steps to identify existing problems, review available solutions, and determine potential opportunities, it's time to think strategically about whether your organization can meet the needs of the marketplace, and if so, how.

You need to have leadership that encourages and supports taking risk and allows for some failures, and a culture that embraces untested waters—like SurePayroll. You need to know your industry better than your members, prospects, or your competition—like HIMSS. You need to anticipate needs based on diligently keeping track of trends—like Encyclopaedia Britannica. And you need to be open to changing things that may have been around forever, if those changes will benefit members (and make the association more profitable) —like the MMS.

And you need to incorporate the recommendations in this chapter into your strategic planning process. I cannot stress enough that the perspective on "failing" must be altered; every successful company can show you a list of projects that failed before the company found success with a new solution, business model, or product. It's not that you are actively planning to fail. Rather, you are welcoming the risks that necessarily accompany a potential failure—or a potential success. Is the glass half empty or half full?

At the same time, you don't want to set yourself up for an unsuccessful venture, either. To minimize the risk of failure, consider the following questions to determine whether the new idea is poised to succeed:

• Will the program or product serve a large audience segment? Size matters when it comes to investing time and resources in a new product or program. If the need is great but the audience is small, the new product may simply be too costly to develop and too expensive to sell. The group membership model was a viable solution for medium and large health care organizations because the Massachusetts Medical Society could offer a significant discount based on participation requirements that it could set. The organization could offer their member employees a valued benefit (membership and a personal subscription to the *New England Journal of Medicine*), and the Society could gain market share without losing money on the transaction.

• Does the program or product solve a problem? New products and programs fail for many reasons, but one of the most common is that they do not solve a problem; rather, they just provide an alternative that is no better than existing products. SurePayroll succeeded against tough odds because it solved a problem that small business owners experienced when using existing payroll services. HIMSS Analytics provided health care executives with the data they needed to make good decisions. Both organizations provided a solution that, when used, improved the lives of those who purchased it.

• Does the program or product leverage the strengths of the organization and provide something that members cannot achieve on their own? Even good products fail if the organization that develops them is not able to tap into existing channels or internal strengths. Encyclopaedia Britannica could have tried to compete head-to-head with Wikipedia. Instead, they chose to leverage their strengths and fill a gap in the marketplace for high-quality, reliable information that is easily accessible and affordable.

• Will your idea adapt to advances in technology or delivery channels? Some organizations focus on a new delivery tool, such as an app, instead of focusing on the problem and how their product will provide a solution that will result in a positive outcome. The best solutions are adaptive to changes in behavior or technology.

• Does the idea focus on the member or the organization? When building new programs or products, you must consider both market forces and member needs. The new group membership program at the Massachusetts Medical Society is a perfect example of this in action. It isn't a traditional "product," but it does focus on the needs of the member and the changing workforce.

Action Steps

1. Conduct an environmental scan and update it on an annual basis. This is such a simple idea that is rarely executed, because it is connected to forecasting future events rather than addressing today's problems. Most environmental scans include data on the political, economic, social, and technological events or trends affecting an industry. They could also include human resources or personnel, population or general demographics, and science. The purpose of conducting a scan is to gain insight into issues or market forces that could potentially affect your industry.

2. Develop a market research plan that incorporates the collection of data through multiple touch points. Too many organizations rely on a membership survey conducted every year, or every few years, as their primary source for information on the needs and interests of their members. I recommend deploying a market research strategy that includes polls, one-page monthly surveys, and experience evaluations. Asking members how likely they are to recommend membership, education, or resources on an ongoing basis will help you take a steady pulse on whether or not you are meeting or exceeding expectations.

3. SurePayroll conducts a two-minute small business survey with its members on a regular basis. These surveys are easy to complete and include an incentive to participate, and the data is shared with customers and the media. In fact, SurePayroll recognizes that benchmarking data and information collected on small businesses is of interest to their customers. They offer a Small Business Optimism Outlook and a Small Business Scorecard to show trends in hiring and wages.

4. Ask members questions about their current challenges when they join—and when they renew. After the member has paid his or her membership dues, ask three to five questions related to his or her job and the profession. Avoid the temptation to ask what you could offer to make the membership more valuable or provide something they do not currently have. It is your job to identify the problems and challenges and then come up with solutions.

5. Look back at the history of your organization and your industry. Begin the process by asking the question, "How did this happen and how did we get here?" Create a historical document of your organization and your industry that is updated annually. HIMSS created a Legacy Workgroup to develop a document that provides a detailed and factual description of its history with annual updates. The stated objective of this exercise is "to provide the anchor for a work-in progress history." HIMSS leadership firmly believes that it is important to understand how and why the Society began and how it evolved. To further support this recommendation, I recommend reading an article that appeared in the December 2012 issue of *HBR*, "Your Company's History as a Leadership Tool" (Seaman & Smith, 2012). The authors state that "leaders with no patience for history are missing a vital truth: A sophisticated understanding of the past is one of the most powerful tools we have for shaping the future" (para. 2). To illustrate their point, Seaman and Smith use the recent acquisition by Kraft Foods of the British confectioner Cadbury. Many Cadbury employees expressed feared that the acquisition would damage the beloved brand. To ease the transition, the senior management at Kraft created an intranet site that showed there were more similarities than differences between the two companies. The article further states that "business leaders must think like historians" and that "history also impels us to think about the long term—another strength of the best leaders." The bottom line, according to the article, is that by looking at your organization's history, you will gain a perspective that will help "cut through management fads and the noise of the moment to what really matters" (para 2).

6. Use existing data to identify future needs. Data mining is commonly used by organizations that wish to identify patterns and trends that will help them build predictive models. For example, an organization may examine the characteristics or traits of members with the highest lifetime value in order to determine which types of prospects have the greatest likelihood of joining and renewing their membership year after year. Data mining can also be used to examine conference attendance and product sales by identifying members whose past behavior shows they are most likely to attend future events. By tracking and analyzing the data you collect on members and customers, you should also be able to differentiate between a short-lived trend and a major change to how individuals or companies are responding to existing programs and products.

■ ■ ■

One of the best ways to look to where your members are going is to identify their challenges and problems and offer them solutions, not programs and products. In Chapter Eight you will learn how to transform your communications and connect with members and prospects in a more meaningful way.

PART THREE

SELL
YOUR
ORGANIZATION

8

Be a Problem Solver

A FEW YEARS AGO, while training for the Boston marathon, I injured my iliotibial (IT) band. It is a common knee injury found in runners who train on a track or who haven't warmed up properly before a long run. Although I knew the injury wasn't too serious, it was only four weeks until my race, and I was concerned I wouldn't heal in time. I knew that I needed to address the problem as soon as possible.

With a referral from my doctor, I immediately made an appointment with a physical therapist. Within a few minutes of my arrival, my physical therapist reviewed my medical history and examined my symptoms. She assessed the situation by asking me some questions about what may have caused the injury. She also assessed my flexibility, strength, balance, and coordination. Before she created a plan for treatment, we discussed my goals and what it would require to accomplish them. She told me that she could help me during my appointments but that I needed to continue the work at home in between appointments.

Over the next three weeks, my physical therapist continued to ask questions, assess the situation, and adjust our treatment plan. Fortunately, by working together, we reduced the pain and swelling and I was able to run in the marathon. It's not surprising that I've gone back to her each time I've had a new injury—or that I've recommended her to many friends in my community. She helped diagnose my problem, she created an effective treatment plan, and she helped me reach my goal.

Imagine, however, if instead she had begun my appointment by trying to sell me a compression wrap or other product before discussing the problem and the cause and assessing my unique situation—in other words, if she had tried to sell me a solution before understanding the problem. Yet associations make this mistake every day. They sell their products without understanding the problems that members face. Associations tend to suggest solutions before they understand the needs of each audience segment.

As I've discussed in earlier chapters, individuals join organizations for a variety of reasons. Some join to obtain information; others join to expand their network or earn continuing education credits. And some join because they believe in the mission or the advocacy work being done on behalf of the profession. Regardless of why they join, they all have at least one thing in common: they are seeking a solution to a problem. Think about this in even the most minor way, with even the seemingly most minor problem, and it makes sense. You need a new pair of shoes so that you are not walking around barefoot and risking injury to yourself daily, so you pick a style you like and you purchase your new pair of shoes. You are hungry and you need food to sustain your life, so you buy something to eat. Clearly, this idea is not new.

The term "solution selling" dates back to the 1970s, when a man named Frank Watts, who was working at Wang Laboratories at that time, developed a sales process to which he gave that name. Once he felt he had perfected the process, Watts turned to consulting in 1982 and began teaching his method via workshops to sales forces in companies large and small, one of which turned out to be Xerox Corporation. A Xerox employee at that time, Michael Bosworth, went on to embrace the method, subsequently starting his own company, called Solution Selling, in the 1980s; Bosworth has since written his own books about this idea. In 1999, Bosworth sold the intellectual property to one of his affiliates, Keith Eades, currently CEO and founder of Sales Performance International, and he went on to . . . you guessed it: write his own book about solution selling; he then authored a revised version in 2003, and today he blogs about it.

As sure as there are many consultants who subscribe to this formula, there are numerous takes and twists on solution selling overall. However, the core philosophy is that sales efforts are most effective when they are focused on identifying and developing solutions to the customer's points of pain. It requires that the salesperson be curious enough to get to the bottom of the problem, have a keen sense of listening to what the customer is actually saying, and be able to offer a variety of options to solve the problems.

In the past few years there has been discussion in the sales community about solution selling, with a good amount of that chatter positing that it had run its course. In fact, *Harvard Business Review* addressed this notion in its July/August 2012 issue, with an article titled, "The End of Solution Sales" (Adamson, Dixon, & Toman, 2012). The authors start out indicating that "Customers don't need you the way they used to. [Solution selling] worked because customers didn't know how to solve their own problems, even though they often had a good understanding of what their problems were" (para. 1). However, I found many threads on LinkedIn discussions about the death of solution selling, and interestingly, most people do not share the authors' view.

For associations, I also do not agree with Adamson et al.'s stance. Individuals go through many stages and transitions in their lives. During the transitions, new problems arise that may create both challenges and opportunities. While there is plenty of free information available on the Internet, I believe there is a greater desire to find a community or resource that can point individuals toward relevant and meaningful solutions. There is security in knowing that other people have gone down a similar path and that the solutions your organization offers have a track record for helping individuals experience a smooth transition. One of the best ways to communicate this value—which is unique to associations, because of the vast community of like-minded people who share similar interests and are willing to help one another—is by connecting membership benefits (solutions) to problems (challenges or transitions).

In the conclusion of the *HBR* article, Adamson et al. nearly contradict themselves by opining that sales people may still be selling solutions, but more broadly, they're selling insights. To me, that is just a matter of semantics—and Robert Kear, CMO, agrees with me, in a Solution Selling blog post. On July 10, 2012, Kear said that "if a customer has already assessed their needs, the probability of winning their business is very low . . . And we've always taught that the best salespeople (eagles) insightfully 'educate' customers about critical business issues that are not perceived as needs or problems yet" (Kear, 2012, para. 6).

What Kear suggests in his rebuttal of the *HBR* article is, again, just what associations have been about all along. Salespeople (that is, the association staff) have insightfully educated their members and, more important, their prospective members about issues that quite possibly are not even seen as needs and/or problems yet.

Association members (and prospective members) are in need of solutions—call them insights, if you must—and it's up to you to essentially know this even before they do. They may not be seeking solutions to every problem, or even the most pressing problems they face in their daily lives, but they are looking to their professional organization to be a solution provider, based on the following individual perceptions and criteria:

- The primary role of an organization
- The unique advantages and opportunities the organization offers
- A reputation for quality and/or effectiveness in solving specific problems

Start Selling Those Solutions

Once again, when individuals are making a decision whether to join, renew, register, or make a purchase, they are making a decision regarding your association's ability to solve their problem. Unfortunately, many organizations don't *sell those solutions.* They don't position themselves as problem solvers. Instead, organizations frequently market their conferences, events, webinars, publications, and other resources. They sell membership, programs, and products.

When an individual considers joining an organization, there is a risk involved in the decision. There may be some doubt as to whether or not the organization can solve their problem. It's this uncertainty that can lead to failed expectations and low retention rates of first-year members. There is another group of individuals who may not realize they have a problem, or they may believe they have the resources they need to solve their problems. They are your prospective members.

To provide you with another analogy, consider the following products and the problems they solve:

- You don't buy shampoo—you buy clean, shiny hair.
- You don't buy a gym membership—you buy a slimmer, stronger body.
- You don't buy a luxury car—you buy prestige, comfort, safety, a reward for being successful.
- You don't buy insurance—you buy peace of mind.

To solve problems, you need to understand where your members are today and where they want to be in the future. Of course, this will vary based on many factors, and you will need to create a variety of different profiles based on different types of members. You start this process, however, by asking individuals to describe their current situation. At a granular level, this may include type of work, title or position, work setting, education, certifications, professional recognition or achievement, rank or status, income level, and debt load. You should also explore past challenges and recent accomplishments.

Once their current situation is defined, it is important to understand what your members hope to accomplish as well as the goals they hope to achieve within the next twelve months. Sometimes organizations reach too far into the future and ask members about their plans for the next three to five years. Years ago, this was a common practice. Today, however, things change far too quickly to make that time frame of any value. By focusing on the next twelve months, you can identify immediate concerns and provide real solutions. Are they happy in their current position, or do they hope to receive a promotion? Do they need to gain experience before moving ahead or are they simply waiting for an opportunity to come available? Are there skills they need to obtain, a degree or certification they need to earn, or do they need to expand their patient, client, or customer base? These questions, among others, will help you understand the different career paths for your members. Additionally, you will determine what is needed for them to move up to the next level.

There will be some individuals who have achieved their goals or obtained a senior position in their industry. So what's next for this group? If there are a good number of years before they intend to retire, they may be asking the same question. If those individuals are nearing retirement, they may want to understand how best to transition into retirement or semi-retirement.

Career Transitions Provide Opportunities

In fact, one of the best ways an association can serve the needs of its members over the lifetime of their entire career is to be there for the transitions. Regardless of the profession, individuals go through many transitions throughout their professional careers. Each transition creates a new set of problems or challenges: finding a job, finding clients or patients, setting up a practice, managing the office, obtaining a license or certification, obtaining a promotion or a new job, new responsibilities, adapting to changes in the profession or advancements in technology, and so on. Providing solutions to these problems will help your organization create meaningful and long-lasting relationships with members. It will also support your efforts to prove the value of membership.

A few years ago, I worked with a small specialty association that proudly boasted a market share in the high 90th percentile. When individuals graduated in this field, they almost always joined the association. Although there were other organizations that provided relevant content, education, and information, this association was viewed as the only organization that focused exclusively on this field. Market share was high, but engagement and attendance at educational conferences were declining. After reviewing the market research conducted with members from various audience segments, their value proposition became very clear: they would be there over the entire lifecycle of their members' careers. From graduation through retirement. We had a very small budget, but we knew it would be important to communicate this value to all members.

We created a membership brochure that would be mailed to all members—not just new ones—that highlighted the offerings (and therefore benefits to the members) based on various transitions. Instead of promoting *publications, education, networking,* and *advocacy,* we focused on the following audience segments:

1. Just starting out?
2. Well established—Now what?
3. Know it so well you can teach it?
4. Ready for your second act?

One advantage of creating a marketing piece that highlighted each stage of the member's professional lifecycle was that we could increase awareness of programs and products that would help them today and let them know that the association would help them through each transition.

Regardless of your members' goals, it is important to find out the answer to the question, "Why is this important?" For example, you may discover that one segment of your membership is unhappy with their current position. Their problem is: I need a new job. For some members, expanding their network in order to learn about new opportunities can solve the problem. Others may lack the skill set, credentials, or experience needed to obtain a new position. A third group may feel overwhelmed, overworked, or unhappy with their employer. Understanding both the problems and the various resources you offer that can help solve problems is critical.

The difference between where members are today and where they hope to be is a gap your association can help fill. You become a problem solver when you present your programs and products as solutions. The insight you can gather on your members can provide you with the Holy Grail in marketing: the psychological triggers that will motivate individuals to respond to your marketing messages.

Just Say No (Except Don't)

If you are a designer, installer, or technician in the information technology systems (ITS) industry, there's a good chance you've heard of an association called BICSI (Building Industry Consulting Service International). Headquartered in Tampa,

Florida, BICSI's membership comprises twenty-three thousand ITS professionals from nearly one hundred countries worldwide. Its members provide the fundamental infrastructure for telecommunications, audio/video, life safety, and automation systems. Its credential program and professional development offerings provide a level of assurance to the industry and to consumers that an individual is knowledgeable and qualified to perform his or her job. To obtain any one of the credentials BICSI offers, individuals must meet certain requirements and pass a rigorous exam. Unfortunately, the exam pass rate was typically very low.

A good friend of mine, Greg Fine, served as the director of membership and communications at BICSI in 2005, when exam results were coming back low—again. When Fine started off for work one beautiful, hopeful spring morning that year, he was happy and ready for the day. However, his demeanor was immediately dampened once he walked into his office and looked at the faces of his team. He didn't have to ask: he knew that BICSI had just released the results from the latest credentialing exam. The mood in the room was considerably lower than the week before, and many of his colleagues were visibly down. At BICSI, Fine's team was in charge of sharing the bad news with those members who had taken the exam and were anxiously waiting to hear how they had done.

"One day, I was walking out of my office and I heard one of my staff members having yet another difficult conversation with a member who had just taken the exam. I stood there for fifteen minutes and just listened," Fine told me (personal communication, February 1, 2013). "I could hear the pain in the voices, or maybe it was indifference, because they had given so much bad news, they had steeled themselves for it. The words I kept hearing over and over were, 'I'm really sorry, but no.'"

It was at that moment that Fine decided to outlaw the word 'no' in the organization. He told his staff that, while they certainly could (and would at times need to) convey the message of "no," they could not use the word "no" itself. Although this proclamation was initially met with some confusion and even frustration, his staff agreed to the challenge, and they began answering the calls with a different tone. Once this change was in place, BICSI's customer service staff began to uncover new opportunities for the organization to serve its members. With longer, more in-depth conversations with exam-takers, a number of questions were raised regarding how BICSI could better prepare individuals who were interested in taking the exam. From products to programs, BICSI realized it could create stronger relationships with its members by solving some of their problems.

"Once we outlawed the word 'no,' we really changed how we spoke to our members and customers. It helped us turn around perceptions of the organization," Fine said. "Once we started listening to our members and prospective members, we realized we needed to change our product and program offerings." The impact of this change was widespread. BICSI experienced an increase in the number of members who renewed, especially newer members, with whom they had a much lower retention rate. In addition, BICSI changed the way it sold its products.

> First we aligned our products with problems. We also evaluated our products to make sure we offered what members needed. In some cases, there were gaps, and we needed to create some new programs. By creating this feedback loop between the frontline staff and the other departments, we were better able to meet our members' needs—and provide the assistance they needed to move forward in their careers. Then we transitioned our staff from sales people to career coaches. As a result, we saw an increase in sales of our products and programs. We also received less complaints and had happier members and customers [Greg Fine, personal communication, February 1, 2013].

Fine firmly believes that you cannot have a member-centric culture—one that is responsive to member needs and solves members' problems—unless the CEO and senior staff value the staff as much as they value the members. Fine was cognizant of the important role the frontline staff played in communicating with members and relaying their concerns to the rest of the organization.

It's been nearly ten years since this change took place at BICSI, and Fine has moved on to other organizations, yet this sentiment is a guiding force in the culture he builds at his current organization.

When he arrived at the Turnaround Management Association (TMA) last year, one of the first issues he needed to address was the relationship between TMA's chapters and its headquarters office. His first action was to, once again, ban his staff from saying the word "no" to chapter volunteers and staff. Prior to his arrival, the headquarters staff had begun most conversations with chapter staff and leaders by stating what they couldn't do until they were convinced they should say "yes" to their requests. In the past year, with the creation of chapter affiliation agreements, TMA staff now begin conversations with a positive "Let's get this done" attitude, unless there are truly justifiable reasons they must say no. "We have a formal contract now," Fine told me. "It's a declaration of what we have a responsibility to do for the chapters and what they have to do for us. In the past it was open revolt. Now we make promises to our chapters that we can keep, and the relationship has improved dramatically."

Fine realized it was easier to "sell" a solution to a problem than the benefits of your offerings.

An Example: ASAE: The Center for Association Leadership

What are the most common problems that membership in your organization will solve for members and prospects? Table 8.1 shows how ASAE: The Center for Association Leadership could connect its programs, products, and services to the problems many of its members face. The Problem describes the situation. The Features/Offerings identify the programs or products ASAE currently offers. The Benefit/Outcome should identify *what will happen as a result of using the offering.*

A Two-Way Street: Gather and Offer Information

Associations have unique opportunities that are not available to most companies or businesses. They collect a significant amount of demographic data through their membership applications. In addition, they can create social and behavioral profiles based on data they collect from online interactions and

Table 8.1.   Problem—Feature—Outcome

Problem	Features/Offerings	Benefit/Outcome
Declining membership	Periodicals including *7 Measures of Success* Membership articles in *Associations Now* Collaborate: Online community of membership professionals you can ask questions in real time; share files Models and samples of membership strategies and campaigns Educational programs on membership topics E-newsletter	Membership growth Increased retention rates Increased market share Increased engagement New membership models
Need a new job	Online job board (CareerHQ) CAE certification Networking opportunities at conferences and by serving on councils or committees Career coaching services Leadership training ASAE University (face-to-face and online programs) Local idea swaps and brown bag events	Expand your network Demonstrate knowledge and differentiate yourself among job applicants Expand your knowledge and skill set Get advance notice on job openings Obtain a new job

(Continued)

Table 8.1.   (Continued)

Problem	Features/Offerings	Benefit/Outcome
Declining revenue from industry supporters, sponsors, and advertisers	Obtain advice from a community of peers Content on ASAE website and *Associations Now* Educational programs	Increased revenue New sources for revenue New opportunities to obtain support
Low attendance at the Annual Conference	Decision to Learn research Business of Meetings certificate program Marketing Membership Communications conference 199 Ideas books Professional development courses at ASAE Annual Conference, Great Ideas Conference, and other conferences	Increased attendance Improved return on marketing investment Increased satisfaction, returning attendees and positive word of mouth

past purchases (education, publications, and products). Plus, many associations have built a greater level of trust with their members than most for-profit organizations. Although most big businesses have the means to leverage the vast amount of data they collect, often these relationships are purely transactional in nature. To ensure that your organization takes advantage of this unique position, you need to create and implement a data collection plan.

Recruitment

During the recruitment phase of your organization's relationship with an individual, the more information you can collect on that prospect, the greater the likelihood that you will deliver relevant messages that address your prospects' most pressing issues. Before you begin your recruitment efforts, you should identify opportunities to exchange content for personal information. For example, if your organization generates content from its magazines, journals, and books, you can repurpose the content into smaller white papers or reports that highlight some, but not all, of the valuable content. Once you've created the unique content that will be valuable to a prospect, you can offer it in exchange for personal contact information. You can offer it on your association's home page or purchase ads on other sites and social media platforms such as LinkedIn. By developing a content marketing campaign that requires prospects to answer questions about who they are and what they need, you will be able to build a more robust database.

Another way to build a robust prospect database is through highly targeted campaigns that offer free webinars to prospective members. The two main reasons to offer the free webinar are to (1) identify prospects who are interested in a topic your organization covers, and (2) collect more information about them.

Onboarding Tactics

Once a prospect makes the decision to join, you should have a strategy in place that will help you learn more about the new member during the first ninety days of the relationship. Most experienced marketers will tell you that you should simplify the process of joining your organization and avoid asking too many questions on the membership application. While I agree that the application should be brief and easy to complete in order to join the organization, there are other ways to collect information at the beginning of the relationship. For example, once you've identified all of the different data points you wish to collect on new members, you should develop a multi-stage plan that encourages new members to share as much information as possible during the first ninety days (see Figure 8.1).

A new member joins the association. Within the first twenty-four hours, send a new member survey, then a welcome email. Within the first thirty days, send a personalized welcome letter. Finally, send a new member welcome packet/kit. Within the

Figure 8.1.   Onboarding Timeline

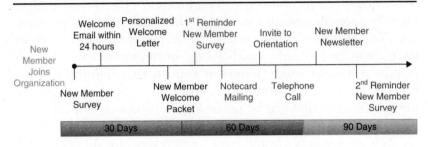

first thirty to sixty days, if the survey has not been completed, send a reminder. Send a postcard—not selling something. Use the postcard to just remind the member that the association is there. Send or email an invitation to a new member orientation. Staff makes a personal phone call to check in. Within sixty to ninety days, send the member a new member newsletter that is designed specifically for a new member; this should not be a newsletter that goes to everyone. Follow up again on the survey, either reminding the member to take it or thanking them, if they have completed it.

■ ■ ■

One tactic you can use includes offering additional free downloads of information, reports, or past issues of publications in exchange for personal information. You can also encourage new members to complete a census survey by rewarding them with points or other "free gifts." Another way to collect data is to invite new members to join a panel. The invitation to the panel should give the impression that you are inviting a select group of new members to help build new programs and identify new products that will help them succeed. The panel may include two hundred or two thousand new members. But again, the key to gaining participation is to make it feel exclusive, provide an incentive, and ask this invitation-only group to participate in surveys that take less than two minutes to complete. Finally, if your association offers many valuable resources on its website, you can build a marketing campaign that encourages and rewards members who complete their online profile.

All of these steps will provide your organization with information that will help with future marketing segmentation efforts. Why is this important? In marketing, you have two choices. You can develop an ongoing campaign that includes many generic touch points with prospects and members—and most likely yields low response rates. Or you can invest your time and money in collecting information that will improve your chances of marketing the right messages to the right people. Unless your advertising budget is large enough to support both a mass marketing campaign and a highly targeted campaign, I recommend focusing your efforts on developing different messages and campaign materials based on the different problems that need to be solved.

Ask Why Multiple Times

Before you can begin to solve your members' problems, you need to answer a few questions. Based on the problem, what is the desired outcome? When asking this question, you may need to ask, "Why does that matter?" at least five times. The 5 Whys, originally developed by Sakichi Toyoda and used by the Toyota Corporation (Liker & Meier, 2005), is a technique used by marketers to identify and understand the root problem and the desired outcome at the deepest level. If you ask why only once, you will identify only a symptom, or perhaps a few symptoms, of the larger problem. However, when you ask "Why is that important?" after each answer, you will eventually get to the root of the problem—and gain a greater understanding of how to solve it. Some people have called this applied common sense; it is also referred to as "root cause analysis." here's an example, plucked from the association world:

Why did you join ASAE?

Answer: Because my boss told me it was a good idea.

Why would your boss feel belonging to an association like ASAE would be a good idea for you?

Answer: She found it to be a good resource and suggested I would as well, because I can meet and learn from other people in the same field.

Why do you want to meet other association executives?

Answer: Because they share many of the same challenges at work—different challenges from my friends who work at for profit companies.

Why is it important to be connected to other people who "get" what you do for a living?

Answer(s): Because they can relate to the challenges I face when dealing with volunteers. Because I can learn things from another association CEO that I cannot learn anywhere else. Because I don't have a colleague I can turn to in my office who understands or can provide advice when I need it.

Why would it be helpful to learn from others who deal with similar challenges?

Answer(s): Because I don't always need to reinvent the wheel. I can achieve my goals (recruit or engage more members, grow revenue, attract more meeting attendees) and invest my time and money in solutions that have worked well for others.

You also need to determine whether the problems you are trying to solve are aligned with your organization's mission and vision. Some problems, although important to members and rightfully so, are simply not aligned with the organization's priorities. When an association tries to solve problems that no longer fit into an organization's role and purpose, it is difficult to provide meaningful solutions.

Finally, you need to assess whether your organization will be perceived as a source for solutions or you will need to educate members and prospects about your strengths and abilities. Sometimes organizations are unable to attract new members because the organizations are not perceived to be the primary organization that provides solutions to members' problems. If this is the case, you will need to invest time and money in building awareness of your unique strengths and qualities.

Integration of Marketing Efforts

Once you've defined the your members' problems and the solutions you can offer to help solve them, it's time to think about how to integrate your marketing efforts.

One association I worked with measured the success of their direct mail, email, telemarketing, print, and online advertising as independent marketing tactics. The print and online advertisements showed very little, if any, positive return on the investment. Our analysis revealed that print and online advertising depleted a good portion of the budget. Yet there is a risk in assuming that each tactic worked independently of the others. In some cases this may be true, if there isn't a connection or integration of messages. However, when a marketing campaign integrates all of the different touch points and reinforces a clear and simple message, the lines between the different tactics become a bit more blurred.

Case Study: Electronic Retailers Association Tells Stories to Enhance Brand Image

Direct-to-consumer companies rely on a combination of direct-response marketing tactics and consumer confidence to sell their products. Therefore, having a favorable landscape that allows companies to bring quality products and services to consumers is essential to the future of this industry. Representing this $300 billion market is the Electronic Retailing Association (ERA). Founded by nine company members as the National Infomercial Marketing Association in 1991, ERA today represents more than 450 companies in 45 countries. Although ERA had experienced steady growth over the past two decades, the association decided it was time to try some other marketing strategies, and so it turned to its own members.

When Dave Martin, ERA's vice president of marketing and content, and his team embarked on the initiative to clarify the association's brand and synchronize its messages, he defined his goals as follows:

- To realize the association's vision of being the universally recognized authority, resource, and voice for electronic retailing

- To clearly communicate ERA's value proposition to its constituents
- To lead members and association staff to "live the brand" at all touch points
- To promote universal adherence within the electronic retailing industry to a common code of ethics relating to integrity, good business practice, and respect for the rights of clients, employees, and suppliers

ERA members typically market to their companies by using case studies, in which a problem is laid out, followed by how the company solved the issue. ERA decided to take a page from this book and incorporate a series of case studies into its marketing efforts to clarify the ERA brand. To achieve their goals, ERA determined that it needed a threefold strategy:

1. *Let members do the talking.* Develop member success stories that would incorporate testimonials to showcase the ERA brand.
2. *Connect content to brand attributes and features.* Instead of using clichéd terms that appear inauthentic at best, and empty at its worst, ERA focused on connecting its content from a variety of sources to its four key brand attributes.
3. *Create targeted communications.* ERA developed campaigns that were targeted to prospect segments to ensure efficient communications and avoid email fatigue and, in addition, low open rates.

In determining these goals, and the strategies to address them, ERA felt it could leverage one of its proven strengths. That strength is that ERA has a membership that could share stories based on more than twenty years of experience with the association. For example, Katie Williams and Peter Spiegel understand the value of membership and how it provides exposure and access to potential business partners in the industry. With over twenty-five years of combined multichannel marketing experience, Katie and Peter are responsible for more than $3 billion in sales worldwide. Their company, Ideal Living, markets fitness, wellness, and health products through direct response and home shopping TV, online, at major retailers, and through catalogs.

Like many companies trying to sell products to consumers, Ideal Living experienced a decline in sales due to the recession in 2008 and 2009. While some companies were unable to survive the recession, Ideal Living made two strategic moves that helped it regain its position in the marketplace and increase sales. First, according to Williams, "We got back to the basics by fine-tuning our marketing efforts to increase lifetime value" (Electronic Retailing Association, n.d.a, para. 5). And second, they expanded their partnerships with others, most of whom they found through their involvement in ERA. Williams also reported, "Relationships with partners have always been important to me and even more so, during the recession" (para. 6).

This story and three others are an integral part of ERA's marketing efforts, referred to as SupERAchiever Success Stories. When the organization talks about sharing *best practices*, it connects its offerings to real challenges that members have experienced. In other words, ERA proves—in members' own words—how it offers its members solutions that really work. To promote the four main tenets of membership—advocacy, self-regulation, wisdom, and access—ERA promotes its SupERAchiever Success Stories.

They spread the word by using multiple channels, including their website, digital and print marketing collateral, and advertisements. In these ads, ERA uses the tagline "ERA Stands Behind Every SupERAchiever." The opening ad goes on to explain precisely what a SupERAchiever is: "An industry powerhouse who's used their ERA membership to get to the top" (Electronic Retailing Association, n.d.b, para. 1). So the promotion of these individual ERA members points out the fact that their membership in the association has directly led them to be a leader within the industry. The case studies themselves put forth a challenge, the objectives and a result (see Exhibit 8.1).

Exhibit 8.1. Electronic Retailing Association Membership Campaign

6 / WE PROTECT AND GROW MARKETING'S BEST SELLERS   ACCESS²

ERA HAS TAKEN ACCESS TO THE NEXT **POWER,**
AND NO TRADE ASSOCIATION FOSTERS NETWORKING QUITE LIKE WE DO.

"While we develop many products in-house, at least 20% of our revenue stems from products we've developed with partners, most of whom we have found through ERA."

—

KATIE WILLIAMS
PRESIDENT,
IDEAL LIVING

—

Access²

Our members associate and work side-by-side with their peers, offering invaluable opportunities to expand their businesses; in fact, many members say that they sell their entire year at ERA shows. Along with our many events, we offer two additional ways for our members to network. Every member is included in and receives a copy of Gold Book, our annual industry directory. Every member also has access to MyERA, an online networking community that allows members to easily connect with one another, share ideas and content, find new business leads and much more.

Access² SupERAchiever Katie Williams

Ideal Living develops innovative consumer brands, specializing in health, wellness and home environment. The recession presented many challenges, and President Katie Williams continued to turn to ERA as an invaluable resource to open more doors and reinforce existing partnerships. "So much of my business has been built on relationships," she says. "And every single ERA event is a great opportunity to strengthen these relationships." Katie's involvement in ERA's Board of Directors and various committees has strengthened Ideal Living, and helped her forge domestic and international partnerships through networking.

Action Steps

1. Write a complete list of problems or challenges your members face. Tap into market research with your members. Conduct focus groups with members at your next meeting.
2. Identify how and why the problem occurs. Are there certain audience segments more affected by the problem than others?
3. Identify all of the solutions available to the member—including both the solutions you offer as well as those offered by other sources.
4. Identify the areas where your association offers the best solution based on a variety of factors, including perceived quality and cost.
5. Look for opportunities to bundle different offerings to create a unique or more robust solution.
6. Collect feedback or testimonials from real members who have used your offerings to help solve their problems or challenges. Identify the different outcomes that have resulted from using your offerings. (More information using effectively using testimonials within marketing messaging appear in Chapter Nine.)
7. Develop program or product profiles that connect the problems, solutions, outcomes, and testimonials.

■ ■ ■

Once you've identified your members' problems and created solutions, you need to make your case for why they should turn to your organization to help them achieve positive outcomes. In Chapter Nine, I will demonstrate the power of proof.

Prove It!

A FEW YEARS AGO, I was invited to give a half-day marketing workshop for a state association located in Milwaukee, Wisconsin. The workshop had originally been scheduled to take place in Milwaukee, which, in addition to being the headquarters city, was home to many of the attendees. But the workshop had been moved to Wausau, a city situated in the northern half of Wisconsin a good three hours away from Milwaukee.

The original location was far more ideal for many attendees because of the close driving distance; they could even have returned to their offices in the afternoon. When the new location was announced, many of the attendees had to choose between arriving the night before, thus also incurring a hotel expense, or getting up at the crack of dawn and driving three or more hours in order to arrive for the 9:00 AM session. The new location deterred some individuals from attending altogether. In the face of all of this, I felt that I needed to exceed expectations for those who chose to attend. Once you considered the time and the added travel expenses, the workshop had to deliver considerable bang for the buck.

When the workshop was over, I walked over to the executive director to say goodbye. At the same time, one of the attendees approached us and thanked us for putting together the workshop. She then said, "This was worth getting up at 5:00 AM and driving halfway across the state to attend." I happily thanked her for the feedback. As she left, I turned to the executive director and told her that she should incorporate this into her promotional materials about the value of their educational programs.

The marketing copy that the association currently used to promote its education said: "We put on eight half-day educational programs featuring expert speakers on cutting-edge topics." Imagine if instead they said: "We host educational events that are worth waking up at 5:00 AM and traveling halfway across the state to attend." Not only is this a more compelling reason to register and attend their events, it incorporates a testimonial into the marketing copy as "proof" of their value.

Take the Words Right Outta Their Mouths

Testimonials have long been a part of many associations' membership recruitment efforts. They appear on brochures and websites and are sometimes included in direct mail or email campaigns. Yet many testimonials don't feel authentic. And they often include very generic references rather than specific examples. To prove to members and prospects that your organization can solve its problems, you need to obtain and share authentic testimonials. Your members should relate to the individuals and the words being shared in the story.

Here are some of the testimonial mistakes I often see:

• *The association lacks attribution to a real person.* A testimonial from an unnamed source—such as "A senior executive," "A sole practitioner," "A young professional"—is rarely believable. Most people assume the quote was created by the organization and was never actually spoken by a member of the organization. Anonymous testimonials lack credibility.

• *The testimonials are too long.* A testimonial that takes more than thirty seconds to read is simply too wordy. Attention spans are getting shorter, and there are too many distractions to take a chance that your members or prospects will read a long statement. Most copy can be cut in half without losing the main points that need to be expressed. This is true for both written and video testimonials.

• *Testimonials feel contrived.* Those that include words or phrases not commonly used in everyday conversations create a sense that the statement was developed by the organization and not by the individual. When the attendee came up to me after my session in

Wausau, Wisconsin, she didn't say: "Thank you for providing professional development and cutting-edge information that will help me succeed back at the office."

- *Testimonials lack specificity.* It's easy to include clichés or general statements to describe the overarching value of membership—yet when they lack specifics, they also come across as hollow or, even worse, they become invisible.

Focus on Problems, Solutions, and Outcomes

Testimonials should provide proof of your statements that your organization provides top-notch education, information, or networking opportunities. They should focus on a specific problem, the solution to the problem, and the eventual outcome. When testimonials include emotional statements, they are also highly memorable. Good testimonials highlight the benefits to the audience in very specific ways.

Recently, one of my clients shared an interesting story about how her association came to use an outbound calling center to bring lapsed members back to her association. It started when she attended a membership session at the ASAE Marketing, Membership, and Communications Conference that focused on how to regain lapsed members. During the session, one of the methods the presenter recommended using to encourage lapsed members to rejoin was collaborating with a calling center. Based on the information she learned at the session, my client added this tactic to her marketing mix and was very happy with the results.

After using the service for just two months, her association was able to bring back 20 percent of its lapsed members, which translated into more than $15,000 in dues revenue. The testimonial of my client could easily be used by the calling center vendor as a way to demonstrate their value and show proof of the value of their services. However, it could also be used by ASAE, because it was at that meeting that my client gleaned the information and example to try this type of marketing. For ASAE, her testimonial could be convincing proof that the association's education offers "unique lessons to help you develop the right blend of marketing, membership and communications for powerful results!"

Every organization should be able to find stories such as this one. However, not every organization makes it a practice to actively collect this information and, further, to incorporate it into their marketing messages. So I am going to make it easy for you to utilize this method.

First, I will describe a variety of options for collecting testimonials. I will also provide you with a worksheet you can complete to help you plan ahead and collect valuable feedback. Finally, I will recommend ways to incorporate the feedback into your marketing materials.

Collect the Proof

Sometimes members and customers will share positive experiences even if they have not been prompted by an organization. But this is the exception rather than the rule. When it does happen, the person on the receiving end of the "compliment" is often unlikely to take any action other than to thank the person(s) for the feedback or tell them that they are glad they were very satisfied with the experience. To show the proof—and to provide a compelling reason to join your organization, purchase a product, or attend a meeting—you must take an active role in collecting this feedback.

First, the marketing department should manage and coordinate efforts to collect feedback on an ongoing basis. If your organization does not have an entire department dedicated to marketing, or if marketing is decentralized, I recommend assigning the responsibility to one individual who will be held accountable for ensuring that these efforts are made. As with pretty much any initiative, if you don't assign someone the responsibility for making sure efforts are made to collect feedback, it simply won't get done. Due to the crossover between various departments and the need for online and automated feedback forms, collaboration is needed to build a feedback loop into the ongoing activities of the organization.

Once a point person has been assigned responsibility for collecting the information, the next step is to create a calendar of organization activities. This should include in-person and online events, new product launches, networking events, and the release of publications including your magazine or journal (see Table 9.1).

Table 9.1. Organization Event Calendar for Member Feedback

Activity	Date, Time, and Location	Audience Segments	Description	Format
Chapter networking event	Feb. 5 11:30 AM–1:30 PM Cleveland, OH	Local members Attorneys, business owners, brokers, CPAs	Members-only educational event on the topic of xxx Expected attendance: 40 people	On-site
February issue of magazine	Print and digital editions arrive the first week in February	All audience segments	Leadership and management issue	Brief online survey/evaluation form
Midwinter conference	March 2–4 Orlando, FL	Volunteer leaders Senior level executives	Education and networking event Expected attendance: 350 people	On-site interviews, evaluations, and follow-up emails
March issue of magazine	Print and digital editions arrive the first week in March	All members	Technology issue	Brief online survey/evaluation form

Women's group dine-around	April 21 6:30–8:30 PM Chicago, IL	Women All career stages (young professionals, mid-careerists, leaders/partners)	Women-only networking event	On-site
April issue of magazine	Print and digital editions arrive the first week in March	All members	Business development issue	Brief online survey/evaluation form
Webinar	May 2 11:30 AM Online	Entry-level or young professionals	Introductory course for continuing education credit	Online survey/evaluation form
Release of new book	May 20 Book release July 20 Follow-up	Solo or small practice members	Description of books contents	Email and online survey follow-up two months after book release

Feedback forms need to be created by the responsible staff member. These should be brief, yet specific; avoid the temptation to ask too many questions regarding needs and interests. Keep in mind, the feedback tools should focus on gathering testimonials or proof that your organization helps members achieve their goals. Therefore I've listed a few sample questions you may want to include in your efforts to collect feedback (just don't use all of them):

- On a scale of 0–10, how likely are you to recommend [product name/event] to a colleague or friend?
- In your own words, how would you describe [product name/event] to a colleague or friend?
- Identify one or two ideas you learned from using or attending [product name/event].
- How, specifically, did [product name/event] help you?
- What problem were you facing that [product name/event] solved?
- Has [product name/event] made your work easier? How?
- What did you find remarkable about [product name/event]?
- What part of your experience with [association name] makes you want to [renew your membership/purchase a product/attend another event]?

Once you've created a feedback loop, you then need to create a process for incorporating the data into your marketing messages. This is critical, because without a process, it is much easier to collect the information and store it on the proverbial shelf than to incorporate it into your marketing materials. Don't let this happen; make sure that all the work devoted to collecting the feedback yields useable marketing material for your organization.

One way to ensure that all of your marketing efforts show the proof behind your claims is to create a checklist of required elements in all communications. The elements that typically appear on all communications include your name, logo, website, and social media links and icons. Just add your proof to the required elements list.

Another way to ensure that feedback is incorporated into your messaging is to conduct a semi-annual audit of your communications. Engaging in an assessment like this ensures that all the communications your organization puts out align with its mission, market opportunities, and member needs. At the end of an audit, an association should be able to see how to craft tangible messages that clearly and consistently illustrate the problems the association can solve and why prospective members need to belong to that association. An audit should also reveal how your association communicates (or fails to communicate) how it is different from the competition. As part of this process, you should make sure that the claims you make in your communication vehicles are substantiated with proof and that the messages are up-to-date.

Finally—and this may be the most focused way to build a feedback loop that is tied to your communications—develop a process that rewards departments and individuals based on the positive feedback they receive. For example, each month the marketing department could give an award to the individual or department that collects the most creative or positive feedback. You can even reward departments that collect helpful criticism that is used to improve a program or product. Rewards may include small items such as coffeehouse gift cards. Another option is to purchase a trophy that is passed along from one department to another. A larger annual prize could be awarded to the department that receives the best feedback as voted on by their peers.

Be Unforgettable: Play the Numbers Game

One big hairy audacious goal for associations should be to create marketing messages that not only resonate loudly with the intended audience but also are memorable. We probably can all name popular advertisements that are truly unforgettable, sticking with us for years and even decades:

Melts in your mouth, not in your hands. (M&Ms)

Tastes great, less filling. (Miller Lite)

Like a good neighbor . . . (State Farm Insurance)

There are some things money can't buy. For everything else, there's MasterCard.

And if you grew up in the 1970s and '80s, you may remember the advertisement slogan of Trident gum: "Four out five dentists surveyed recommended sugarless gum for their patients that chew gum." Trident didn't claim that dentists believe that chewing gum was good; rather, that chewing sugarless gum was preferred over regular gum. The slogan worked well, and Trident became one of the top-selling and best-known sugarless chewing gums on the market. Although the slogan has been parodied over the years, the makers of Trident gum not only had the data to support their claim from an independent study but also earned the American Dental Association Seal of Approval following the submission of scientific evidence.

Today, stating that your association is the *leading provider* or the *premier organization* may just make your marketing copy invisible or irrelevant to young professionals who have grown up in a world oversaturated with inflated statements and false promises. People have become so immune to bold claims that they ignore them unless there is actual proof that is credible. Fortunately, it isn't difficult to obtain the proof if you know how to collect it and incorporate it into your marketing and communications in the form of testimonials. Again, testimonials validate your claims because they provide an independent endorsement of your organization and its offerings.

You can get prospects to take notice and actually remember your association by incorporating agreement statements, in which you ask members to share their level of agreement with statements based on your mission, vision, and strategic plan. Consider the following scenario as an example of how to do this.

The Turnaround Management Association is an international nonprofit association dedicated to corporate renewal and turnaround management. With more than nine thousand members worldwide, TMA's members share a common interest in strengthening the economy through the restoration of corporate value. Members include attorneys, financial advisors, accountants, lenders, investors, and other related professionals. Their vision is to be globally recognized as the community that brings together individuals from a variety of disciplines in the industry to associate, market their services, and develop their professional skills.

To support their vision statement and their messaging around the value of membership, we assisted the organization in conducting a survey with members to measure their agreement with a variety of statements. We asked members: *What is your level of agreement with the following statement?* (Scale of 1 to 5; 5 = Strongly Agree)

TMA provides valuable networking opportunities for business development.

The response? Approximately three out of four members agreed with this statement. In addition, nine out of ten members believed that the value they receive from their membership is equal to or greater than the cost of membership. If TMA were to incorporate these findings into its messaging, the organization could, supported by data, make this pitch: "Three out of four of your peers, and competitors, turn to the Turnaround Management Association to grow their business, open new doors, or learn about potential deals. Isn't it time for you to join this community?"

One more way to incorporate research findings or program evaluations into your messaging to support your statements and show proof is to identify a percentage of past attendees who believe that your annual conference (or another conference) had more impact on their professional growth than any other event they attended in the past year. To obtain the proof that your organization provides the *resources and tools that members need to succeed,* you need to ask your members and then share this information with the rest of the industry.

Then they'll tell two friends . . . and they'll tell two friends . . . and so on, and so on, and so on . . .

100 Billion Can't Be Wrong

On April 15, 1994, McDonald's executives announced they had reached a milestone: more than one hundred billion hamburgers had been sold (Over How Many Billion Served? 2010). It was time to change the famous sign under the golden arches to read *Billions and Billions Served.* Why did Ray Kroc erect the original sign that stood in front of the first McDonald's: *McDonald's Hamburgers— Over 1 Million Served?* It helped bolster the restaurant's image by promoting the popularity of its burgers.

Impressive statistics, such as *Over 1 Million Served* or *Billions and Billions Served,* help to build an emotional response and assure potential customers they will be satisfied with their purchase. This is mainly because the company, association, or any entity can prove that others before them were satisfied. Using statistics to reinforce your message is a good way to show potential members that you are not just claiming to be the *leading provider of education or information* on a topic, but that many individuals or companies within your industry agree. It's the proof behind your statements.

Backing up claims with statistics is effective whether you are trying to win over burger eaters or an association's prospective members and/or members thinking about whether to pay their dues year after year. If you use surveys to evaluate your programs, products, or even satisfaction with being a member, then you have data that can be used to promote membership. After each event, as recommended with the Feedback Calendar, you may want to ask members if they would recommend your networking events or education to a friend or colleague.

And, similar to the TMA story, which dealt with how members felt about the organization's mission, another way to get at credible and interesting testimonials is by asking members to share their level of agreement with any of the following statements:

- [Association and conference name] is a must-attend conference for [your industry professionals].
- [Association name] is the leading provider of professional development.
- [Association name] provides networking opportunities that are useful to growing my business.
- [Association name] brings leaders together from across the field.
- [Association name] provides market intelligence that will help me grow my business.
- [Association name] is a trusted source for data and intelligence.
- [Association name] serves as an authoritative voice for the industry.
- [Association name] is a leading publisher of research that advances the field.
- [Association name] is the global leader in [your industry or field].

If your organization represents a significant percentage of your industry, you can use either a number or a statistic to bolster your claim. If you are a trade association, you can showcase the logos of your members on your website. Socialmedia.org is a community for social leaders of some of the largest brands in the world. The organization promises members—from Zappos to Kraft to Southwest Airlines—that they will have access to best practices, actionable advice, and solutions in a vendor-free environment. When they say they are an instant advisory board of the heads of social media at the world's biggest brands, they back it up by displaying the logos and naming the brands represented in their community. The combination of the visual proof and the list of well-known name brands strengthens their claims.

Socialmedia.org takes this one step further by displaying a photograph on their website from one of their meetings showing the real people at their event. The image includes the names of individuals and their companies including General Motors, H&R Block, AT&T, and UnitedHealth Group (see Figure 9.1).

The following list provides some ideas for finding some impressive statistics within your own organization.

• The number of individual members, both current and past, who have belonged to your association. For example, if you add up all past members and current members, you may be able to make a statement similar to the one made by McDonald's regarding how many individuals you've served during the history of your organization. This number may be significantly higher than your current membership. Indeed, that is what you're going for: an impressive statistic. However, it is important that you clarify that it's a cumulative figure.

• Does your organization have a large portfolio of publications, reports, and whitepapers? Could you impress prospective members with the number of pages, articles, or books you've published over time? If you add up all of the pages published from your magazine and journal, would it be over twenty-five thousand? Or fifty thousand? These are impressive numbers and could be shared in a statement to bolster your claim that you are a leading authority on a subject matter.

Figure 9.1. Socialmedia.org Promotes Its Membership

• If your association can claim that individuals from your industry's largest or most prestigious organizations are members or past conference attendees, consider promoting this by identifying these organizations by name. For example, a health care organization could potentially claim that members come from nine out of the top ten leading health care institutions in the country, including the Johns Hopkins Hospital, MD Anderson Cancer Center, the Mayo Clinic, UCLA Medical Center, and Massachusetts General Hospital.

• Use statistics from an internal research study or a reputable third party, such as Pew Research Center or Nielsen to demonstrate a growing need or a lack of resources or information available on a topic.

Zero Moment of Truth

In 2011, Jim Lecinski changed the way many marketers viewed the sales cycle with his Google ebook, *ZMOT Winning the Zero Moment of Truth.* As a consumer, you have already experienced this moment. It happened when you checked out the reviews on Amazon before buying a book, or when you looked up and compared products on your mobile phone while standing in a store aisle.

More than a million times a day, a new decision-making moment occurs when an individual is exposed to a marketing stimulus such as an advertisement, email, or direct mail. It is often at that moment, or soon thereafter, that the majority of Americans conduct some form of research before making a purchase (Lecinski, 2011). It was Google that coined the term "Zero Moment of Truth." Before that, the big moment was the First Moment of Truth (FMOT), when the consumer decided to choose one brand over another at the point of purchase. A Second Moment of Truth (SMOT) occurs when the individual uses the product or has an experience based on the purchase. If the experience exceeded expectations, then brand loyalty begins to form and an emotional connection occurs (see Figure 9.2).

Figure 9.2.   Zero Moment of Truth

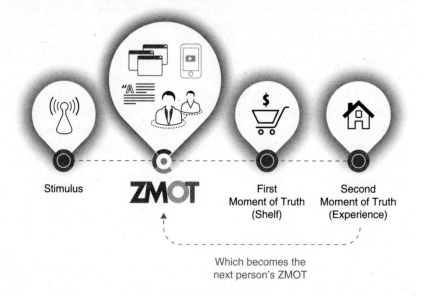

Stimulus   ZMOT   First Moment of Truth (Shelf)   Second Moment of Truth (Experience)

Which becomes the next person's ZMOT

Today there is a new step in the decision-making process. It happens after the stimulus and before the First Moment of Truth. And according to the author of the ebook, this isn't happening just with consumer products. So what can this mean for associations? Prospective members are more likely to make their decision to join based on a combination of the following factors:

1. Access to information, to better understand the personal and relevant value proposition
2. The experiences of others, based on reviews, testimonials, and other methods for sharing opinions
3. An urgency or reason to act today, based on incentives or special offers

When individuals belong to more than one association, or if they pay for their membership dues out of their own pocket, there is even a greater likelihood that a ZMOT (Lecinski, 2011) will occur. That's when, if there are alternatives or if cost is a consideration, prospective members will look for some proof that they are making the right decision in joining your organization.

Fortunately, associations typically have stronger relationships than consumer brands do, because they have not just customers but members—ideally, loyal members. By developing the tools that will allow members to *review* the organization and its offerings, an association can help a prospective member make his or her decision whether to join. Additionally, there is an overwhelming amount of research supporting the fact that most reviews are positive. Finally, associations have members who share similar traits with prospects. This therefore increases the confidence in the decision made by a prospect. Consider this: if the single most influential factor for many of your prospective members, in their decision to join, is an endorsement, shouldn't you be actively collecting and sharing this information?

Although word of mouth and reviews are important, your association can also, by sharing case studies and engaging industry thought leaders, prove to prospective members that the value of joining exceeds the cost. (This is precisely what the Electronic Retailers Association did, as referenced in Chapter Eight.)

Today, one of the best ways to share these stories is through YouTube videos. As the second largest search engine on the Internet, YouTube is being used by B2B and consumer organizations to connect real-life stories to its brand. Online videos do not require a significant investment to create; in fact, some of the most authentic videos are made with amateur equipment. From the chapter level to the national and international level, associations can easily tap into a cadre of volunteers and staff to capture the stories behind the members that are captivating yet also provide real and tangible examples or proof that there is value in belonging to the organization.

As mobile phone and tablet usage increases, it becomes increasingly important to ensure that your case studies and videos are accessible on these platforms. In the consumer world, much has been written about shopping cart abandonment. For associations, the same thing can easily occur if the ZMOT (Lecinski, 2011) is a failure.

Avoid Failure

What can you do to reduce the likelihood of a ZMOT failure?

- *Engage a diverse group of members in the process.* Although it may be easier to enlist the aid of active volunteers, leaders, and rising stars, look for members who join for a variety of reasons.
- *Make sure your case studies are easy to find and access.* If you've created a series of videos, adapt some to digital formats so that they can be downloaded onto a laptop or desktop. Purposefully format some to be viewed on a tablet.
- *Connect your case studies, video testimonials, and reviews to membership information.* Provide additional information and links to help prospective members better understand the value of joining. Share statistics you've gathered from marketing research or program evaluations to further support your claims.
- *Connect prospective members to current members.* Ask your members to serve as ambassadors for your organization. Reward their efforts by recognizing them (with badges or icons) and encourage them to connect with prospective members.

Membership Meets the Press

An independent endorsement from a credible source, such as a major news outlet or institution, can provide additional proof that there is value in belonging to your organization. Many academic institutions will promote a top ranking that appeared in *U.S. News & World Report.* If a consumer brand is profiled in a positive light on CNN or *60 Minutes,* the company website will feature a video clip or promote the story because it lends credibility to their claims. In some instances, your organization may have received a favorable mention from a mainstream publication, an industry trade, or even a well-known blogger. When this occurs, you should be prepared to incorporate the news coverage into your messaging.

Most of the time, however, you will have to use other techniques to support your claim and connect your organization to credible sources. For example, if your association focuses on the needs of physicians within a specialty area, such as dermatology, cardiology, or urology, and a specific top doctor related to your industry has been discussed in the media, you most certainly have an opportunity to connect your organization, your members, and your content to the media sources discussing the topic. Here are some other ways to use the media as an endorsement of your organization:

- Recognize members who have appeared in the media on your website.
- Conduct an annual state of the industry study.
- Connect your industry experts to reports through www.helpareporter.com.
- Plan ahead and make sure your members are ready and available to the media when a local or national issue becomes mainstream news.
- Create a robust online media room, including videos, white paper downloads, timelines, backgrounders, phone numbers, and email links to your staff and trained volunteers.
- Use Twitter to request testimonials. You can then retweet these to your own followers, or repurpose them in marketing materials, on websites, and so on. The reach is exponential, and it costs your association a total of nothing monetarily and very little time or effort.

You may already be incorporating some or even all of the suggestions I've listed here. However, are you connecting these efforts to your organization in a way that strengthens your promise to members and prospects? Are these efforts visible on your website? If prospective members check out your *About Us* page, will they see examples that you are actively working on the behalf of the industry? It's one thing to say you serve your members, the industry, and the public; it's another to prove it. If you just post mentions of your organization and your members on a press or media page, you are missing an opportunity to showcase your efforts in the areas where prospective members are looking.

How Do You Measure Up?

Sure, you can claim that your organization offers more bang for the buck. You can easily create a marketing piece that says, "We provide more value than the cost of dues!" And you can certainly make a statement that your industry's leading experts are, in fact, your members. However, it is far more effective if you can actually prove these claims through side-by-side comparisons with your competitors. Companies that wish to show customers that they offer more features than their competitor for the same price frequently use this tactic.

Because associations compete with for-profit companies that offer education or publications of interest to their members, this may be a great way to demonstrate or show proof that membership provides more value than just being a customer.

Another concept used as a way to influence others, called "social proof," entails using experts or celebrities to reinforce your claims of quality or excellence. In the consumer world, celebrities may include well-known television or movie stars, politicians, or members of the media. For associations, celebrities may be your experts and include authors, professors, speakers, researchers, and industry leaders. If your organization's board of directors includes some of the most prestigious and respected figures in the field, don't hide them on the *About Us* page of your website. Promote their names and organizations in your membership marketing materials.

As I hope you have learned in this chapter, there are myriad ways to provide proof that your association is worth the price of membership. It may take a little creativity, brainstorming, or just reading a book that details some effective ways to do this.

Case Study: ACG Mines Testimonials for Gold

Testimonials, statistics, and reviews help bolster marketing claims, but if you can demonstrate actual results, you've got gold. The Association for Corporate Growth (ACG) knows that the best way to market the organization to prospective members is to promote the results of the relationships that are built among members. Founded in 1954, ACG is a global organization with more than 14,500 members whose business involves middle-market growth. Throughout its marketing collateral—including digital and print brochures, its website, and social media communities—ACG frequently names individuals who are part of their community.

In a research study I conducted on behalf of the organization, we discovered that 75 percent of ACG members report they have done business with fellow members. This statistic appears as a headline in its membership brochure and on its website. The statistic is a way to showcase the results of membership. ACG understands that their members care about the return on their investment—and this fact is highlighted throughout their messaging regarding joining the association.

To augment their claims that ACG provides opportunities to network with more than two thousand dealmakers in the industry at their primary event, InterGrowth, they promote "Who's Coming" with a link to a frequently updated attendee list.

ACG doesn't just claim to be Driving Middle-Market Growth; they prove it.

Action Steps

1. Develop a plan to capture authentic testimonials from a diverse audience. This should include many different age groups, work settings, specialties, and other audience segments. Coordinate your efforts so that every department is included in the plan. Identify one individual who will take ownership for collecting and incorporating testimonials into all marketing materials, including, but not limited to, membership promotions, professional development, publications, and advocacy.

2. Develop a series of questions that can be used to collect testimonials and feedback. Create an online feedback form that prompts individuals to provide feedback after they've had an experience with the organization. This may include a combination of tactics, such as the use of online surveys with open-ended questions and follow-up emails to meeting attendees or individuals who have purchased a few products from your organization. You should also create a form on your website that encourages visitors to provide feedback.

3. Conduct mini surveys with your membership to quantify the impact of, and level of agreement with, the big statements your organization makes to market its membership. Once you've collected the data, craft marketing messages that are thought-provoking and will help your organization stand out in a cluttered, saturated media world.

4. Ask members for specific feedback and examples rather than general observations or statements. Ask members to share the initial challenge they faced and to provide feedback on how the association helped solve the problem. Ask members how much time or money was saved by using your offerings. And don't forget to ask about any outcomes that occurred as a result of membership or attending one of your meetings.

5. To increase authenticity, include real names and other contact information with the testimonial. Glowing praise from "Sheri J." will not have the same credibility as a statement from Sheri Jacobs, CAE, president and CEO of Avenue M Group.

6. Create a combination of brief testimonials and longer case studies to help demonstrate the real benefits and outcomes of joining your organization.

7. Obtain written permission. This is extremely important if you wish to use photos, names, or other points of identification with the testimonial.

8. Help prospective members find the information they need during the Zero Moment of Truth. Connect your membership offers to (1) relevant content, (2) reviews and testimonials, and (3) a sense of urgency and an incentive to act today. Don't forget to make sure your efforts are viewable on mobile and tablet devices.

9. Identify and promote impressive statistics or information about your organization and the industry. This may include impressive numbers, individual names, organizations, or companies. Identify opportunities to incorporate this information into all of your marketing materials to help support your claims and show proof that you are the most important or most helpful organization in your field.

10. Show results. When you make a claim, prove it, and then show the results with case studies, statistics, and stories. Match each of your message points with one of the tactics included in this chapter.

Showing proof will help make the decision to join or renew easier because you've help instill confidence that the individual made a good decision. Not everyone, however, will be ready to respond. You may not have answered every question on a prospect's mind; as a result, you may be unable to make the sale. In Chapter Ten I will discuss how to overcome the common objections that remain barriers to growth.

PART FOUR

PERSONALIZE THE PROCESS

10

Overcome Objections

WHEN I WAS GROWING UP, my parents would often tell me that I should think about becoming a lawyer. Nearly every time we had a disagreement, I would argue my case with facts and information mixed with a little emotion. I frequently won these arguments because I always had a plan. Before I would approach them to ask for their permission to do something new, I tried to think through every possible reason they would say *no*, and I would be ready with a solid rebuttal. Although this happened on many occasions, one incident stands out among the others because I needed them to change their perceptions about a number of pretty big issues.

When I was a junior in high school, I had an opportunity to take part in an exchange program with high school students from Strasbourg, France. During the first two weeks of the program, we would stay with a host family. We would then travel to Nice and on to the Loire Valley and then make our way to Paris. The trip would last five weeks, and the cost included everything but airfare and spending money. My two best friends signed up for the experience, and I desperately wanted to join them. Only a few obstacles stood in the way. Although the program was very reasonably priced, it wasn't free. So price was an obstacle. Additionally, I was a mediocre French student at best. Therefore, if I wanted to impress upon my parents that I would take advantage of the educational benefits of the program, I needed to overcome the perception they may have held that I saw this opportunity as a grand vacation, rather than an educational experience in a foreign country. I also figured they would ask questions about the supervision, safety, and overall logistics of the trip.

If I was going to sell my parents on the idea of allowing me to participate in the student exchange program, I knew I needed to come up with an intricate plan. Because cost was sure to be an obstacle, I found a few part-time jobs to help share the expense. Next, I turned to one of my friends who also was planning to go on the trip and who had earned an A in the previous class. I asked her to tutor me over the semester so that I could raise my grade from a C to a B. Finally, I developed a list of questions I thought my parents would ask about the logistics of the trip; I had already found the answers from my French teacher along with a packet of information I requested that I felt would aid my case. I asked my French teacher to share the names of other students who had taken the trip in past years so that I could possibly have my parents talk to their parents about the experience. When I finally made my request, I felt that I had an answer to every question my parents could possibly ask, and I even provided additional information above and beyond. I promised to improve my grades, and I took the actions needed to make sure I could keep my promise. I presented the facts, answered their questions, and even used a bit of emotion in my appeal. It may sound like I went a bit overboard in my efforts, but in this situation the payoff was big, and it was worth it.

My parents agreed to my request and allowed me to have this once-in-a-lifetime experience. I had overcome my parents' objections and fulfilled the promises I had made.

Over the years, I didn't win every argument, but there were more marks in the "W" column then in the "L" column. And I didn't become a lawyer; I became a marketing professional. (I did marry a lawyer, however.) But the lessons I learned early in my life about overcoming objections have helped me sell membership over the years. I learned how important it is to set expectations and keep your promises. I learned that selling requires raising potential objections and overcoming existing perceptions. If I didn't "fill in the blanks" with reasonable and believable information, my audience (in the case of my high school France trip, my parents) would make assumptions based on their existing knowledge and perceptions.

We live in a time in which people are skeptical of statements or claims that promise to solve their problems, make life better, or improve a current situation. They are bombarded with so many messages and sales pitches that an internal defense mechanism usually advises them to question advertising claims, marketing messages, or sales pitches. In the Global Trust in Advertising and Brand Messaging Survey (Nielsen Company, 2012), of more than twenty-eight thousand individuals surveyed, it was revealed that 92 percent trust information from earned media sources, whereas less than half trust paid advertisements (direct mail, print or digital ads, TV ads).

Unfortunately, associations cannot build all of their recruitment efforts around word-of-mouth marketing. With that in mind, you need to build trust by addressing prospective members' concerns up front and proactively overcoming objections. Unless they are moved to join or become active in your association because they want to advance a mission or influence legislative actions, most people will try to determine whether what you offer meets their needs, for the right price. Remember, it isn't always a matter of the price being so high that they can't afford it; it may be that (1) the perceived value does not equal the cost, or (2) the value is there, but any of a number of factors prevent the individual from using or taking advantage of the membership. Some marketers may argue that price is not a barrier in their industry, because membership dues are low and their target market can easily afford membership. This may be true, but no one wants to waste even one dollar. The key word is "waste"—people want to feel they are paying for something that is worth it.

"I Will Not Join (or Renew) Because . . ."

When I was on the staff at the Association Forum of Chicagoland, each year toward the end of the renewal period we would make phone calls to lapsed members in an effort to get them to rejoin the organization. As the chief marketing officer and director of membership, I was responsible for creating the scripts we used for our calls. The renewal call script contained all of the typical elements you'd expect to find, including a list of objections we could hear. We also had a number of suggestions for how to respond to various objections, such as:

- Dues are too expensive.
- I am no longer employed (out of work, in transition, retired).
- I thought I had paid my membership dues.
- I don't have time to take advantage of my membership.

Sound familiar? Developing a list of objections and suggestions for how to respond is a common tactic when making telephone calls to prospective members or lapsed members. Yet this tactic is rarely used to recruit and engage members. I believe it can be effectively implemented for this audience as well.

In this chapter, I will go over some common objections to joining and provide suggestions for how to overcome them. I will also help you identify other objections that may be unique to your industry or field. Finally, I will provide ideas for how to incorporate this information into your communications.

Objection #1: Dues Are Too Expensive

Responding to this objection through mere mathematics probably won't persuade many people. I've seen some associations break it down into a daily rate by stating that "dues are only a few cents a day." This usually does not resolve the issue. Even if dues are only pennies a day, most associations ask members to pay their entire membership fee in one lump sum. For some individuals, the fee may be too high to pay at the moment they are asked to join or renew. For example, individuals who are just starting out in their career most likely have a large student loan debt, others may be in transition between jobs, and still others may be experiencing a lifestyle change (mortgage, children). A few hundred dollars may be just too much for some to manage, even if the value is there.

I also noted in an earlier chapter that many individuals belong to more than one association. Those who work in the health care, legal, or financial industries may belong to their local, state, national, and special interest societies. A few hundred dollars may seem like a fair price; however, many people who belong to multiple associations consider the total sum of their membership dues when deciding if they can afford to pay.

Further, when you tell members and prospects that membership is only "a few cents a day," this resonates only when you can actually offer an installment payment plan. The American Occupational Therapy Association (AOTA) went in this direction when they realized they could attract more members and increase retention rates if they provided a more affordable way to pay for membership dues. The result was a monthly installment plan called the Easy Pay Option.

The regular annual membership dues for an occupational therapist are $225. This works out to less than $1.00 a day, but for some it's a lot to pay at once. However, an individual may participate in the Easy Pay Option and pay only $18.75 a month. The Easy Pay Option is offered to both occupational therapists and occupational therapy assistants. Through the Easy Pay Option, the member agrees to a monthly credit card charge for one year, with no service fees. If a credit card is declined for any of the monthly charges, AOTA reserves the right to cancel the membership.

After offering this option to prospective members and renewing members, AOTA experienced an increase in its membership.

"In our first recruitment test, individuals who were offered an opportunity to join through the installment plan had almost a 50 percent better response rate than those who did not receive this offer. When those same members came up for renewal at the end of their first year, our retention rate was approximately 25 percent higher for those on the installment plan compared to those who paid a one-time annual fee," Chris Bluhm, AOTA's chief operating officer, shared with me (all Chris Bluhm quotes are from personal communication, January 20, 2013). "Remember, one of the key points of the installment program was auto renew. We agreed to not charge any 'fees,' but, at the same time, the member agreed that the association would continue to charge for membership until we were contacted directly to cancel. Since this first effort, the numbers have started to become less pronounced/normalized, but we still hold better recruitment and retention of new members with the installment plan option."

A big surprise for AOTA came when they looked at the audience segment with the highest response rate to the offer to participate in the payment plan. It wasn't what the association had anticipated.

"While we thought this offer would entice newer, younger members, in fact, the group that seemed most interested was the forty-five-to-fifty-four-year-old demographic," said Bluhm. "We also looked at it from a 'household income' perspective and saw only modest improvement in affiliation in the $50K to $80K range. Our hypothesis is that the credit card choice is one of convenience as much as one of financial necessity."

If you've seen an infomercial, you have probably heard the sales pitch, "Just four easy monthly payments." This tactic, commonly used to sell products on TV, works because it takes an expensive item and makes it affordable. Companies and organizations have experienced such high success rates with this approach that it is no longer just a gimmick used to sell products on the Home Shopping Network. In fact, even luxury brands like Dooney & Bourke, a company that sells expensive leather goods such as handbags and wallets, offer an easy pay option to customers.

On the other hand, when an individual says that dues are too expensive, the truth may be that there simply isn't enough perceived value for the price. If this is the case, in order to overcome the objection of price, you need to do more than just provide options to make it more affordable.

You could, for example, compare the price of joining your organization to other methods for achieving the benefits you provide to members. (This is based on the "prove it" mentality I discussed in Chapter Nine.) If one benefit of membership is *staying informed on issues related to the industry*, you could compare the price of membership to what it would cost to purchase industry reports, trends, publications, subscriptions, or other resources.

Another way to overcome an objection to price is to instill confidence by demonstrating how others within your association have received a positive return on their financial investment. Some organizations also use a strong guarantee to help overcome financial objections. This tactic helps remove the risk associated with joining by assuring the prospective member or lapsed member that if they are not completely satisfied, they can receive a full refund on their membership dues.

One for-profit company that initiated this type of guarantee is Athleta, a clothing brand that offers athletic clothing for women. Athleta is owned and operated by Gap (along with Old Navy, Banana Republic, and Piperlime shoes). On the company's home page, front and center, they state their unconditional guarantee: try working out in their clothing, and if you don't love it, you can return it, no charge. And this is not just lip service.

A friend of mine ordered a pair of workout pants from Athleta online; the pants appeared to be a navy blue color, which is what she wanted. When she received the pants in the mail, she loved the fit, but the color was actually purple rather than blue. However, she is a busy person (like all of us), and she didn't have time to return the pants immediately. Plus, Athleta didn't have another blue option. So, she wore the purple workout pants several times and washed them several times. A few months later, she was visiting the Athleta website and happened to see that a new color had been developed in the same style pants: navy blue, her original choice. She took the old, worn-and-washed pants—with no receipt other than her credit card charge—to the store. The Athleta employee first apologized for the color discrepancy, then handed her a new pair of navy blue pants. No questions asked.

Athleta opened a new store in California in December 2012, and several of the customers at the grand opening said that a large appeal of the brand is its "love it or return it" guarantee. One woman stated, "The guarantee is wonderful. If you wear it and it doesn't feel right, you can return it. I love that!" (Rabinovitz, 2012, para. 4).

Obviously, associations cannot implement a "Wear it or return it" guarantee, but a simple twist would work: "Try us on for size. If we don't fit, we'll refund your money." Some associations are offering this. The Association of Corporate Counsel, based in Washington, DC, states, "We guarantee our membership with a money back refund if you are not satisfied" (2013). The Chicago-based American Association of Individual Investors words it this way: "You risk nothing, because all first-year memberships are backed by our full, no-questions-asked, money-back guarantee" (2013).

Finally, consider this: price is a set amount that is paid in exchange for something received. When the item that is being sold is viewed as a commodity (even when there are points of differentiation, regardless of being well understood), price is subject to supply and demand. In marketing, it's generally understood that value lies in the perceived benefits received divided by the price paid, or value = benefits/cost.

If the features offered by an organization do not provide relevant value, then price has very little influence on the decision to join or renew. Understanding which audience segments cannot afford to join and which ones just don't find enough value in membership is an essential part of recruitment and retention. You can overcome the objections of individuals who cannot afford to join your organization, but want to. You cannot overcome the objections of those who find no value, unless you achieve one of the following:

1. You change your value proposition.
2. You change perceptions about the value you deliver in a way that positions your organization as an essential membership.

If your organization frequently hears the complaint that dues are too high, address the issue head on. Preempt the objection; bring it up before they can. If you don't, then your members will continue with their assumption. A simple way to do this is by creating a page on your website titled *Debunking Myths* to demonstrate value in tangible and intangible ways. Communicate with members who choose not to renew, sending a link to the home page and other web pages that contain authentic testimonials and case studies, with the headline: "Did you know?" What is *not* an option here is ignoring the objection.

Objection #2: I Already Belong to Another Association That Provides Similar Benefits

Associations cannot be all things to all people. They can, however, be the experts in their primary focus area. Understanding this idea means accepting the fact that your members will most likely belong to more than one professional association in order to meet their needs. Do you know where your organization fits into this equation? Do you try to be everything to everyone? Do you emphasize what is unique and different about your organization and recognize, publicly, that you fill one specific need? (Of course, you'll need to continually reemphasize how darned good you are at that singular thing.) Do you admit, publicly, that if there are other things a member needs, there are other sources? As crazy as this sounds, having laser-sharp focus on what you do best not only strengthens your brand but also sets the stage for ensuring that you can deliver on your promises. It helps improve retention rates because you are less likely to attract members who are unsatisfied with the experience or what they receive in exchange for what they paid.

One way to determine where your strengths lie within your industry is to survey members. Find out if they consider your organization to be their primary or secondary source for areas such as education, information, networking, volunteering, advocacy, career advancement, or other industry-specific areas. When raising this question, it is also helpful to find out what other organizations they turn to in order to meet these specific needs. You may discover that your unique selling point (USP) isn't your focus area, but rather the education you provide within that focus area. Or it could be the networking opportunities you create for individuals within this focus area. And of course, different audience segments may turn to your organization in different ways, based on their demographics or attitudes.

Another way to identify and measure your value is to start by identifying the market segments you wish to serve. I have found that value differs based on different market segments. Next, look at your closest competitor. What do they charge for programs and products that solve similar problems? Even if their offerings are different, if they address the same issues, you should conduct a comparison between your organization and your competitor. Next, it's time to consider the benefits associated with your offering's features. What are the outcomes members can expect if they join, attend or purchase one of your products? Once you've completed these steps, you will have a better understanding of where your organization excels, based on what is valued by members and available in the marketplace.

It is unrealistic, and frankly careless, to believe that you are the only organization that delivers the benefits you promise. Other organizations will offer some of the same benefits to your members, and there may be a perception that your organization basically offers the same offerings that the others do—offerings as universal as information, education, networking, and career advancement. It is up to you to demonstrate that it isn't an "apples to apples" comparison, because what you offer is not a commodity. Drill down into your benefits. What is unique about your information, education, networking, certification, or career advancement? It could be the audience, the topic, the expertise, or the results. Once you are able to distinguish the major difference or differences between your association and others, you need to incorporate it into every message. It should become part of your brand so that it is impossible to separate the brand from the differentiating point. There may be overlapping programs, products, or services, but something about your offerings must be different from other organizations, and you must figure out what that is. Sometimes you just need to spell out the differences and the results or outcomes of those differences. To overcome this objection, you could build a campaign around the idea that there "simply is no comparison." This will help to both raise and address a common objection.

Another tactic is to build your messaging around how your organization is *the missing piece.* With this approach, you accept that there are other organizations that meet some of the needs of your members, but another organization will not meet *all* of their needs. Your organization is their missing piece.

For example, if you belong to ASAE and you work in media or publications, you are a prime candidate for membership in Association Media and Publishing (AM&P). What's holding you back from joining the organization, however, may be the perception that your needs are already met by ASAE. To overcome this objection, I developed the following messages to be used by AM&P to position itself as the missing piece in your puzzle:

- We're people like you. We are publishers, editors, art directors, and others. We love to share our experiences. (Show the similarities they will find among members of this organization.)
- We fill the gap. We are your true peer network of individuals who have been there and done that. (Show how this unique audience, of which they are a part, can help them because of their experience.)

Objection #3: I Just Don't Have Time to Take Advantage of Membership Benefits

Over the years, I've discovered one very common reason that people do not respond to calls for volunteers or invitations to events to join an organization: a *lack of time.* Lack of time is a real issue in today's 24x7 world. In some surveys, when respondents are asked to define their primary challenge, a high percentage tell us it is finding work/life balance. Typically, issues related to work/life balance can be traced back to not having enough time to accomplish everything that needs to get done and a sense of being overwhelmed by the quantity of work.

Yet "save time, save money" is one of the most overused advertising slogans. It's become such a cliché that the words are likely to be invisible to the prospective reader. You need to do more than just promise to save people time (and money).

Some individuals may say that they just don't have enough time to invest in another membership organization or networking community. Or that they just didn't take advantage of their membership during the past year and therefore they will not renew. Everyone has too much on his or her plate right now, and the idea of trying to fit in one more relationship is just too big an obstacle to overcome.

Address this issue up front in your messaging. Acknowledge that there isn't enough time in the day to accomplish everything on a to-do list, or even on a wish list. In fact, you can say this in your headline: Not enough time to join one more organization? Not enough time to volunteer? By addressing the issue, you will immediately relate to the person to whom you are speaking. Reinforce the idea that your association understands that time is the most precious thing we all have, want, and need.

When I worked at SurePayroll, we didn't just say "using our service will save you time." Rather, we explained how and why prospects would gain back time that they now must set aside to do a variety of tasks involved with paying employees. Part of our story was to identify the different pain points for small business people when it came to processing payroll. We offered a comparison between our approach and the traditional ways of running payroll. We painted a picture that was easy to understand and, at the same time, clearly showed how we saved small business owners time.

It's not a stretch. Associations save people time in many different ways. They just need to illustrate their claims with stories that create an emotional connection to members (or prospective members). To collect the stories on how your association has saved members time and made a significant difference in their ability to find some work/life balance, you could create a campaign that encourages members to answer this question: Did you spend the time you saved by

- Using our online resources rather than searching the millions of unqualified resources on Google?
- Attending our conferences and expanding your network?
- Accessing our journal or magazine on your tablet?
- Using any of our hundreds of educational tools offered online?
- Referencing our benchmark studies?

You can create a contest or invite members to submit stories and images to an online community. Once you've collected the stories and images, share them through other media channels, including your website, marketing collateral, and in-person meetings.

Objection #4: I Receive All of the Education I Need Through Another Organization or My Employer

This objection is somewhat similar to an earlier one; however, I've singled out education because it is one the core functions of many associations and a major selling point as well. One of the benefits promoted by many organizations is free or low-cost continuing education (CE). Because some industries require individuals to obtain a specified number of CE credits within a given timeframe in order to maintain a license, providing CE is viewed by many organizations as a way to educate practitioners, help professionals stay up-to-date, and ensure that practice standards are met.

Years ago, organizations had very few competitors when it came to providing CE. Today, associations not only compete with other nonprofit organizations but also have to go up against vendors or suppliers and even members' employers. In some cases, the education is very similar to the ones offered by the association. As a result, it is not uncommon for individuals to no longer value the "benefit" of education from the association, because continuing education can easily (maybe even more easily) be obtained elsewhere.

How do you overcome this objection? Begin by evaluating your current educational offerings. Do your programs consistently receive high ratings for the caliber of the faculty and the quality of the content? Can you differentiate your education by promoting statistics that strengthen your claims of providing education that is significantly better than other suppliers? Do your continuing education programs provide more than just *information*? This is a good start, and may persuade some individuals, but it may not be enough. If an individual can find an educational program on a relevant topic that is "good enough," they may not respond to your argument that your education is of higher quality. Therefore you need to identify gaps in your current educational offerings and create programs or courses that could fill those gaps, rather than compete with existing programs. Using this approach, you could use a variety of analogies that show items that are incomplete—missing some vital element. Highlight the differences in your education, don't just talk about how you provide high-quality education. You can create an ongoing campaign that emphasizes that you offer *more than just information*. This should become part of your brand identity.

The bottom line is that you shouldn't try to hide the fact that there are other options out there. On the contrary, you should call attention to it, then emphasize why *your* option is more valuable than others. You need to be able to openly ask prospects "Why choose our continuing education when you can obtain credits from your employer, a vendor, or another association?" and then tell them precisely why they should choose your organization's offering. Address the objection in specific and tangible ways.

Objection #5: My Employer Will Not (or Will No Longer) Reimburse Me for My Membership Dues

When individuals make this statement, they are essentially saying that they do not believe that membership in your organization provides enough value for them to pay their dues out of their own pocket. For some organizations this has always been a challenge, because a majority of their members already pay their dues out of their own pocket. For others this is a new and growing issue, as budgets are cut or changes in the workforce have resulted in a different process for reimbursement of membership dues.

In this case, it's about justification or rationalization. Members or prospects are looking for tangible benefits that can justify the investment of their money (or time). Although most sales pitches should include a combination of emotional and logical reasons "to buy," there are times when you need to help justify the purchase. You also need to consider that the individual member is not the only buyer. Sometimes the employer needs to evaluate the return on the investment from their vantage point.

A good example of providing the logic to justify the cost can be seen in the change in how luxury cars are pitched to potential buyers. BMW of North America has used the tagline, "The Ultimate Driving Machine" since the 1970s (BMW of North America, 2013b). Even when they've incorporated other campaigns into their advertising efforts, they have not abandoned what many people consider one of the best taglines ever created. It's memorable and meaningful and instantly conjures the image of a luxury vehicle driving down a rain-slick road in a beautiful setting. When the recession was in full swing, however, advertisements appeared with additional messages emphasizing the value of a BMW. A prospective buyer can visit the BMW website and learn that included in the price are well-equipped models that include no-cost maintenance and fuel-efficient engines. The website suggests to visitors:

> When comparing costs, the competition may appear to offer lower monthly payments, but that's before factoring in their true cost of ownership. This "true cost of ownership" factors in the various charges incurred over the years for routine maintenance and premium services.
>
> With BMW you get a well-equipped model, as well as scheduled inspections, brake pads, oil service, roadside assistance, and many other valuable services with our no-cost maintenance program—and with many models, our no-cost BMW Assist™ Safety Plan—for the first four years or 50,000 miles. Not to mention a selection of vehicles that consistently receive top honors from the automotive press.
>
> So when it comes to peace-of-mind, your BMW is well equipped, at no added expense to you. So when comparing costs, a competitor's low monthly payment may not be so low after all. Run the numbers [BMW of North America, 2013a].

BMW works hard to overcome any objections and prove they provide more bang for the buck by allowing website visitors to *compare vehicles*. On the BMW website, you can select a BMW model and compare it to other luxury cars using unbiased and impartial comparison data from an independent third party. Although the decision to buy a luxury vehicle is clearly one that is emotional and not completely logical, BMW makes the decision easier by providing logical reasons to feel good about the decision.

Although it may seem scary to go down the path of openly comparing your organization to others, this approach gives you an opportunity to present any number of benefits in a way that is most advantageous to your association. Plus, if you believe your members and prospects are making this comparison anyway, why not frame the discussion in a way that leverages your strengths and identifies the weaknesses of others?

Another aspect of this objection may come from the prospective member's employer, who essentially may be the final decision maker. If you suspect this is the case, you need to create messages that speak to everyone involved in the decision-making process, or create a variety of messages and tailor each to the intended audience segment.

When the Urgent Care Association of America (UCAOA) changed its dues structure in 2012 to accommodate industry changes, the organization quickly realized it needed to change how it sells membership.

Jami Kral, membership manager at UCAOA, said, "Selling membership has shifted from solely individual benefits to building proper member value objectives of why it is a good business decision for urgent care centers and owners. We used to sell membership to individuals with a health care background. Now we sell to corporate owners who come from a different world. You have to convince a corporate world that there is value in belonging to a health care association" (Jami Kral, personal communication, January 18, 2013).

If there has been a significant change in who is paying membership dues to your association, you must address the issue head-on. Try asking: Has your employer stopped paying for your membership dues? And move the discussion forward by saying: Let us justify the investment. Then proceed to support this with all the tangible ways membership will save members money or have a positive impact on their life or business. Another way to support your statement that membership *pays for itself* is to provide concrete data or statistics to illustrate your claims.

Objection #6: I Just Don't See the Value

If your organization is trying to recruit individuals who work in positions or industries that are outside your core audience, you may hear this objection frequently. If you use an outbound calling center to make recruitment calls, there is a good chance that a prospect may have asked, "What do you offer that is specifically geared for me?" If the caller responds with the typical list of offerings, "You will receive our award-winning magazine, discounts on educational programs, networking and volunteer opportunities with others in the profession . . ." these words may fall on deaf ears, because it just isn't specific enough. The person on the other end of the phone doesn't feel like it applies to him or her. And for a good reason.

This objection needs to be addressed with a different approach. You need to be up front and honest about the opportunities. Don't forget, as I said in Chapter Three, you don't need to offer a long list of benefits in order to provide value. You just need to offer a few things that people can't get anywhere else or do for themselves. In some cases this may be just one or two items. Again, you can't be everything to everybody. Think about how refreshing it could be for a prospective member who never considered joining your organization because they held a perception that it offered little value. Now, if you can pinpoint even one unique offering that will provide a relevant benefit to the prospective member, you not only may be able to recruit him or her, but you may also increase the likelihood of retaining that individual for years to come.

Consider the many associations that struggle to recruit government employees. If the organizations are able to get them to join, unfortunately the retention rates are usually much lower than they are for individuals who work in private practice or for companies. I have found this to be true for many industries, including finance, legal, health care, and engineering.

So, how do you attract this group if you believe it is important for them to be a part of your community? First, conduct some research to identify the challenges they face that are both unique, in some way, to their situation but also, in a broad sense, common in the industry. Next, conduct an asset audit to match your benefits to their areas of interest (see Chapter One). Finally, select the one or two benefits that provide real value to this particular group, then develop messages focused on government employees, their unique challenges, and the things your association offers that will enhance their professional lives. While this seems obvious, it has been my observation and experience that very few organizations follow through on all of these steps. Yet this is essential if you wish to recruit this audience or other audiences that find only a little bit of value in joining your organization. If you emphasize that "little bit," it actually translates into making a real difference for them.

Objection #7: Someone Else in My Practice or Company Is Already a Member

When this objection is voiced, the individual is most likely telling you that he or she views membership as a transactional relationship, one that will provide a discount on programs or products. As such, these individuals don't view membership as necessary to achieving personal goals. They may believe in and support your mission, along with the advancement of the industry or field, but they are content with their current status as a nonmember and occasional customer. They have not heard a compelling reason to join.

To overcome this objection, you will need to consider whether your organization offers enough exclusive and valuable benefits that are available to members only. From exclusive networking events to career assistance, associations can play a vital role if they can provide something that is unique and important. If these benefits exist, you can overcome this objection by highlighting these special features and provide examples of how members benefit from belonging to the organization. Providing examples of outcomes may also support your claims that membership plays an essential role in succeeding in your industry. Case studies or testimonials are good tactics to employ for this type of objection.

If your organization does not offer members-only benefits that are unique and valuable, the best way to encourage someone to join the organization (rather than share a colleague's membership) is to offer pricing incentives that demonstrate the return on their investment.

Action Steps

1. Identify all of the reasons an individual or employer may object to your request to join, volunteer, register, or participate in association-sponsored programs and events. I've listed some of the reasons I've heard over the years. Now it's your turn to expand this list. Ask your colleagues for their input. Ask your current members for their feedback. Ask your former members to chime in. And don't forget to include your frontline staff, who may have the most interaction with members. This may include customer service representatives, membership coordinators, meeting and registration staff, and administrative assistants.

2. Develop emotional, logical, and authentic responses to the objections. Be specific! Don't provide responses that are too generic or clichéd. The suggestions in this chapter are a good starting point, but they will resonate more with prospective members if they include specific information and references to your industry or association.

3. Raise the objections and answer them throughout your marketing and communications. From recruitment through retention, it is important to provide answers to the questions on the minds of your audience. Conduct an audit of all association touch points and interactions with prospective members. Identify opportunities to continue the discussion, even if it is an electronic conversation via your website, emails, or a download of a PDF outlining the objections and your responses. If you do not provide answers, your members and prospects will look elsewhere for the answers or make assumptions based on potentially erroneous information.

4. Conduct market testing with different audience segments to measure their responses to your statements, acceptance of them, or any questions they raise. Are your statements believable? Do they resonate? Will they move people to action or change perceptions? If not, make changes and gather additional feedback. It may be—in fact, it should be—an ongoing process.

5. Engage your advocates in the process. Conduct focus groups with your most loyal members to find out how *they* would answer these common objections if they heard them when they asked their peers and colleagues to join. They may provide some new responses or answers that will resonate with prospective members.

6. Reevaluate the situation every two to three years, or sooner, if major changes occur in your industry or environment. Create a living document that is frequently evaluated and updated to ensure that you are providing timely and relevant answers.

7. Track responses over a two- to three-month period. With this type of gauge, you have the chance to discover some opportunities you are not currently leveraging or even some weaknesses in your organization.

■ ■ ■

Understanding the motivations and drivers behind the decision to join is an important part of the recruitment process. But it may play an even bigger role in the overall health and sustainability of the organization if you understand how to apply this information to the retention process. In Chapter Eleven, I will provide a framework for creating a successful onboarding program.

11

Engagement, Onboarding, and the First Ninety Days

FEW EXPERIENCES ARE MORE AWKWARD than the first day on a new job. You're excited and nervous about meeting new coworkers. You're anxious to learn more about the environment where you will be spending roughly forty hours a week. Sure, during the interviewing process you got a quick glimpse of the culture, but it's impossible to know precisely what it will be like to work for a company until your first day of work (or actually the first few days). It's possible you will have a steep learning curve as you become familiar with the company's products, the industry, and the clients. At this point, you have high expectations that the job will be interesting and challenging and help you advance in your chosen field. But past experiences and anecdotal evidence tells you that this isn't always the case.

Although the recession has slowed down the national average turnover rate, according to recent data, more than 25 percent of the U.S. population goes through some type of career transition each year. Unfortunately, not all of these changes are successful. In fact, according to a report by the Society of Human Resource Management (SHRM) Foundation (Bauer, 2010), half of all hourly workers leave new jobs in the first four months, and half of outside hires for senior positions fail within eighteen months.

To reverse this trend, employers are beginning to make a deeper investment in helping brand-new employees transition into their new position. By all accounts, the sooner new employees feel welcome and understand the culture, mission, products, and clients, the greater the likelihood they will succeed—and also stay with the company. By helping new employees during the first ninety days of their employment, it is that much more likely that they will feel invested in their job and the company.

Starting a new, compensated position as an employee at a job and becoming a member of an association are very similar activities. In both cases, an individual hopes to advance his or her career, learn new skills, and feel part of a community. Consider that some members are similar to telecommuters. They may work remotely and connect with their colleagues via email and the Internet; however, they still have the same needs as new employees who work on-site. Regardless of their employer or work setting, in both situations, it is imperative that an organization uses a variety of tactics during the first ninety days to help individuals feel welcome and ensure their long-term success.

The Secret to Long-Term Relationships

If you want to create long-term relationships with your members, as is true for the companies and the trends just cited, your association must invest in an onboarding program that spans at least the first ninety days. Research I've conducted with current and lapsed members revealed that a key predictor of retention is creating a second meaningful interaction between the member and the association within the first three months of joining the association. (The first meaningful action, of course, is the member's actually joining the association.)

What Is Onboarding?

"Onboarding" is a term used by human resource managers to describe the process of helping new employees transition into a job and assimilate into the organizational culture. Not too long ago, employees used to attend a brief—perhaps one-day or even one-hour—new member orientation, and then they were expected to sink or swim. Today, companies of all sizes are beginning to realize that in order to build a successful relationship between an organization and an employee, they need create a formal process that will make a new employee feel like an organizational insider.

One approach to building a successful new employee onboarding program is to address four distinct levels: compliance, clarification, culture, and connection (Bauer, 2010). In many cases, compliance (basic employee policies and rules) and clarity (job descriptions and expectations) are provided. However, culture and connections are frequently left out of new hire training. Successful onboarding programs address all of these four stages during the first ninety days of employment.

An onboarding program for new members of your association is similar, in many ways, to onboarding new employees. Your ultimate goal is retention, but that is a long-term goal. Simultaneously, you need to set short-term goals that will lead to retention and a high lifetime value. Such short-term goals should include:

1. Get to know new members, based on their interests and needs—not yours.
2. Create customized communications based on the new member's needs and interests.
3. Create at least one meaningful interaction with every new member during the first ninety days.
4. Deliver highly satisfying experiences, as measured by a new member survey delivered during the first ninety days.
5. Generate high levels of awareness of your programs, products, and services.

Take Time to Get to Know New Members

In Chapter Two, I discussed how important it is to get to know your members on a much deeper level than just their demographic information. I introduced the idea that individuals join for a variety of reasons, despite their similarities in terms of age or generation, career stage, interest or specialty, or employment setting. Although it would be ideal to gather this information during the application process, it is unlikely that you will be able to do so, because you don't want to create additional barriers to joining. Therefore, getting to know new members should be a top priority immediately *after* they join. Unfortunately, many organizations skip this step and go right to selling the individual other products and services.

I found a good example of this situation in a story my friend Mark told me recently. Mark had received a call from his industry's professional society, asking him to join the organization. He had been a member years before, but he had let his membership lapse once his dues increased from the *young professional* rate to the *full member* rate. At the full price, he just didn't see enough value based on his needs and the field he had entered. However, the representative for the association made him an offer he couldn't refuse: join today and you will receive six months of membership for free. At the end of the six months, he would receive an invoice; he could either pay it, thus becoming a full member, or choose to ignore it and no longer receive the benefits of membership.

During those initial six free months, he would receive all of the benefits of membership, including access to members-only resources and members-only special discounts on programs and products. Although Mark was skeptical, because he was still unaware of any specific benefits that might be of interest to him in his position, he decided to join. The incentive of a free membership period resonated with him.

Within two weeks, he told me that he started to receive a number of mailings. Each communication promoted a different program, service, or product with special member pricing. Although the organization was trying to engage Mark by offering him discounted rates on their offerings, there were two problems. First, Mark perceived these activities as ways to try to sell him other products; in other words, in order for him to receive something, he would need to pay a fee. And second, Mark wasn't interested in the products, because they were not relevant to his work. After the six free months were up—six months of receiving various sales pitches for a variety of programs and products that held little to no value for him—when the invoice arrived in his mailbox, Mark decided not to join the organization as a paid member.

Unfortunately, this was a missed opportunity. If the organization had invested the time and money in getting to know Mark and his specific interests and needs, they could have customized their messaging and significantly increased the likelihood that he would have found value in joining the organization as a full member. Alternatively, had they discovered that his interests were not aligned with what they offered, they could have applied this knowledge to future efforts to recruit new members who would have a greater likelihood of joining and renewing.

Imagine if a different scenario had taken place within those initial free months. If the association had developed and implemented tactics to learn more about Mark's needs during the first thirty days, the outcome could very well have been quite different. In this alternative scenario, the association could have used the initial phone call to confirm Mark's basic demographic information and preferences:

- Career stage (years in practice)
- Work setting
- Field or area of practice
- Preference for print or digital communications

Within a week of joining, Mark could have received a special invitation or incentive to log in to the organization's website. At this stage, the organization would not try to sell him anything. Instead, they would put time and effort into providing him with a reason to visit their website and log in for the first time. Because the organization does not yet know Mark's primary interests, the best approach would be to let him pick one item from a variety of free offerings. The key here is that *Mark is choosing*, and, by seeing that choice, the association now has a small snapshot of Mark's interests. What he is offered could include a free webinar, free publication of his choice, or a free white paper. Although the organization is offering these items to Mark for free, they should not be items that are free to all members. By showing him the actual value of the items, and a limited time frame for him to select one to receive for free, there is a greater incentive for Mark to respond during the first thirty days. There is one catch. In exchange for receiving the free gift, the organization should ask Mark to log in to their website and answer three questions about his interests and preferences.

Of course, it is possible that the exercise will show that Mark is not be interested in any of the items offered to him during the first stage of the onboarding program. This is a possible outcome.

However, if this is the case, and he doesn't respond, it is still important to attempt to collect more information about his needs in order to customize other communications. Therefore, other tactics should be developed that will encourage new members like Mark to provide more information about their needs and interests. Therefore, during the first thirty days of your onboarding plan, your organization should develop a series of tactics that are focused on collecting additional information about the new member. I will detail several ideas for doing this within the next few pages of this chapter.

Have It Your Way

Do you remember the jingle used by Burger King in the 1970s?

Hold the pickle, hold the lettuce;

Special orders won't upset us.

All we ask is that you let us serve you your way!

Even if you can't sing along to the jingle, we hope you will understand the reference. Burger King highlighted their point of differentiation, their flexibility, in order to try to sway consumers to choose their restaurant rather than McDonald's. Flexibility, or the ability to customize your burger, was a great selling point because it put control back into the hands of the consumer. With advancements in technology, associations have nearly limitless options to help them when it comes to customizing communications based on the expressed interests and preferences of their members.

An easy place to start is with the creation of a unique landing page just for new members. The very first time an individual logs on to an association's website, he or she should be directed to a new member landing page. The purpose of the page is to actively encourage members to take advantage of the benefits that are most relevant to them. Links to the page should be included in the new member email and letter as well as subsequent emails within the first ninety days. It is very important that this page be different from the member benefits page that may be viewed by everyone. It should be accessible only to current members, and it should include a headline that specifically welcomes new members. The landing page should also include the following messages:

- Just joined? Tell us about your interests or needs and we'll point you in the right direction. (Link to new member survey.)
- Have a question? Contact our staff. (Link to staff contacts.)
- Looking for a local event? Click here to join us for an upcoming event. (Link to map to connect to local chapters or communities.)
- Interested in volunteering? Click here for a list of short-term and long-term opportunities. (Link to a page describing open volunteer opportunities.)
- Looking for the information on a specific topic? Check out our members-only resources. (Link to a trend report or magazine or journal articles.)
- Looking for a new position or a new employee? Visit our job board. (Link to a job board.)
- Got a question? (Identify and then list the Ten Questions Most Frequently Asked by New Members.)

By creating a landing page specifically designed for new members, you can accomplish two goals. First, you help new members assimilate and find their own place in the organization based on their needs. Second, you can collect data on their interests and track their movements to create more customized offerings in future communications.

You already know that segmentation is essential if you wish to generate higher response rates and long-lasting connections. This step will help you move in that direction. If the new member hasn't responded to previous requests for more information, don't give up. Continue to ask him or her to spend one or two minutes completing a profile so that you can customize future communications based on the individual's needs.

Once you've collected the information, it's time to customize your communications based on how the new member responds to these questions. Resist the urge to add new members to every email and mailing list. Bombarding them with information is not likely to make them more engaged. In fact, as in my friend Mark's experience, information overload and constant sales pitches can be a turn-off, so much so that the new member decides to decline paid membership. Continue to nurture the relationship during the first ninety days by sending customized messages that provide ways for them to learn more about the organization and find solutions to their needs. No price tag attached.

Alternative Approaches to Engagement

Once your association is able to capture unique information about each member, it's time to turn to technology. Advancements in technology provide many opportunities for organizations to connect with new members based on their needs, interests, and even preferred communication channels. Many new members may sit at a desk for most of the day, but others spend more time away from their office, visiting clients, customers, or patients. So it is important to offer new members a variety of opportunities to connect. Some may prefer to learn about the organization through an online video that they can access when and where it's convenient for them. A good example is the one created by the Wisconsin REALTORS® Association (WRA, 2013): https://www.wra.org /Resources/Video_Center/WRA_Member_Benefits_Video/.

With nearly thirteen thousand views, the WRA member benefits video has received more than five times as many views as the next most popular video on their website. This video is so effective, in part, because WRA does not require new members to sit through the entire eighteen-minute length in order to learn about the various offerings and benefits of membership. Instead, visitors can view different segments based on their interest. For example, vignettes are available on the topics of education, the WRA legal hotline, WRA publications, industry news, advocacy, conferences and events, sales tools, and exclusive WRA group benefits.

Although the vignettes offer flexibility to new members based on their interest and time, some new members will still prefer to attend a live event. Providing a monthly live webinar held during the lunch hour (and repeated for different time zones) should help meet the needs of new members who have questions and wish to connect with others soon after they join.

Case Study: AHIMA Centralizes Its Engagement Efforts

The American Health Information Management Association (AHIMA) represents more than sixty-seven thousand professionals who are involved in health information management (HIM), one of the fastest growing fields in health care. Celebrating its eighty-fifth anniversary in 2013, AHIMA promotes and advocates for high-quality research, best practices, and effective standards in health information. Its goal is to ensure quality health care through quality information. Over the last few years, as the big data revolution expanded into health care and an explosion of data created an increasing number of challenges in the industry, AHIMA's staff and volunteer leadership recognized that it would play a central role in ensuring that its members had access to the information they needed to succeed. As efforts to grow the organization began to match the growth in the industry, staff became concerned that retention rates could drop. Similar to many associations, for AHIMA retaining first- and second-year members at the same rate as other members has always been a challenge.

To address these concerns, AHIMA made the decision to centralize its member service functions in order to improve its focus on engaging members at all stages of their membership. The goal was to provide new members with a personally relevant and professionally fulfilling experience as they become more familiar with the organization. As part of this process, staff created a new member orientation guide and five different two-minute training videos to help individuals make the most of their membership. They also made these resources accessible at any time on the AHIMA website.

The new member guide, titled *You're the Boss—Put Your AHIMA Membership to Work!* provides a five-step process to onboard new members (American Health Information Management Association, 2013). The first step is a template to be completed by the new member to help them identify their top personal and professional goals and connect them to the resources at AHIMA. In Step 2, AHIMA challenges new members to match the opportunities provided by the organization with the values held by members (see Exhibit 11.1).

Exhibit 11.1.   American Health Information Management Association New Member Orientation

Know AHIMA's Benefits and Opportunities (2013)

Think you know everything AHIMA membership brings you? Challenge yourself by matching each AHIMA opportunity with its corresponding value from the list that follows. Fill in the blank with the value letter.

Your Value

1. Be a leader by keeping up with the latest advances and best practices. _____

2. Influence health care issues affecting you and your career. _____

3. Encounter valuable opportunities to increase skills through web-based training. _____

4. Gain professional insight and network with peers from around the world. _____

5. Build skills through the latest books and audio seminars. _____

6. Exchange ideas with local peers. _____

7. Update personal information and select communication preferences. _____

8. Increase resources by exploring articles and data. _____

9. Stay current on the electronic health record (ICD) and ICD-10. _____

10. Advance your career opportunities through searching job opportunities. _____

11. Demonstrate knowledge and expertise. _____

12. Add professional recognition to your list of accomplishments. _____

13. Share the benefits of AHIMA membership with others. _____

14. Serve as an inspiration and source of information to a new HIM professional, or be paired with an experienced professional. _____

AHIMA Opportunity

A. Career Assist: Job Bank

(Continued)

Exhibit 11.1.   (Continued)

B. Public and Government Relations

C. *Journal of AHIMA*

D. Distance Education Campus

E. AHIMA Body of Knowledge

F. AHIMA Communities of Practice

G. Certification

H. Component State Associations (CSA)

I. Volunteers

J. Bookstore

K. My Profile

L. HIM Resources

M. iShare Member Referral Campaign

N. AHIMA Mentor Program

In Step 3, new members are encouraged to complete a worksheet that will help them identify their top goals and the action steps needed to achieve them. A sample goal may be to increase professional expertise, and the suggested action steps could include attending an in-person meeting, reading the *Journal of AHIMA*, and networking with peers. The worksheet is a template that provides space for the new member to write out his or her goals and action steps.

Steps 4 and 5 help new members connect with the organization and other members and plan for the year ahead. Included in the kit is a list of ten ways to connect, including tips and techniques used by other members who have made the most of their membership. The new membership guide works because it includes an involvement device, not just information. AHIMA clearly understands that individuals need to customize their membership in order to find value in their investment. The organization provides the information and resources as well as the tools to design a membership based on the member's unique personal and professional goals.

New member orientations are not a new concept. It is time, however, to revisit this task and consider a variety of approaches based on the changing needs of members and advancements in technology. It is important to include a variety of approaches if you wish to connect with the changing needs and interests of professionals within your industry.

The Biggest Myth in Member Engagement

The secret to increasing retention rates for first-year members is simple: create at least one meaningful interaction during the first ninety days of their membership. It is during this time frame that most decisions are made regarding the perceived value of the membership and the decision to renew. That said, meaningful interactions will vary based on the new member's needs and interests. Although many people may assume that in order for an experience to be meaningful, an individual must attend an event, accept a volunteer position, register for an educational event, and more, this isn't the case. That is, unless one of those activities relates to the specific reason that person joined the organization.

As I alluded to in Chapter Five, there is a myth often perpetuated in the association industry that organizations must move members up the engagement ladder. You'll recall that I subscribe to the belief, based on research and experience, that not all members need to or want to move up the typical engagement ladder in order to be highly satisfied with their membership. Associations define engagement as volunteering, contributing, attending, or actively participating in the advancement of the field. The dictionary, however, defines engagement as any of the following: to involve a person intensely; to draw somebody into conversation; to participate; to draw in; and, my favorite, to win over or attract or occupy the attention of.

So what's more important is whether members' attention is being occupied and attracted by the association. Are they getting what they want from an association? And once they do receive what they want, are they satisfied? Likewise, are they willing to continue to pay the price of membership?

This should become clear when you consider what we all have experienced with association members: many people will never attend an in-person conference or volunteer, yet they have meaningful interaction with the association, or else they would not continue paying their dues invoices. Meaningful interaction could be any of the following activities:

- Download a useful tool, resource, or report from the association website.
- Read and/or share a magazine or journal article.
- Purchase a product or publication.

- Review a product, program, or article.
- Opt in to receive email newsletters.
- Participate in a new member orientation or event (online or in-person).
- Attend a webinar or online learning program.
- Attend a local, state, or national conference or event.
- Participate in an affinity program.
- Participate in a focus group, interview, or research project.
- Volunteer at the local, state, or national level.
- Join a shared interest group.
- Join an association-sponsored LinkedIn group.
- Participate in a private community discussion.

You may have many other forms of interactions that attract your members' attention that you could add to this list. Customize this list based on your own organization. Identify specific activities and opportunities under each heading. For example, identify all of the tools and resources, by various audience segments, that new members may find useful based on what is most read by others in the organization. Promote and provide links to your most commented and most read resources over the last twenty-four hours, seven days, and thirty days.

The next step is to monitor new member activity. Each week (or at least once a month), identify members who have joined within the last ninety days but have not had any form of interaction with the association that left a trail. Develop a plan to encourage them to take advantage of a free association offering. You can still actively promote your annual conference or program or a course that requires a registration fee; however, you should identify some items that are included with membership for no additional charge.

This is the point where it is critical to humanize your communications. Avoid sending generic emails loaded with images and links but no real message. Include the new member's name and, if possible, other identifying information such as the date they joined or the name of their employer. Ask them to be your guest at an upcoming networking event or give them early access to a soon-to-be-released white paper. Use a conversational yet professional tone. If your organization's culture embraces humor or a more casual approach to its communications, then incorporate this into your emails. Try to be less institutional and more approachable. After all, in most cases you're talking to an individual.

This is also a good time to encourage volunteers and brand ambassadors to take a more active role in communicating with new members. An email from a staff person does not carry the same weight as an email from an active member, sent from his or her own email account. One association I recently joined did a very successful job of communicating with me during the first three months of my membership because they had a local volunteer send me an informal welcome email. The message was only two or three sentences. It didn't promote all of the benefits of membership, nor was it formatted using HTML and images from the organization. Rather, it was sent in a regular text format. The sender, the local volunteer, welcomed me to the organization and stated that she hoped to see me at a local event next month.

I've already mentioned how important it is to incorporate storytelling (via testimonials or case studies) into your marketing. It is equally important to include actual storytelling tactics in your efforts to engage new members. A variety of stories showcasing how membership leads to successful outcomes will resonate more than platitudes and clichés. Social media platforms such as LinkedIn, YouTube, Facebook, and private online communities or microsites provide low-cost opportunities to showcase authentic success stories.

Experiences Are Meant to Be Shared

I'll never forget the first shared interest group (SIG) meeting I attended soon after becoming a member of the Association Forum of Chicagoland (Forum). I was new to associations, marketing, and membership. I had recently graduated from Indiana University with a dual degree in journalism and history, and my prior experience was limited to working in the marketing department of a small college.

Within weeks of starting my first professional job at an association—the American Academy of Implant Dentistry—my boss encouraged me to attend the SIG meeting hosted by the Association Forum because the topic was *How to Recruit New Members*—and, truthfully, I had a lot to learn. At this time, the Forum was located in a relatively small office in the Civic Opera Building in Chicago. Because there was just enough room to fit about fifteen individuals around the conference table, I immediately felt part of an intimate group. But I was also somewhat nervous about what I could add to the discussion. Prior to this point I had never visited the Forum's office, and when I walked into the room I didn't see any familiar faces.

Within minutes, everything changed. The chairman of the SIG walked up to me, introduced himself, and welcomed me to the meeting. All the people there were invited to introduce themselves and provide one or two reasons why they had chosen to attend the meeting. The event made a long-lasting impression on me because of the warm welcome and inclusive attitude displayed by those in attendance. By the end of the meeting, I felt connected to the association community and to the Forum. Within a few weeks of the meeting, I received a phone call from the SIG chair encouraging me to attend another meeting and, if I was interested, to get more involved in helping to organize future events.

Looking back at this experience, I realize that many of the actions that took place over the first few weeks of my membership in the Forum could easily be replicated and expanded with the variety of tools, resources, and technology available today. At its core, what cemented a long-term relationship with the Forum was an opportunity to learn, feel connected to others, and expand my network.

Action Steps

1. Segment your messages based on behavior. Individuals learn about an organization through a variety of different methods. Some decide to join to take advantage of a member discount for a conference. Others join during a local or state chapter event. A third group may join based on the recommendation of a colleague, peer, or mentor. And some will join through the proactive efforts of an organization, including direct mail, email, or telephone solicitations. There are many different routes to an organization. Tag or identify how members came to your organization, and segment your messages based on this information.

2. Customize your messages based on location. Individuals who live or work in urban areas may have access to more resources, networking, and educational events or employer sponsored programs. On the other hand, individuals who live or work in more rural areas or in other countries may have less of an opportunity to access resources, information, and events.

3. Ask new members to opt in or out based on their needs and interests. If everything else fails, you can send a simple, personalized message to new members asking them to either opt in or opt out of future emails and promotions based on their interests. This simple and direct approach may appear risky. What if your new members wish to opt out of your emails? That may happen if you don't provide a strong enough incentive and meaningful content that will encourage them to opt in to at least some of the communications you plan to send. You may also want to state that even though opting out, they will still receive other communications such as a monthly email, print mailings, or special invitations.

4. Thank new members for joining the organization, and show your appreciation by offering them a gift. Make it something that doesn't require paying a fee to receive. I once worked for an association that sent all new members "association bucks." The bucks were in the form of a certificate for $25 off any upcoming event or program. The problem I had with this gesture is that it required the recipient to pay money in order to receive the gift. Eventually I was able to convince my boss that we should offer them a gift card for a free program rather than the association bucks. The goodwill we created and the increased participation in our events easily covered the incremental cost for allowing an additional person to register without paying for an event or program.

5. Provide new members with helpful tools, worksheets, or guides that are interactive and not just informational. To increase engagement, include an involvement device that requests the active participation of the new member.

6. Include a variety of tools and resources, including video, social media, in-person events, microsites, surveys, and interactive new member guides to engage new members in their preferred format.

7. One of the most important aspects of developing a successful onboarding program is to keep your word. If you ask a new member to share his or her interests and preferences, you must respect the individual's wishes and not bombard them with emails and mailings that are not relevant. It will weaken your value proposition and decrease the likelihood that they will renew their membership.

Exhibit 11.2. Best Practices for Onboarding New Members

- Create a ninety-day onboarding program with thirty-, sixty-, and ninety-day milestones.
- Define success within the first thirty, sixty, and ninety days.
- Engage all departments in onboarding efforts.
- Use a variety of channels and methods to engage members, including microsites, video, phone calls, emails, chapter involvement, surveys, new member welcome guides, and gifts.
- Identify ways to make new members feel welcome.
- Survey new members to identify their personal needs, interests, and preferences.
- Customize communications to increase the relevancy of messages.
- Use incentives with a sense of urgency to encourage engagement during the first three months.
- Follow up with new members to collect their feedback and respond to questions.
- Track efforts and results to make changes or improvements.

Table 11.1.   Onboarding Planning Worksheet

Goal	Tactics	Communication Tool	Staff Responsibility	Timing
Identify needs, interests, and preferences	1. 2. 3. 4.			
Deliver value	1. 2. 3. 4.			
Create social and emotional engagements	1. 2. 3. 4.			

Build awareness of offerings and benefits	1. 2. 3. 4.			
Track, monitor, and measure efforts and success	1. 2. 3. 4.			
Collect feedback and respond or make changes	1. 2. 3. 4.			

■ ■ ■

Sometimes, even the best-laid plans and policies have unexpected consequences. A formal set of rules for engaging new members may set expectations and help ensure consistency across an organization; however, it does not take into account changes in the economy and environment. In Chapter Twelve, you will learn the importance of creating a sense of flexibility to adapt to a changing environment.

12

Be Flexible

WHEN I SIGNED UP FOR THE ASAE Marketing and Membership Symposium in 2002, I had every intention of attending. I booked my flights and hotel room early to ensure that I could take advantage of the best rates. I registered during the early bird sign-up period so that I could pay the lower registration fee. I even adjusted my work schedule so that my time out of the office wouldn't disrupt a few projects that were in progress. And then disaster struck. First my one-year-old daughter came down with the stomach flu. She proceeded to pass it on to my husband. Although I was able to avoid catching the bug that was traveling around my house, my plans had to be put on hold while I stayed home and cared for my family. Everyone recovered, but I had to cancel my trip just twenty-four hours before I was to hop on a plane and fly to Baltimore, Maryland.

When I realized I would not be able to attend, I called the airlines, the hotel, and ASAE. The airline would offer no refund; the company first charged me a fee to change my ticket, then said I would have to use it for a future flight. The hotel, too, charged me for one night because I had paid a nonrefundable deposit for the first night. I could have paid a higher rate to the hotel that would have allowed me to cancel, but I took a risk when I booked the room, and I fully understood the terms. I had no problem paying the fee. When I called ASAE, I was surprised to learn I had two options. I could receive a full refund or I could apply the registration fee to a future conference. Although it was only two days before the start of the conference, ASAE's flexibility created a lasting impression. I was thrilled that I could attend a future conference, using this money toward that registration fee. ASAE had not overtly stated that this was their policy regarding cancellations. In fact, I had never looked at their policy. I just called someone in the meetings department, and this individual was empowered to make a decision and provide me with two options.

Over the years, I've attended more than thirty ASAE conferences and events, purchased many books, and served as a volunteer. This experience cemented a relationship that has lasted many years and I expect to continue for many more years to come.

Will Rogers once said, "You never get a second chance to make a good first impression" (Forbes, 2013). In most cases, the first impression doesn't happen when a new member joins an organization. It happens when members actually start using their membership. It is that Second Moment of Truth (SMOT) I referred to in Chapter Nine. This may happen immediately, or it may happen one month into the membership, or, for some, it can take up to six months. It occurs when the member first logs in to an organization's website or when he or she registers for a conference. It takes place when members attend their first networking event, read the journal or magazine for the first time, or call the organization because they have a question. When a new member evaluates the value of membership, he or she will consider both the benefits and the overall experience.

When members talk about an organization in a positive way, it is often the result of an experience that had unexpected, successful results. To achieve this level of satisfaction among your membership, it isn't enough to meet their needs and expectations. Just the word "expectation" should tell you that they expect their needs to be met; they believe you when you tell them they can attend a conference or read a magazine article. No, you have to do better than just meeting those needs. You must exceed them. This happens when your organization is flexible, adaptable, and member-centric.

To master the art of membership, you must master the art of being flexible, of bending without breaking, of being able to adapt to changing circumstances without becoming so weak that you come apart.

If you look up the word "flexible" in the *Merriam-Webster Dictionary*, you will find the following definition: "Flex-i-ble *adjective \flek-si-bl* 1. Capable of being flexed: Pliant, 2. Yielding to influence: Tractable, and 3. Characterized by a ready capability to adapt to new, different and changing requirements" (Merriam-Webster, 2013). Flexibility is also defined as "capable of being turned, bowed or twisted without breaking." When flexibility is mentioned, it is commonly used in terms of an individual's physical well-being. Many people understand the link between flexibility and the prevention of injuries and serious illnesses like cardiovascular disease. However, the benefits of increased flexibility also apply to associations.

In sports (as you know by now, I am fond of turning to sports for analogies and life lessons), coaches use a *playbook* to guide them through various situations so that they can help players (and themselves) reach their ultimate goal of winning the game. For organizations, the playbook geared toward "winning the game" is referred to as a *strategic plan*. You've heard of them, written them, sat through day-long meetings about them, helped implement them, seen them sit on shelves and collect dust, and so on. However, for both sports and associations, there is a belief that in order to stay focused, leverage organizational strengths, and take advantage of an opponent or competitor's weaknesses, it is essential to plan ahead. And I agree with this philosophy. Yet just like in sports, where players must learn to be flexible and adapt to ever-changing situations on the field or court, associations must learn how to build flexibility into their strategy, policies, and practices.

Show Off Your Flexibility

One of the greatest challenges individuals face today is not a lack of options when searching for a solution. Rather, it's a lack of flexibility. A 2012 survey of more than 3,100 U.S. online shoppers revealed a direct correlation between overall satisfaction and an easy-to-understand and convenient return policy (comScore, 2012). In other words, the more flexible the return policy a company offered, the better the overall customer experience. This doesn't necessarily mean that a customer will return an item, it just means they want to know the various options available should a return be inevitable. The survey points to the fact that a customer will express satisfaction with the company even if he or she returns a product. For associations, there are many more opportunities to provide a more flexible environment, beyond a convenient and generous return policy.

The story behind the success at Zappos has been retold many times because of the unique and friendly culture created by its CEO Tony Hsieh. Yet it isn't just the company culture that makes Zappos a favorite place for millions of online shoppers. Hsieh understood that in order to create an exceptional shopping experience and overcome some obvious objections to buying shoes online, his policies needed to be flexible. Zappos customers have 365 days to return unused items. Plus, Zappos pays for shipping both to the customer and for returned items. You'll also recall the story I told about Athleta, the sportswear store for women, and its unusually generous return policy. A customer can take something back to the store, even if it was purchased online, even if she has washed it, even if she has worn it, even if it's six months after the purchase. A refund is issued with a smile.

A third example is Target. The back of every Target receipt states that a customer has ninety days to return an unused, unopened item. Some items carry a less generous policy, but the receipt says that such items will have a clearly marked "Return By" date so that there is no confusion for the customer. Finally, Target also offers a simple return transaction, stated on the receipt: "We promise to attempt a return on every item purchased by scanning your receipt, packing slip, offering receipt look-up . . ." (Target Brands, 2013, para. 1). This works! You do not have to dig through your wallet to show the Target employee your credit card; you don't have to swipe it yourself. By scanning your receipt, Target simply searches for your original payment method, and, if you paid by credit card, the company automatically credits back the same card. It's very easy for the customer, and it's explained clearly.

Although the stories I've shared references online and corporate retailers, the concept of creating transparent, flexible, and adaptable policies should be adopted by all organizations. In addition, there is one area that seems to be frequently overlooked. Even though many companies are starting to pay attention to the increasingly important role of providing excellent customer service, they still need to establish policies that enable and empower staff to be flexible when interacting with prospects, members, and customers.

Be Categorically Flexible

For many years, it was fairly common for organizations with stringent eligibility requirements to develop a set of policies to ensure that applicants are knowledgeable and qualified to work in the industry. These policies elevated the organization's brand image by creating a sense of exclusivity and professionalism. At that same time, they also created unnecessary barriers to growth. The more rigid the policies, the less likely the organization will be able to create a strong bond during the first phase of an individual's career. In fact, if an organization cannot provide valuable assistance early on in a member's career, it becomes an even greater challenge for the organization to demonstrate the value of membership once a credential has been earned.

In response to this dilemma, I examined the structures of twenty associations that require members to earn a credential, in order to qualify for full or active membership. The overall trend among these organizations is to provide support to individuals during their educational and early careers, which proves beneficial to the profession, the industry, and all allied components (such as credentialing affiliations and membership organizations). Additionally, by allowing students and early careerists the opportunity to join an organization, it's expected that they will develop stronger connections with industry professionals during a critical point in their career. In other words, in the beginning of a career, individuals generally need more interaction and networking, mentoring and examples.

My research revealed that those associations serving professions who require a license or credential were able to attract young professionals and increase retention rates, but there was an important variable to consider. The organization had to be more flexible with its membership categories. Some organizations made the leap and created new membership categories to address the needs and interests of students and early careerists. Others created programs and services geared toward these two audience segments, even though they did not offer an actual membership category for individuals who had not yet earned an industry credential.

At the Other End of the Spectrum

When my friend's father retired and sold his dental practice, he was excited to begin the next chapter in his life. He was still relatively young and was looking forward to spending more time with his grandchildren and pursuing a few interests he had never had time for during the many years he was serving patients. He had been a very active member in his local dental association, but the relationship ended as soon as he announced his retirement. Yet it wasn't his choice to no longer volunteer for the association; it was theirs. When my friend's father changed his membership status to "retired," the organization sent him a letter thanking him for his years of service and, for all intents and purposes, said goodbye. My friend asked his dad why he no longer volunteered; his father shrugged his shoulders and explained, rather sadly, that he didn't feel that there was a place for him in the organization. Indeed, he had been made to feel that way. But unnecessarily so.

Retired members create a unique opportunity for organizations to be engaged with members throughout the various life stages. Some individuals may retire from a profession long before they retire from working; others may retire from fulltime employment but are still very much interested in staying actively involved and taking on a larger role as a volunteer. When you think about it, who has more spare time than a retired potential volunteer? At the same time, they most likely have decades of experience in the industry and with your organization as well. In short, they have a lot to offer—and a lot of time.

Although a retired member may not pay the same amount as active members, organizations may have more to gain—a lot more—from increasing the amount of opportunities to engage this group rather than reducing their involvement. If your organization offers a category for retired members, consider conducting an audit of your association's eligibility requirements, fees, opportunities, and communication policies. Are they too restrictive? Is your organization flexible enough to allow ways and means to stay engaged and involved to members who are no longer actively practicing?

When a member retires, an organization should make a personal phone call to the individual to thank him or her for contributions over the years and ask if he or she wishes to stay engaged. This can easily take place via email communications; however, this audience will be much more receptive to the personal interaction. Some members may be ready to move the next phase in their life and consequently may be ready to end the relationship. And that's okay. But don't leave behind the ones who wish to continue their membership just because their employment status has changed.

The Fine Print

Have you ever been excited about a special offer, only to have your hopes dashed because of the rules outlined in the fine print? This may happen when you receive a special offer or coupon for a discount or a free item. It can also occur when you sign up for membership or register for a program and then realize that you need to pay additional dollars for the items you were most interested in receiving. For this reason, you should try to avoid creating a situation in which the *fine print* damages your association's brand. Consider the story behind the Association Forum of Chicagoland's membership gift card.

One issue that nearly all associations struggle with is how to communicate and encourage members to renew. By the time members receive their invoices, they already know whether they'll renew their membership. So at this point, an inspiring, benefit-identifying, graphically beautiful letter will do little to convince someone that your organization provides value if you've failed to communicate this successfully throughout the year.

Successful renewal programs should focus, instead, on ways to increase the number of early renewals. As director of membership at the Forum, I decided to take a different approach to this challenge. One thing I didn't change in my approach was that members should still receive invoices announcing it was time to renew their membership. Unlike in years past, however, we didn't offer a gimmick or special incentive to encourage members to renew. We simply asked them to pay their invoice. Once the member renewed, he or she received something unexpected but valuable: a gift card similar to the ones sold at Barnes & Noble (see Figure 12.1). However, Forum members didn't have to pay any additional fee to receive it. The gift card was sent with a card thanking them for renewing their membership. The gift card could be used for any half-day educational program offered by the Forum during the next twelve months.

This campaign worked for several reasons. First, because many of our members worked together and knew others in the Chicagoland association community, word of mouth about the campaign spread quickly. We gave members a second reason to feel good about renewing their membership, along with a first reason to talk about us. As a result, this prompted a higher-than-average response rate to our second renewal mailing. The goodwill we created by offering members something extra could have evaporated had we not implemented a flexible policy for how the gift cards could be used.

Figure 12.1.   Association Forum of Chicagoland Gift Card

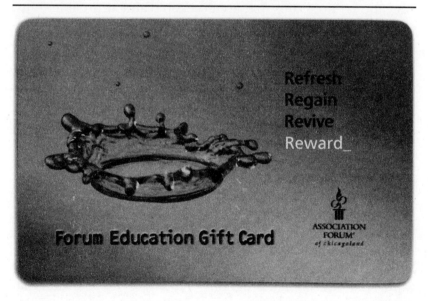

When the gift cards were sent out, I highlighted the fine print (actually in a very readable 12-point font), which included the following rules:

- Gift cards may be used for *any* half-day educational program or webinar.
- Gift cards *are* transferrable to friends or colleagues.
- If you lose your gift card, call us and we will provide you with a redemption code so that you may still enjoy one free educational program.
- One gift card per person may be used during a twelve-month period.
- Gift cards may not be exchanged for cash.

Essentially, we wanted to let our members know that we understood that times were tough and budgets were tight. We also wanted to reinforce our message that we were there for our members to help them achieve their goals. And we were thanking members for being members, for sharing themselves with the Forum and other members, and for paying their dues year after year. Part of our value proposition is that we provide high-quality educational programs that are accessible and affordable. Plus, everyone who renewed received the free gift. The gift card program was a big success because it increased the rate at which we received our renewals—which was our goal.

Adding to the success of increased renewals was the fact that, by and large, the feedback we received about the campaign was extremely positive. Our members loved the idea and spread the word to others. They appreciated the flexibility we offered because, for some members, the gift card allowed them to send someone from their team to a Forum educational event. (Clearly, this was yet another benefit for the Forum by way of expanding our reach and heightening our brand identity.)

A year after the program was launched, we surveyed the members who had used the gift cards and learned that 100 percent had *not* used the gift card to pay for a program they would have attended even if they weren't able to attend for free. In other words, our educational program revenue did not take a hit that year because members were using the gift cards rather than paying for programs. Instead, we saw a significant increase in attendance for our half-day educational sessions.

In addition, the flexibility of the program allowed prospective members to try out one of the benefits of membership, because some of our members transferred the gift card to their nonmember colleagues. The bottom line is that this campaign would not have been as successful if we hadn't allowed for some flexibility in how it was implemented.

Be an Enabler: Empower Your Staff

Being flexible requires more than creating a set of policies; it also calls for empowering your staff to make decisions. By giving staff additional responsibilities and entrusting them with making decisions—at every level—you will create a greater sense of ownership from within the organization.

The Ritz-Carlton Hotel Company offers a good example of how a company can empower its staff to reinforce a brand image. To support its efforts to fulfill every guest's needs, the company permits every employee to spend up to $2,000 to make any single guest satisfied. The policy is in place because the company views each employee as an extension of its brand. The Ritz-Carlton understands that it isn't just the product—in their case, the hotels and resorts—it's the brand itself and the experience a person has when staying at a Ritz-Carlton. (Think back to all the early stories about Starbucks as a brand, and you'll remember that it's the experience, not the coffee.) The hotel relies on staff to deliver a brand experience that ensures an outstanding experience each and every time. Ritz-Carlton's "About Us" page on its website talks about gold standards and offers a motto and credo (much like a mission and vision statement). It then goes into detail about the service values of the hotel itself and, by extension, its employees.

In addition, the Ritz-Carlton offers a promise to its employees: "At The Ritz-Carlton, our Ladies and Gentlemen are the most important resource in our service commitment to our guests. By applying the principles of trust, honesty, respect, integrity and commitment, we nurture and maximize talent to the benefit of each individual and the company. The Ritz-Carlton fosters a work environment where diversity is valued, quality of life is enhanced, individual aspirations are fulfilled, and The Ritz-Carlton Mystique is strengthened" (Ritz-Carlton, 2013b).

There are many ways to measure success, but for the Ritz-Carlton, one of the most important measurements is voluntary turnover. The company hires only about 2 percent of the people who apply for jobs, and they provide extensive training and career opportunities for advancement. The Ritz-Carlton entices prospective employees by stating that working with the hotel "Could be the start of a life-changing experience" (Ritz-Carlton, 2013a). Imagine what you could achieve if all of your association staff felt that working for your organization was a life-changing experience and that they were empowered.

We've Always Done It That Way!

With advancements in technology, shifts in the workforce, and the changing needs of new generations, it is important for organizations to be flexible in how they develop new programs, products, and services. Unfortunately, this is easier said than done, and that's an understatement. Many organizations do one of two things: they either overtly state their resistance to change or just quietly resist it, because there is a feeling that things simply cannot be altered due to the age-old, and frankly tired, statement: "But we've always done it that way!" or, even more negatively, "We've tried it another way and it failed, so we went back to the way we've always done it."

History is filled with stories of companies that no longer exist, or are a shadow of their former selves, because they were unable to adapt to the changing environment. One of the most recent, and interesting, examples I came across was the hiring of the new Chicago Bears head coach Marc Trestman. A March 10, 2013, *Tribune* story is titled "Trestman's Redemption" (Pompei, 2013). In short, Trestman was hired by the Bears in 2013, after holding thirteen other coaching jobs in the previous thirty years. He had been fired seven times—several times just after he had done some pretty amazing things, such as getting a team to the Super Bowl.

Why? "Part of it was bad luck," the article states. "He didn't always fit in. There were conflicts." Trestman, the article explains, was the type of coach who didn't engage with people very much; he would focus on the game and the plays, but not the human factor. This would prove to be a major element of himself that he could change—and did change. Trestman did not look back on his career and think, "Well, I'll just keep on going, perhaps it's bad luck, but I cannot change that." Rather, he changed himself. He began "to look at his firing as opportunity." He started to read more about what it takes to be a leader; he "retraced the steps of his career." And he changed. In his first interview as head coach for the Bears, a question was tossed at him: "Based on the pieces you have in place, do you anticipate any major changes by bringing in a new defensive coordinator?" Trestman replied, "With all due respect, they are not pieces. They are men who love football. During my transformation, they will never be pieces again. They are valued people." Proof that an old dog can learn new tricks.

Similarly, in order to adapt to changes, your organization must constantly reexamine itself, by looking at your offerings and the value of your benefits. Innovation, a word that is tossed around by many organizations but rarely achieved, is possible only when an organization becomes more flexible and is open to change.

Case Study: Rotary International Focuses on Flexibility

Rotary International (RI) is a volunteer organization with thirty-three thousand clubs in over two hundred countries and geographical areas. Perhaps most widely known for its efforts to eradicate polio, Rotary's main objective is service—in the community, in the workplace, and around the globe. The 1.2 million Rotarians who make up more than 34,000 Rotary clubs in nearly every country in the world share a dedication to the ideal of Service Above Self. To live out that ideal, Rotary International initiates humanitarian projects that address the challenges affecting the world today, such as hunger, poverty, and illiteracy.

RI has been around for over one hundred years. The organization could very well be satisfied with its lengthy and successful history of doing good things and its dedication to service. The brand is well known, and its reputation is stellar, among members and the public. Yet in 2010, the organization's new strategic plan included, as one of its top priorities, "to support and strengthen clubs." Furthermore, one of the major ways RI felt it could achieve this goal was by fostering club innovation and flexibility.

"Rotary is looking to be more inclusive, be appealing as much as possible from the broadest range," said Jennifer Deters, manager of membership research and programs. "We have taken the perspective that we want to test new and creative ideas in a methodical manner. We want to make sure that changes clubs make can be widely applied across our movement and organizational structure."

Feedback from surveys and focus groups showed that prospective qualified members and younger-aged Rotarians wanted and needed more flexibility in order to become or remain involved with a Rotary club. With that in mind, and to coincide with the strategic planning goals, the organization launched several new pilot programs allowing Rotary clubs to experiment with flexible memberships and club operations. Each pilot program was designed to improve recruitment and retention, allow for flexibility in club operations and structures, and give Rotary clubs an opportunity to explore new and innovative ways to promote member diversity—all of which, again, are goals of the Rotary International Strategic Plan.

"There are two hundred clubs per pilot," explained Deters. She said the clubs that were chosen to participate were told, "Change one thing about your club and let's see the impact. Rotary gave them the freedom to try these things with the support and structure of the organization. Once the pilot is launched, we are in constant contact to find out what's working, what's not, and what recommendations they have to make if we were to deploy this worldwide." In this way, everyone is making the best and more informed decisions.

Three of the pilot programs are satellite club, associate member, and innovative and flexible Rotary club. Each is an experiment in offering members flexibility, both with ways to belong to the organization as a whole and overall rotary club management and operations.

Satellite Club

Rotarians in a "satellite club" will belong to a host club but will meet at their own time and location and can have their own projects. The idea behind this pilot program is flexibility for members' time and personal schedules, in order to attend meetings and stay connected to Rotary. Clubs can conduct multiple club meetings during a week, each taking place at a different location, on a different day, or at a different time, then determine which was best attended.

Associate Member

This type of membership will be something akin to a trial period. Rotary's pilot program will be a tool for teaching prospective members about the club and the expectations of membership before they join. Clubs will determine the length of time a person can remain an associate member before becoming an active member. The goal is to let potential members who may otherwise be uncertain of the commitment involved with membership get a taste of membership and see all the benefits. This type of membership allows people to get acquainted with a club's members, programs, and projects, thereby increasing retention.

Flexible Rotary Club

The third pilot program reminds me slightly of the story I shared in Chapter Two, about the Whitney Museum of American Art, in that it positions membership as something an individual can customize. Essentially, this program allows clubs to change one element of their format or structure as an experiment. The Rotary program allows clubs to self-determine their operations to better fit with the needs of their members and community. It was also designed to encourage clubs to conduct numerous tests to

- Try out different meeting logistics (time, date, location, online, use of social media, club event or social activity, and so on)
- Improve club leadership and oversight

- Create relevant and creative membership qualifications and requirements
- Update Rotary terminology to current language
- Shift the focus from meeting attendance to member engagement

The common idea behind each program is flexibility. It's about allowing different clubs to conduct diverse activities and encouraging individual members to experience membership uniquely. The premise, as Rotary International sees it, is to encourage clubs to be fun, dynamic, diverse, resilient, tolerant, interested in trying new things, member driven, inspirational, and relationship rich.

The outcomes from the pilot programs have been interesting, to say the least. "When we started to pilot the idea of frequency, we had expectations that clubs would love it," Deters explained. "There were anecdotes from other clubs that it works. Other volunteer clubs meet with less frequency than Rotaries. So we thought clubs would love meeting only twice a month. The experience for the clubs was a mixed bag, which is good. Some clubs loved it, and it helped them accommodate the needs of their members, while others felt the change caused them to became less connected. Because we gave them the flexibility, we have varying, different experiences." Deters said that ultimately they may recommend to their board of directors that neither solution is ideal for all clubs across the board. They have found that the flexibility to set individual own schedules is what clubs want.

"Our key learning was that we were glad to run the test," Deters said. RI felt that the Associate Member pilot program would go over very well, mainly because it was a low-pressure way to introduce people to a club. The association thought it would "make membership more appealing. Yet the opposite has happened. What we've learned so far," explained Deters, "is that not every club may want to have an associate program." But some should. Every club is different. Again, what emerges from this trial is that being flexible allows you to be accommodating. As always, RI is "still evaluating, and when the pilot closes, we will make decisions," Deters said.

The notion of creating pilot programs is "a systematic, reliable method of testing something within everyone's comfort zone,"

Deters explained. The board is happy that new things are being initiated, tested and evaluated. At the same time, the clubs "feel excited to be innovative, trying new things. It helps staff evaluate based on key measurables that we set out at the beginning. We can determine the right direction to go. Our advice is, you don't know what you don't know until you see it in practice."

Action Steps

Earlier in this book and referenced again in this chapter, I told the story of how my friend was able to exchange a pair of workout pants even though she had worn them and washed them several times. The store had a very liberal return policy because it wants customers to be thrilled with their products, tell others about the experience, and return frequently to make other purchases. And why not buy from them? There is absolutely no risk involved. An association can offer a "love it or return it for any reason" policy on everything it offers. To create a more flexible, member-centric organization, take the following action steps:

1. Offer a no-risk membership guarantee. Allow members to request and receive a full refund on their membership dues, up until the very last day of membership, if they are not completely satisfied and your organization has been given the opportunity to make things better.

2. Allow companies to transfer membership to new employees. If an employer calls and requests that a membership be transferred to a new employee because the member is no longer with the company, do it! Provide the company with a complimentary membership until the end of the term. This will allow the current member to retain their membership and the employer to "transfer" the membership. Everyone wins with this scenario, because the organization keeps one member and gains a new one, and the employer does not lose their initial investment.

3. Make it a policy to make exceptions. Every organization must have a set of operating policies and procedures. Some of the policies, however, should be considered guidelines. By empowering staff to make exceptions based on individual circumstances, the organization will create a tremendous amount of goodwill.

For example, many organizations offer a dues waiver to members in good standing whose circumstances have created a financial hardship. These policies typically offer a full waiver for one year. Instead, consider allowing the member to select the type of waiver based on their individual needs. It could range from 25 percent to 100 percent. Recognize a variety of financial hardships, including loss of job, disability, catastrophe, parental leave, or illness. Also, allow staff to extend the waiver beyond a year if requested.

4. Share testimonials from members who have benefited from an organization's willingness to be flexible. This will remove any lingering doubt about whether or not prospects should join the organization or register for an event. Sharing stories about how you've resolved an issue by using a testimonial from an actual member will create a sense of authenticity and help humanize your organization. No one gets it right every time; that's impossible. However, it's the way you resolve issues when they arise that makes the biggest difference to prospective members.

5. Empower employees to ensure that members' needs are met every time. Train employees to be responsive to member needs and, whenever possible, resolve problems. Create "wow" experiences members will never forget and, quite possibly, will share with others.

6. Allow chapters, components, and committees to pilot new programs that will enhance the organization's ability to attract new members through added flexibility.

References

Adamson, B., Dixon, M., & Toman, N. (2012). The End of Solution Sales. *Harvard Business Review*. Retrieved from http://hbr.org/2012/07/the-end-of-solution-sales/ar

Albert, L. R., & Dignam, M. (2010). *The Decision to Learn: Why People Seek Continuing Education and How Membership Organizations Can Meet Learners' Needs.* Washington, DC: ASAE: The Center for Association Leadership.

American Association of Individual Investors. (2013). 20 Benefits of AAII Membership. Retrieved from http://www.aaii.com/membership/member-benefits

American Health Information Management Association. (2013). You're the Boss: Put Your AHIMA Membership to Work! *AHIMA Membership Guide.* Retrieved from http://www.ahima.org/downloads/pdfs/membership/MX6889-MemberGuide.pdf

ASAE: The Center for Association Leadership. (2006). *7 Measures of Success: What Remarkable Associations Do That Others Don't.* Washington, DC: ASAE: The Center for Association Leadership.

Association of American Medical Colleges. (2012). AAMC Physician Workforce Policy Recommendations. Retrieved from https://www.aamc.org/download/304026/data/2012aamcworkforcepolicyrecommendations.pdf

Association of Corporate Counsel. (2013). Membership. Retrieved from http://www.acc.com/aboutacc/membership/index.cfm

Athleta. 2013. Retrieved from http://athleta.gap.com/?

Avenue M Group, LLC. (2010–2012). Membership Needs Assessment Surveys.

Avenue M Group, LLC. (2010–2013). Research Database.

Bauer, T. Y., Ph.D. (2010). Onboarding New Employees: Maximizing Success (p. 2). *Society of Human Resource Management Foundation.* Retrieved from https://www.shrm.org/about/foundation/products /Documents/Onboarding%20EPG-%20FINAL.pdf

Berry, T. (2008). Understanding Your Pricing Choices. Palo Alto Software. Retrieved from http://articles.mplans.com /understand-your-pricing-choices/

BMW of North America. (2013a). Exceptional Value. Retrieved from http://www.bmwusa.com/Standard/Content/Owner /nocostmaintenance.aspx

BMW of North America. (2013b). We Only Make One Thing: The Ultimate Driving Mchine. Retrieved from http://www.bmwusa .com/Standard/Content/Innovations/onething.aspx

Cauz, J. (2013). Encyclopedia Britannica's President on Killing Off a 244-Year-Old Product. *Harvard Business Review.* Retrieved from http://hbr.org/2013/03/encyclopaedia -britannicas-president-on-killing-off-a-244-year-old-product/ar/1

Chernev, A. (2012, May 29). Can There Ever Be a Fair Price? Why J.C. Penney's Strategy Backfired (para. 4). In *HBR Blog Network. Harvard Business Review.* Retrieved from http://blogs.hbr.org/cs/2012/05 /can_there_ever_be_a_fair_price.html

Collins, J. (2006). 7 Measures of Success: A Summary. Retrieved from www.mla.lib.mi.us/files/7%20MEASURES%20OF%20 SUCCESS_0.doc

comScore. (2012). Online Shopping Customer Experience Study, pp. 5–15. Commissioned by UPS. Retrieved from http://www.comscore .com/Insights/Presentations_and_Whitepapers/2012 /Online_Shopping_Customer_Experience_Study

Dalton, J., & Dignam, M. (2007). *The Decision to Join: How Individuals Determine Value and Why They Choose to Belong* (pp. 1–6). Washington, DC: ASAE: The Center for Association Leadership.

Dalton, J., & Dignam, M. (2012). *10 Lessons for Cultivating Member Commitment: Critical Strategies for Fostering Value, Involvement, and Belonging.* Washington, DC: ASAE Association Management Press.

Disney. (2013). *Runner's World* Challenge. Retrieved from http://www .rundisney.com/disneyworld-marathon/#runners-world-challenge

Duggan, M., & Brenner, J. (2013). The Demographics of Social Media Users—2012. *Pew Research Center's Internet & American Life Project.*

Electronic Retailing Association. (n.d.a). Access SupERAchiever—Katie Williams. Retrieved from http://www.retailing.org/membership /superachievers/access-superachiever-katie-williams

Electronic Retailing Association. (n.d.b). ERA Stands Behind Every SupERAchiever. In *Membership*. Retrieved from http://www.retailing .org/membership/superachievers

Forbes. (2012, March 16). What Is a Thought Leader? (para. 8). Retrieved from http://www.forbes.com/sites/russprince/2012/03/16 /what-is-a-thought-leader/

Forbes. (2013). Thoughts on the Business of Life. *Forbes.com.* Retrieved from http://thoughts.forbes.com/thoughts /business-will-rogers-you-never-get

Fox, S. (2002, November 17). Data Memo: Findings. In *Online Banking 2002. PEW Internet & American Life Project.* Retrieved from http:// www.pewinternet.org/Reports/2002/Online-Banking-2002 /Data-Memo.aspx

Gladwell, M. (2002). *The Tipping Point: How Little Things Can Make a Big Difference.* New York: Back Bay Books.

Hampton, K., Goulet, L. S., Rainie, L., & Purcell, K. (2011, June 16). Part 4: Trust, Support, Perspective Taking, and Democratic Engagement. In *Social Networking Sites and Our Lives. PEW Internet & American Life Project.* Retrieved from http://www.pewinternet .org/Reports/2011/Technology-and-social-networks/Part-4 /Civic-Engagement.aspx

Henrickson, K., & Scott, J. (2011). Baggage Fees and Changes in Airline Ticket Prices. In J. Peoples (Ed.), *Advances in Airline Economics, Volume 3: Pricing Behavior and Non-Price Characteristics in the Airline Industry.* Bingley, UK: Emerald Group Publishing Limited.

Horrigan, J., & Rainie, L. (2002, June 23). The Broadband Difference: How Online Behavior Changes with High-Speed Internet Connections. *Pew Internet and American Life Project.* Retrieved from http://www .pewinternet.org/Reports/2002/The-Broadband-Difference-How -online-behavior-changes-with-highspeed-Internet-connections /Methodology/Methodology.aspx

International Health, Racquet & Sportsclub Association (IHRSA). (2010). Consumer FAQs. In *Frequently Asked Questions: Research* (para. 6–7). Retrieved from http://www.ihrsa.org/research-faqs/

J.D. Power and Associates. (2012). Press release: 2012 North America Airline Satisfaction Study (para. 2). Retrieved from http://www .jdpower.com/content/press-release/aOGunkG/2012-north-america -airline-satisfaction-study.htm

Kear, R. (2012, June 10). Breaking News: Solution Selling Pronounced Dead—Again. *Sales Performance International Inc.* Retrieved from http:// www.solutionsellingblog.com/home/2012/7/10/breaking-news -solution-selling-pronounced-dead-again.html

Kramer, G. (2012, August 8). 8 Surprising Characteristics. Forbes .com. Retrieved from http://www.forbes.com/sites /realspin/2012/08/08/8-surprising-characteristics-of-winners-at-the -london-olympics/

Lecinski, J. (2011). ZMOT Winning the Zero Moment of Truth (para. 10). Retrieved from http://www.zeromomentoftruth.com/assets /files/google-zmot.pdf

Liker, J. K., & Meier, D. (2005). *The Toyota Way Fieldbook: A Practical Guide for Implementing Toyota's 4Ps.* New York: McGraw-Hill.

Manyika, J., Chui, M., Brown, B., Bughin, J., Dobbs, R., Roxburgh, C., & Byers, A. H. (2011). Big Data: The Next Frontier for Innovation, Competition, and Productivity. *McKinsey Global Institute.* Retrieved from http://www.mckinsey.com/insights/business_technology /big_data_the_next_frontier_for_innovation

Marketing General Incorporated. (2012). 2012 Membership Marketing Benchmarking Report. *White Paper Library* (p. 28). Retrieved from http://www.marketinggeneral.com/resources/white-papers /white-paper-library/

Marvin, C. (1990). *When Old Technologies Were New: Thinking About Electric Communication in the Late Nineteenth Century.* New York: Oxford University Press.

Massachusetts Medical Society. (2012). 2012 MMS Physician Workforce Study. Retrieved from http://www.massmed.org/AM/Template .cfm?Section=News_and_Publications2&CONTENTID=77980 &TEMPLATE=/CM/ContentDisplay.cfm

Merriam-Webster. (2013). Flexible (para. 1). Retrieved from http:// www.merriam-webster.com/dictionary/flexible

Mothers Against Drunk Driving. (2012). Statistics (para. 2–3). Retrieved from http://www.madd.org/statistics/

Munir, K. (2012, February 26). The Demise of Kodak: Five Reasons. *Wall Street Journal.* Retrieved from http://blogs.wsj.com /source/2012/02/26/the-demise-of-kodak-five-reasons/

Nagel, T., Hogan, J., & Zale, J. (2010). *The Strategy and Tactics of Pricing: A Guide to Growing More Profitably* (5th ed., p. 319). Upper Saddle River, NJ: Pearson Education.

Nielsen Company. (2012). Global Trust in Advertising and Brand Messages. Retrieved from http://www.nielsen.com/us/en /reports/2012/global-trust-in-advertising-and-brand-messages.html

Over How Many Billion Served? (2010, April 30). Retrieved from http:// overhowmanybillionserved.blogspot.com/

Pompei, D. (2013, March 10). Trestman's Redemption: Bears Coach Once Was So Caught Up in X's and O's, He Forgot Game About

People. *Chicago Tribune, Sports.* Retrieved from http://articles
.chicagotribune.com/2013-03-09/sports/ct-spt-0310-bears-pompei
-chicago–20130310_1_trestmans-head-coach-bears-coach

Rabinovitz, A. (2012). Fans Flock to New Athleta Store at Valley Fair in Santa
Clara (Photos, para. 4). *Examiner.com.* Retrieved from http://www
.examiner.com/article/fans-flock-to-new-athleta-store-at-valley
-fair-santa-clara

Reichheld, F., & Markey, R. (2011). *The Ultimate Question 2: How Net
Promoter Companies Thrive in a Customer-Driven World.* (rev. exp. ed.).
New York: Harvard Business Review Press.

Reinhardt, A.. (1998). Steve Jobs on Apple's Resurgence: "Not a
One-Man Show" (para. 5). *Business Week Online.* Retrieved from
http://www.businessweek.com/bwdaily/dnflash/may1998
/nf80512d.htm

Ritz-Carlton Hotel Company. (2013a). Careers. Retrieved from http://
corporate.ritzcarlton.com/en/Careers/Default.htm

Ritz-Carlton Hotel Company. (2013b). Gold Standards. Retrieved from
http://corporate.ritzcarlton.com/en/About/GoldStandards.htm

Roper Center for Public Opinion Research. (2006). *Social Capital and
Community Benchmark Survey.*

Satmetrix, Bain & Company, and Reichheld, F. (2010). Retrieved
from http://www.satmetrix.com/pdfs/Satmetrix-DataSheet
-SatmetrixandNetPromoter.pdf

Seaman, J. T., & Smith, G. D. (2012, December). Your Company's History
as a Leadership Tool. *Harvard Business Review.* Retrieved from http://
hbr.org/2012/12/your-companys-history-as-a-leadership-tool/ar/2

Simon, N. (2010, September 20). Curate Your Own Membership: An
Interview with the Whitney's Director of Membership (para.
4). *Museum 2.0.* Retrieved from http://museumtwo.blogspot
.com/2010/09/curate-your-own-membership-interview.html

Stoller, G. (2008, February 18). Airlines Want You to Pack Less—or
Pay More (para. 9). *USA Today.* Retrieved from http://usatoday30
.usatoday.com/travel/flights/2008–02–18-checked-bags_N.htm

Swift, E. M. (1982, December 27). Greatness Confirmed (para. 9). In
Sports Illustrated Vault. Retrieved from http://sportsillustrated
.cnn.com/vault/article/magazine/MAG1126259/index.htm

Target Brands, Inc. (2013). All About Returns. Retrieved from
http://m.target.com/HelpContent?help=/sites/html
/TargetOnline/help/returns_and_refunds/targets_return_policy
/targets_return_policy.html

Taylor, J. W. (2013). The Best Industries for Starting a Business Right Now. *Inc.* Retrieved from http://www.inc.com/ss/best-industries-for-starting-a-business#2

Villarreal, J. (2010). Curate Your Own Membership: A New Approach to Museum Membership at the Whitney. Retrieved from http://www.artdaily.org/index.asp?int_sec=2&int_new=40682#.UVID11s4Vro

Whitney Museum of American Art. (2013). Curate Your Own Membership (para. 1). Retrieved from http://whitney.org/Membership/CYOM

Wisconsin REALTORS® Association. (2013). WRA Member Benefits Video. Retrieved from https://www.wra.org/Resources/Video_Center/WRA_Member_Benefits_Video

Index

predictor of, 223, 233; synchronizing cost and value as key to, 26; of transactional members, 37; of uninvolved members, 26

Rider, Kirsten, 110

Rinie, L., 140

Rising Stars, 35

Ritz-Carlton Hotel Company, 249–250

Rogers, Will, 241

Roper Center for Public Opinion Research, 125

Rotary International (RI), 251–255

S

Satisfaction: with alternative sources, lapsed membership due to, 46; and likelihood to recommend membership, 125; limited value of information about, 7–8; questions about, in brand attributes survey, 48, 49; as reason for renewing membership, 24–26

Satmetrix, 124

Scoring leads, 95–107; attributes of prospects to consider, 96–99; calculating lifetime value (LTV) of member, 100, 106–107; example of model for, 104–105; importance of, 95–96; methods for assigning points, 99–104

Scott, J., 20

Seaman, J. T., 155

7 Measures of Success (ASAE: The Center for Association Leadership), 146

Simon, N., 29

Small business surveys, 154

SmartBrief, 94

Smith, G. D., 155

Smith, Steve, 58, 59, 60

SmithBucklin, 125, 127

Social media: advisory board for heads of, 191, 192; engaging new members on, 239; recruiting members using, 110–111, 112, 115, 117, 135, 171; source of information on trends in, 94; stories on, 235

Social proof, 198

Socialmedia.org, 191, 192

Society of Human Resource Management (SHRM), 222

Solution selling, 160–164

Spiegel, Peter, 176–177

Sports, 137–139, 242

Staff: contact with, during onboarding, 171–172, 228; policies promoting flexibility in decision making by, 244, 249–250, 255; required to eliminate saying "no," 165–168; responsible for implementing group membership, 88–89; unaware of price of membership, 64

Starbucks, 249

Stoller, G., 20

Stories: about how association saves members time,